T0295843

PRAISE FOR *WHY DEFI MATTERS*

"If decentralized finance is one of those crypto buzz words that annoy or scare you, fear not, because Ian Horne's new book will guide you through the history that brought us DeFi, breaking down jargon, and uncovering details that even the OGs might have missed."
Mauricio Magaldi, Head of Product, Midnight, Input Output and host of the Blockdrops podcast

"*Why DeFi Matters* provides a comprehensive, global and inclusive look at decentralized finance. Ian Horne expands the narrative beyond the narrow, store-of-value lens that often limits a real understanding of the depth and breadth of DeFi. The book skilfully captures the story of DeFi, leaving readers with a clear understanding of why money and commerce matters to the global innovation economy."
Cleve Mesidor, Executive Director, Blockchain Foundation and former Obama Presidential Appointee

"This brilliantly informative book serves as a digestible and engagingly written guide, offering clear insights into the past, present and potential future of not just decentralized finance but also digital assets overall."
Erica Stanford, Author of *Crypto Wars*

"*Why DeFi Matters* is a must-read for anyone interested in a holistic understanding of the nuanced conversation around decentralized finance. From addressing the polarizing political climate to financial inclusion, Ian seamlessly blends financial insights, technological trends and philosophical musings, creating a captivating narrative that leaves you feeling inspired and hopeful about the potential of DeFi."
Nicole Casperson, Founder and author, *Fintech is Femme*

Why DeFi Matters

*What cryptoassets, web3 and the metaverse
really mean for finance*

Ian Horne

KoganPage

First published in Great Britain and the United States in 2023 by Kogan Page Limited.

2nd Floor, 45 Gee Street	8 W 38th Street, Suite 902	4737/23 Ansari Road
London	New York, NY 10018	Daryaganj
EC1V 3RS	USA	New Delhi 110002
United Kingdom		India

www.koganpage.com

Kogan Page books are printed on paper from sustainable forests.

© Ian Horne, 2023

The right of Ian Horne to be identified as the author of this work has been asserted by him in accordance with the Copyright, Designs and Patents Act 1988.

ISBNs

Hardback	978 1 3986 1295 2
Paperback	978 1 3986 1293 8
Ebook	978 1 3986 1294 5

British Library Cataloguing-in-Publication Data

A CIP record for this book is available from the British Library.

Library of Congress Cataloging-in-Publication Data
Names: Horne, Ian (Writer on finance), author.
Title: Why DeFi matters : what cryptoassets, web3 and the metaverse really   mean for finance / Ian Horne.
Description: London ; New York, NY : Kogan Page, 2023. | Includes bibliographical references and index. | Summary: "There is a pressing need for a balanced account outlining what DeFi actually means for investors, banks and the finance industry. Why DeFi Matters cuts through the jargon and the hype to help people make more informed decisions in this space. It examines the evolution of DeFi and cryptocurrencies, analysing what it means for investors and the future of finance. It also outlines the developments that truly matter, distinguishing between longer-term trends and fads, and is a must-read for finance professionals, organizations and investors interested in moving into DeFi.Why DeFi Matters explores the rise of DeFi and provides focused, balanced analysis about this alternative financial system that is being built and how it will coexist with banks, institutions and traditional finance. It examines the aspects of DeFi that will materially change financial systems and how they will alter the nature of purchasing, lending, insurance and banking; the role of web3 and the metaverse in the new era of finance; and its role in the democratization of finance" – Provided by publisher.
Identifiers: LCCN 2023031815 (print) | LCCN 2023031816 (ebook) | ISBN   9781398612938 (paperback) | ISBN 9781398612952 (hardback) | ISBN   9781398612945 (ebook)
Subjects: LCSH: Finance–Technological innovations. | Cryptocurrencies.
Classification: LCC HG173 .H66 2023 (print) | LCC HG173 (ebook) | DDC   332–dc23/eng/20230714
LC record available at https://lccn.loc.gov/2023031815
LC ebook record available at https://lccn.loc.gov/2023031816

Typeset by Integra Software Services, Pondicherry
Print production managed by Jellyfish
Printed and bound by CPI Group (UK) Ltd, Croydon CR0 4YY

CONTENTS

ABOUT THE AUTHOR

Ian is a London-based writer and European Head of Content for Money20/20, a cutting-edge international events and content company. In this role, he shapes the agenda for Money20/20's annual fintech show in Amsterdam and can also be found at its US flagship event in Las Vegas. This role offers him a front-row seat to the latest developments in financial technology emerging from banking, payments, lending, insurance and cryptoassets, as well as access to the people behind them.

Ian's fascination with financial technology was sparked during an eight-year stint at financial publisher Citywire, where he led an audience engagement team for the UK financial advice and wealth management market. While at the company, he would launch its wealthtech newsletter, podcast and virtual events, which sought to highlight the many ways that technology could enhance the services provided to clients and improve the operational efficiencies of the firms providing them.

PREFACE

Thank you for picking up this book. Over these next few hundred pages we'll explore the revolutionary, fast-paced, occasionally bizarre and often wild world of decentralized finance, or DeFi. While DeFi's greatest successes and failures sometimes mirror events we've seen before, and things that are inherent to human nature, it is truly an ecosystem like no other. In a short space of time, it has proven to be fertile ground for huge personalities, Ponzi schemes of Bernie Madoff proportions, and missing passwords that have cost people fortunes. But that's not all.

DeFi also represents a change in how we represent economic value. It offers a new representation of money, and it allows us to financialize our assets and lives in new and profound ways. It also offers a value system that can sit outside of government reach, featuring currencies that are barely within regulatory clutches, and it raises unexpected questions about financial stability, international relations, and economic sovereignty too.

The technology behind DeFi is transformative but it's nascent. This nascency is part of what makes it so exciting to discover and follow, as we attempt to figure out what happens next and what it means for you and the world at large. Will decentralized finance underpin the future of all, or some, of our transactions and investments? Will it be the financial plumbing of web3 and 'the metaverse'? And does it give power back to individuals? Power to hold their own assets, execute their own trades, do more with their money and gain greater control of their financial lives?

The analysis provided here will explore DeFi while keeping an attentive eye on traditional finance and the unsteady relationship between the two. This book will also explore some of the biggest declarations about DeFi and crypto (crypto is occasionally used as an all-encapsulating term). Even for a diligent newcomer, there is a lot to pick apart and varying stances that you might take, and these might hinge on your political views, your attitude towards regulators and governments, your feelings towards traditional finance or, perhaps more likely, your personal aspirations. Your opinion might also be contingent on your knowledge of cryptography and code, though please note that this book will not zero in on that.

As to my reasons for writing this, I'm looking to offer clarity on what appears to be the most confusing and exciting financial development of a generation. There are many reasons why this might be relevant to you. You might be considering a switch to DeFi for your next major career move, or plotting the use of DeFi, blockchain or cryptocurrency for a business venture or project. You may even be studying DeFi, or simply be one of the millions of people enraptured by the opportunities and communities that DeFi has conjured. Whoever you are, I hope there is something for you here, and that the mystifying environment of DeFi becomes at least a little clearer.

ACKNOWLEDGEMENTS

I have so many people to thank for making this book happen.

First, the team at Kogan Page, and in particular Isabelle Cheng and Nick Hoar, for championing the proposal and shaping the initial draft. Thanks also to Erica Stanford, for helping me make the pitch and for all your advice (anyone reading this should check out Erica's excellent book, *Crypto Wars*).

I'd like to thank the team at Money20/20, especially Gina Clarke and Micky Tesfaye, for offering fantastic thoughts and ideas. Gina, I couldn't have done this without your support, and Micky, I can't thank you enough for talking through key points of crypto and DeFi and for sharing your expertise.

I'd like to thank everyone who gave up their time for an interview. In no particular order, thanks to Cleve Mesidor, Stani Kulechov, Anthony Day, Max Mersch, Ines Illipse, Rhomaios Ram, Alisa DiCaprio, Ricardo Correia, Tavonia Evans, Christine Parlour, Michael Chobanian, Hugo Hoyland, Charles Kerrigan and Dinesh Goel. Not every interview made it into the book, but every one was incredibly useful and I want to thank you again for making time for me. I'd also like to thank Ruth Wandhöfer, Agustin Rubini, Katharine Wooller and Carlos Martins for offering invaluable insight that helped shape the book.

There are many more people I'd like to acknowledge for being a huge help in my career and for many other reasons too: David Cox, Shan Millie, Frank Dobson, Lawrence Lever, Nadia Edwards-Dashti, Chris Welsford, Simone Koo Ishikawa, Kevin Forbes and Bijna Dasani. Also, everyone who worked with me on the Citywire audience development team.

On a personal note, thank you to my parents for so many things. One of the best parts of this experience was spending more time with you. And thanks to my brother Neil, too, again for too many things to note.

I've also been a nomad through most of this journey, so I want to extend my gratitude to: Sulman and Sophia, Oisin and Jill, Ben and Kat, Daniel Black and Oliver Ware.

A final acknowledgement to anyone who took the time to read the book. Nothing splits opinion quite like crypto and DeFi, and whatever your views I hope it's clear that I worked towards providing a balanced perspective. This industry moves at a million miles per second and I no doubt missed a few things, but hopefully you found this informative and perhaps even entertaining in parts. Despite what's usually written when crypto scandals occur, I think this whole story has a long, long way to go, and there will be so much more to write. It has already changed the face of finance forever.

01

Crypto and DeFi: Why now, and what exactly is it?

Decentralized Finance (DeFi), like any decent superhero, has an intriguing backstory. Before analysing its manifestations and the fruits of what it might become, we should take stock of the context in which it has emerged. This context could span an expanse of history, including the world's first recognized central bank, Sveriges Riksbank, established in Sweden in 1668, or the creation of monetary currency in Lydia in 600BC. From a cryptographic perspective, we could also consider the invention of Merkel Trees in 1987, or the development of hashing in 1958. However, we will focus on 2008, a tumultuous and miserable year for financial institutions, save for the scant few who brazenly (and successfully) shorted the economy.

2008 – The birth of bitcoin and a global financial crisis

2008 is a fine jump-off point for two reasons. Firstly, it was the year of the famous Bitcoin whitepaper authored by the pseudonymous Satoshi Nakamoto, which outlines the benefits of a new, digital, 'trustless' basis for money.[1] This eight-page paper, which did not emerge through an academic journal or university, would give rise to the eventual minting of a digital coin that in 2020 had a market capitalization in excess of a trillion dollars (in the first week of January 2023, it is $330 billion).

The second reason to place emphasis on 2008 is that it was a pivotal year in a global financial crisis. The economic capitulation, starting in the United States and eventually spreading throughout the world, can be directly attributed to major failures of risk management and culture within trusted financial establishments. The crash and ensuing recession would ultimately cost many citizens their financial stability, employment, businesses and retirement plans.

The downturn, the biggest since the Great Depression of 1929, was sparked by predatory mortgage lending (disproportionately targeted at ethnic minorities) and excessive risk-taking by financial institutions, and in some respects was a perfect storm of deregulation and reckless profit-making, tangled up with the dreams of aspiring homebuyers.[2] For borrowers, a lowering of the Federal Funds Rate (in essence the interest rate) from 6.5 per cent in May 2000 to 1 per cent in June 2003 had made mortgages more attainable and attractive, causing a surge in home buying. Simultaneously, there was a boom in the provision of subprime mortgage lending, allowing borrowers with poor credit history, or none at all, to get a foot on the housing ladder. Subprime mortgages had constituted about 7–8 per cent of the US mortgage market in 2000–2003, but their estimated share in 2004–2006 would jump to 18–20 per cent, while mortgage underwriting standards deteriorated.[3] Lending and borrowing had never been easier.

As lenders and borrowers were doing this, investment banks, commercial banks, hedge funds and pension funds had found a way to get in on the action via collateralized debt obligations (CDOs), which started to take off in 2001.

COLLATERALIZED DEBT OBLIGATIONS (CDOs)

CDOs, to simplify somewhat, are financial products issued by investment banks, comprising various fixed-income assets designed to pay investors a regular cash flow.

The underlying assets in CDOs in the US in the early 2000s were typically high risk and high yield, and incorporated the booming market for mortgage-backed securities. Despite the risky nature of these underlying assets, many of the CDOs containing them were assigned an AAA credit grade, a rating reserved for loans that are incredibly unlikely to be defaulted, by the three major ratings agencies: Moody's, Standard & Poor's, and Fitch Ratings. In crude terms, this meant that Wall Street and institutions across the world had invested confidently in investment packages that included hefty amounts of the mortgage debt accumulating across the US – mortgage debt being assigned at increasing speeds, to cohorts with decreasing ability to honour the terms of their agreements. What could go wrong?

As interest rates began to climb and house prices dropped (making it much harder for debtors to release equity to meet their repayments), and as debtors faltered in their repayments, the writing was on the wall. The CDO market began to crumble in 2007, starting a domino effect that would batter the derivatives market, reduce several hedge funds to dust, eliminate global investment bank Bear Stearns, and lead to the famous footage of employees leaving Lehman Brothers – at the time the US's fourth-largest investment bank – clutching boxes of their belongings as the firm filed for bankruptcy. The institutions designed to protect our economies and finances had conspired to do the opposite. Lax regulation, complicated investment structures, and more than a hint of greed, had brought an economy to its knees. It was reported that Americans had lost a total of $3.3 trillion in home equity in 2008 alone.[4]

As we know, this was not solely an American crisis. Many institutions across the globe were exposed to bad credit and contagion from the failure of major establishments, and there was also a drop-off in international trade, which fell 15 per cent between the third quarter of 2008 and the second quarter of 2009 according to the European Central Bank (an issue worsened by the globalization of supply chains).[5] To make matters worse, other nations and regions had lingering economic problems of their own. European headaches, for example, would be compounded by the Sovereign Debt Crisis. First, in 2008, Iceland's banking system collapsed, and the following year there was serious financial instability in Greece, Spain, Ireland, Italy and Portugal. These five nations had borrowed significant sums at low interest rates (there is a recurring theme here) and were unable to pay or refinance these loans when the financial crash took its toll. Also, as members of the Eurozone that shared the Euro currency, none of these nations were able to deploy monetary policy as their economies unravelled. The European Union and International Monetary Fund would end up agreeing to a €750 billion bailout package (at the time roughly $1 trillion), a rescue fund designed to save not only the nations involved, but additionally the goal for a shared currency.[6] €250 million of the package came from the International Monetary Fund, €60 billion from European Commission funding, and the remaining €440 billion comprised loan guarantees from euro area states.

The banks within these nations would be saved by state funding. In the UK, a bank rescue package of £137 billion was issued in the form of loans and new capital. €60 billion was poured into the financial sector in Spain, €64 billion in Ireland, €40 billion in the Netherlands, and €25 billion in Greece.[7] A €12 billion line of funding was made available for banks in Portugal, and Iceland nationalized its banks. As for the United States, many have referred to a trillion-dollar bailout, though attempts to ascertain a correct figure may be futile.[8] In hindsight, the general consensus is that bailout loans and payments were an effective and sensible course of action. It has been suggested that the action was effectively costless since the government loans were eventually paid back, though equally, analysis from Professor Deborah Lucas at MIT Sloan has given a detailed explanation of why the real cost to the US government was likely to be in the region of $500 billion.[9]

In shifting the initial cost from banks to the government, and accordingly the taxpayer, these decisions ensured that the worst effects of 2008 were felt most by those with the least financial security. The financial sector's reputation was further harmed when banks decided to award significant bonuses that year. In the US, the nine major banks who received bailout funds provided bonus pools totalling $32.6 billion, despite reported combined losses of $81 billion.[10] It was argued in some quarters that bonuses were designed to acknowledge the value of key employees to their respective companies, but the bonuses undeniably garnered public backlash while raising significant ethical questions. The same was true elsewhere. In the UK, the highest profile case was that of Fred Goodwin, dubbed 'Fred the Shred' by tabloid journalists, who was the chief executive of the Royal Bank of Scotland (RBS) in 2008. Despite the need for intervention and a bailout for RBS, Goodwin was reportedly paid £2.8 million upon his departure along with a £450,000 annual payout. This sum had been greater before he agreed to relinquish an additional £200,000 per annum, following public outcry.

This analysis is US- and Euro-centric (this book primarily focuses on the impact of DeFi in the US, UK and Europe), yet there were few nations that didn't feel hardship as a result of the crisis. Somewhat unfairly, some of the worst affected nations had little or nothing to do with causing it. According to data from the Carnegie Endowment for International Peace, the five nations who suffered most between September 2008 and May 2009 were Jamaica, Poland, Hungary, Argentina and Ukraine (in ascending order, with Ukraine hit hardest).[11] All five suffered currency depreciation of roughly 20 per cent or worse, and all saw the value of their equity markets halved. Other nations facing considerable economic damage, measured by currency depreciation, equity markets and bond spreads, included Ghana, Russia, Kazakhstan, Bulgaria and Mexico. Staggeringly, the Carnegie research rates the United States as the third *least* impacted nation, behind only China and Japan.

The economic earthquake in 2008, and the events leading to it, raised serious questions about the institutions that we hand responsibility to for our savings, investments and retirement plans. Could we still trust them? And what faith could we have in policymakers and regulators, who in some respects had allowed casino capitalism to run riot? These failures will not have been easy to forgive for some families. Long-term unemployment levels rose in the UK and US,[12,13] and worst of all, research covering Europe and North America directly linked 10,000 suicides to the crash.[14] Time for change?

Enter bitcoin: The first major cryptocurrency

It turns out that the crash was not the only major economic event of 2008. Serendipitously (or so it seems), Satoshi Nakamoto, whoever she, he or they are, published the whitepaper *Bitcoin: A Peer-to-Peer Electronic Cash System* (see page 1). The paper offered a vision of a new version of currency, and the first line of its abstract did a fine job of speaking to the moment:

> A purely peer-to-peer version of electronic cash would allow online payments to be sent directly from one party to another without going through a financial institution.

Satoshi's paper introduces the idea that the functions and authority of financial institutions can be replaced with lines of code, creating what some call a 'trustless' system. And by hosting our currency on a blockchain, rather than depositing it with a bank that has the ability to invest the funds on our behalf, it suggests that individuals can take control of their own financial futures. Satoshi had clearly been thinking about this in relation to the financial crisis. The first block (or Genesis block) of the Bitcoin blockchain contained a hidden message, a headline from an article in British daily *The Times*, dated 3 January 2009. It read: *Chancellor on brink of second bailout for banks.*

> Here, Bitcoin will refer to the blockchain, and bitcoin, lower case, will refer to the currency itself.

The publication of the Bitcoin whitepaper was a landmark moment for digital currency but it did not create the first digital or even cryptocurrency. The honour for first cryptocurrency goes to David Chaum's eCash, launched in 1990, following his 1983 paper *Blind Signatures for Untraceable Payments*. Chaum's pioneering step was to create the concept of a token-based currency that could be safely and privately shared between peers, though eCash would fail to achieve widespread adoption, and its parent company, DigiCash, would go bankrupt by 1998. Several other attempts emerged, including Bit Gold, Hashcash, E-Gold and B-Money. The latter, created by developer Wei Dai, is referenced in the bitcoin whitepaper, demonstrating that previous innovations helped shape the course of digital assets.

Nonetheless, the arrival of Bitcoin blew previous attempts at cryptocurrency out of the water by virtue of being built on blockchain. It also opened a window for decentralization, and although the concept is not spelled out in the Bitcoin whitepaper there are several passages to identify the prospect of a financial world with no requirement for third parties to sign off on peer-to-peer transactions. For example:

> Commerce on the Internet has come to rely almost exclusively on financial institutions serving as trusted third parties to process electronic payments. While the system works well enough for most transactions, it still suffers from the inherent weaknesses of the trust based model.
>
> What is needed is an electronic payment system based on cryptographic proof instead of trust, allowing any two willing parties to transact directly with each other without the need for a trusted third party.

A typical description of DeFi describes decentralization as a shift of power from financial giants to individuals or communities, and as such the Bitcoin whitepaper embodies this spirit. If code can begin to replace the facilities and functions of banks, so the logic goes, then maybe we don't need them in the future.

How blockchain emerged in all but name

The technological advance required to enable this, blockchain, was not originally designed as a financial tool when it was invented in 1991, nor did its creators, cryptographer Stuart Haber and scientist Scott Stornetta, refer to it as blockchain.[15] Instead, their article in the *Journal of Cryptology*, titled 'How to Time-Stamp a Digital Document', would demonstrate an automated method for certifying when a document had been created or changed. Scott Stornetta, who had worked at print and digital corporation Xerox, was inspired to create this solution upon realizing that the future for record-keeping was digital, and that accordingly we were heading to a future where all digital records could be amended or corrupted with no ability to confidently verify an original record, nor the timing of any subsequent alterations to it.[16] And so they set out to create a mechanism that ensures the accuracy and immutability of digital records.

Haber and Stornetta begin their journey towards a solution by outlining a 'naive' centralized 'digital safety-deposit box'. Using this model, when a client needs to time-stamp a document, it is transmitted to a time-stamping service (TSS), which records the date and time that the document is received, along with a copy of the document for safekeeping. The TSS then has the ability to audit any challenges to the credentials of a document by comparing the document with its own records.

This isn't a complete solution. It lacks privacy, as third parties could eavesdrop as the document is being transmitted. Similarly, the client needs to maintain the security of documents under its control and put faith in the TSS to do the same. Another issue, arguably a prescient one, is that of bandwidth and storage. Larger records require more time and expense to time-stamp. A third issue is the scope for incompetence. A copy of a document might be corrupted in transmission, lost in transmission, or incorrectly time-stamped by the TSS. Finally, and this concern becomes fundamental to Bitcoin, there are questions of trust. There is nothing in this model to prevent the TSS from colluding with a client to falsify records.

Two solutions to these problems are put forward:

1   The first is hashing. In cryptography, a hash function is used to reduce a document or message to a 'hash' (or message digest), a fixed-length message a few bytes long. If any aspect of the document is changed, a new hash is formed to represent the new version, making every version of a document verifiable by its hash and nigh-on impossible to amend (the TSS would time-stamp and certify a document's hash, rather than the document itself).

2   Haber and Stornetta also introduce the concept of linking, in which the client includes the previous (or previous sequence of) time-stamped documents when submitting a document, offering strengthened proof of the author's identity.

Hashing solves many issues but leaves one crucial stone unturned, as we remain dependent on the TSS as the sole validator of truth. If the TSS is unreliable, the system fails. Haber and Stornetta's answer to this is 'distributed trust', in which each time-stamp is certified by numerous parties, all of whom are users of the network. This method does not necessarily require 100 per cent agreement across the network, and accounts for a number of users being temporarily unavailable too, but sets a high minimum standard for verification. If most of the network verifies in good faith, the system succeeds. To extend the logic, users are further incentivized to respond truthfully as their own documents pass through the same system. A very similar framework, combining linking and verification along with additional inspiration from Adam Back's Hashcash, now underpins Bitcoin's 'proof-of-work' system for blockchain validation.[17]

The interpretation here of Haber and Stornetta's paper is not comprehensive, but what it shows is the outline of a process for secure, reliable, verifiable and unchangeable message sharing. When we consider that bitcoin and other forms of digital money are an exchange of data – after all, there is no physical bitcoin – then these ideas become incredibly valuable.

> Haber and Stornetta had considered a range of real-life applications for their system. These include verifications of intellectual property and patent claims, and time-stamping of photographs, audio and video. They also suggest its use for 'tamper-unpredictable' business documents, whereby a time-stamped amendment to a document may be incriminating.

How does Bitcoin work?

The challenge Satoshi undertook was to readminister these document verification techniques as the basis for a currency or asset, to be readily and securely exchanged. Blockchain provides a sound base from which to do this, providing the potential to validate and time-stamp transactions, and through time-stamping and hashing, verifiers can easily prevent malicious attempts to 'double-spend' the currency (all cryptocurrencies need to negate the challenge of the same coin being spent multiple times at once). Further, with the addition of new blocks, existing ones become increasingly harder to hack as this creates misalignment with the hash outputs of other blocks. Put more simply, any change to its past needs to be recognized in subsequent blocks, and this has made hacks nigh-on impossible.

There remains a problem. For Bitcoin to be capable of handling transactions at high volumes and speeds, which is a prerequisite for it handling global payments, it needs a suitable transaction validation method. In this respect, Bitcoin has a 'distributed trust' process, and this is called proof-of-work (PoW), a mechanism that was initially designed to counter spam emails.[18]

Proof-of-work in relation to Bitcoin is established through crypto mining, whereby a new block is created roughly every 10 minutes. To achieve this, mining computers (nodes) gather thousands of pending and public bitcoin transactions and collect them in a block (in 2022 this was roughly 1800–2000 per block), and these nodes then compete to find a 'proof-of-work', allowing them to add the block and receive a reward in bitcoin and transaction fees.[19] These rewards incentivize the validators and add new bitcoins to the blockchain.

The proof-of-work is attained via participation in a lottery of sorts. Miners are tasked with generating a hash value that is beneath a given hash target and their computing power is dedicated towards generating random hashes as quickly as possible until this target is met (the difficulty of reaching this target is adjusted every 2016 blocks, which takes roughly two weeks, to keep mining consistent). On occasion, multiple miners will generate valid hashes, and if this occurs the Bitcoin network will decide which miner to honour. This will usually be the miner who has carried out the most work, and therefore verified the most transactions.

The process by which miners succeed is both arbitrary and a game of chance. Even so, this resource-intensive method acts as a deterrent against malicious actors. It also guards against a 51 per cent attack, which occurs when a group of miners control more than half of a network's hash rate, enabling them to alter the blockchain, halt payments, reject new transactions, and reverse transactions that are enacted while they are in control of the chain (this could allow them to double spend coins). In short, the cost of staging such an attack is incredibly prohibitive to any attempt to hack bitcoin, and likely exceeds $10.1 billion.[20] Mining costs also prompt many would-be miners to join collective mining pools and share in the outlays and rewards. Given there are no guarantees of success, going solo often results in a financial loss.

As of 2023, the Bitcoin network is processing roughly three transactions per second (about 95 million per year).[21] By contrast, the Visa payments network processed 192.5 billion transactions in 2022.[22] Owing largely to the proof-of-work validation, the energy outlay required to achieve those 95 million transactions is considerable, too. A 2022 White House fact sheet noted that cryptoassets are responsible for 0.4–0.9 per cent of global electricity usage, with Bitcoin responsible for 60–77 per cent of this.[23] These figures do not account for the methods by which electricity is generated but are concerning regardless. Putting these issues aside, it remains true that proof-of-work provides Bitcoin with the necessary verification system to function as an asset and also, to an extent, a currency.

Why the emergence of Bitcoin is important

Distributed ledger technology, consensus verification mechanisms and cryptography don't trouble the average person's thoughts on a regular basis. Why would they? However, by combining them, Bitcoin opened the door to a new version of money that could radically change people's financial lives. It could change them by providing an internationally recognizable currency that's (notionally) beyond the control of governments and corporations, offering complete user sovereignty (crypto owners can be in full control of their assets). Also, due to its fixed supply cap of 21 million bitcoins, many argue that Bitcoin is anti-inflationary, and therefore does not lose its spending power in the same manner that government-issued fiat currency does.

In being the first cryptocurrency to achieve widespread adoption, Bitcoin also unlocked the promise introduced by earlier crypto efforts and as Satoshi writes in the whitepaper, it is 'a system for electronic transactions without relying on trust'. This shift to 'trustlessness' becomes crucial to DeFi. It implies that the authority of governments, central banks and large financial intermediaries can be eroded, possibly even eradicated at some point. It posits that effective code might immediately, flawlessly and cost-effectively handle functions that had previously been handled by institutions and the people within them.

Satoshi also nods at the future of crypto and how it can be improved, finishing the paper by observing that consensus can be used to enforce any rules and incentives that are needed to uphold the system. While it remains true that the value of Bitcoin is not based on any underlying asset, save for the strength of the network and the amounts that people are willing to pay for it, there have historically been many other currencies to emerge with no backing from any asset of value.

And now to go back to 2008 and its aftermath. It is fortuitous yet fitting that the publication of Satoshi's work and the minting of the first bitcoin block, the Genesis block, should coincide with a generation and industry-defining economic crisis. If we move towards a new system, could there be lasting support for it? In the wake of financial mismanagement, bailouts and bonuses, quite possibly. A 2018 YouGov survey found that 10 years after the crisis, 66 per cent of British adults did not trust banks to work in the best interests of society.[24] In the US, 2021 Gallup polls show that American confidence in institutions (in general) languished, with only 33 per cent of respondents reporting a 'great deal' or 'quite a lot' of confidence in banks.[25] Interestingly, of all the institutions noted by Gallup, trust in banks is one of the few polls that does not skew relative to political views. Although confidence has risen from its 21 per cent nadir in 2012, it cannot be reported that the public is satisfied, nor does it seem that distrust is confined to a particular worldview.

The next decade: Between bitcoin and DeFi

The events of 2008 occur ten years prior to the coining of the term DeFi and mark the start of an unfathomable journey for Bitcoin.

Famously, the first recorded incident of Bitcoin being exchanged for a physical product occurred on May 22, 2010, when Floridian Laszlo Hanyecz purchased two pizzas from a local Papa John's branch for 10,000 bitcoins. This event has become something of an annual celebration for the Bitcoin community, as the current-day value of 10,000 bitcoins in dollar terms has accumulated into the hundreds of millions (its present-day value is updated daily by a Twitter feed). However, Bitcoin's anti-authoritarian streak, and properties, would ensure that its primary use case was far-removed from pepperoni. It would instead find its home on the dark web marketplace, Silk Road, a place where customers could purchase illegal drugs, fake IDs, social security numbers, second-hand credit cards, counterfeit qualifications and 3D printed goods, including guns.[26] It's even said that assassins could be hired.

Silk Road was shut down by the US government in 2013 (subsequent, less successful, iterations emerged), with 144,336 bitcoins belonging to its founder Ross Ulbricht seized in the process.[27] Many consider this incident a crucial landmark in Bitcoin's journey, as it shunted the currency, now proven viable within a marketplace, away from the underworld towards a more sustainable future.

DISCLAIMER

While it would be reductive to claim that the rise of Bitcoin was a direct result of the financial crash, the link between the two offers a valuable and relevant platform for analysis. It is important to consider that crypto and DeFi have arrived at a time of increased technological proficiency and institutional mistrust, not to mention a trend towards lives being increasingly lived online.

The elephant in the room is the soaring price of Bitcoin and other cryptoassets, and the accompanying dreams of riches that brought many to crypto. Whatever the goals and aspirations of those who helped kickstart cryptoassets, and regardless of how incorruptible their beliefs may be, cryptoassets and DeFi are now fuelled and sustained, in part, by dreamers, scammers, gamblers and chancers. DeFi promises Wall Street without regulation. Any speculator might ask themselves if they believe that to be a good thing, and if investing their own assets, whether the odds are in their favour if they speculate within such a system.

Despite this, 2014 was no less jarring and included the bankruptcy of Bitcoin's first major exchange, Mt. Gox, which may have been accountable for nearly 70 per cent of all Bitcoin transactions at one point.[28] The exchange had allowed people to buy and sell bitcoin using bank transfers but was riddled with security issues and almost comical mismanagement (while Mt. Gox encountered legal battles and complaints from customers about months-long withdrawal periods, CEO Mark Karpèles was reportedly preoccupied with launching a Bitcoin cafe at the Mt. Gox headquarters).[29] As its prominence grew, Mt. Gox became a prime target for hackers, who would reportedly take 650,000–850,000 bitcoin from the exchange.[30] In brighter news for cryptocurrency, the price of bitcoin would gradually begin to recover after this 2014 slump, and the year would also mark the launch of Ethereum, which will be discussed in more detail in the next chapter.

Ethereum brought with it the ICO (initial coin offering) craze and the launch of thousands of new cryptocurrencies. These were predominantly failures and many were launched with dubious intentions, yet this was barely a deterrent for new money flowing into the market. By 17 December 2017, the price of bitcoin would reach a high of $20,000, elevating the currency to mainstream status and attracting a new wave of both retail (individual) and institutional investors. Its price would drop 80 per cent from its peak the following year; yet another 'correction' that Bitcoin would recover from. Importantly, the words cryptocurrency and bitcoin were now being discussed in bars, pubs, cafes and internet forums across the globe.

Our attention will shift away from bitcoin and its blockchain now. While Bitcoin put cryptoassets on the map and marks an evolution in digital money, its functionality is limited and does not provide a solid base for an entire system of DeFi. (Even so, Bitcoin can still flow through DeFi protocols in a wrapped format, and its relevance to the overall notion of finance being decentralized remains significant.) Given its notorious volatility, its use as a currency, even, is contentious. Instead, we will focus on Ethereum and the Ethereum blockchain, which enables an entirely new system of peer-to-peer exchange, including lending, trading, savings, and the creation of derivatives. This is where DeFi, the internet's answer to Wall Street, was originally built.

References

1   S Nakamoto. Bitcoin: a peer-to-peer electronic cash system, 2008, www.ussc. gov/sites/default/files/pdf/training/annual-national-training-seminar/2018/ Emerging_Tech_Bitcoin_Crypto.pdf (archived at https://perma.cc/DN3H-XUUH)

2   Economic Policy Institute. Subprime mortgages are nearly double for Hispanics and African Americans, 2008, www.epi.org/publication/ webfeatures_snapshots_20080611/ (archived at https://perma.cc/9E5U-UBJD)

3   M Simkovic. Competition and crisis in mortgage securitization, Indiana Law Journal, 2011, 88, doi:doi.org/10.2139/ssrn.1924831 (archived at https:// perma.cc/D8UV-KTQE)

4   Zillow. Americans lose $1.4 trillion in home values in Q4; more than was lost in all of 2007, Zillow, 2009, zillow.mediaroom.com/2009-02-03-Americans-Lose-1-4-Trillion-in-Home-Values-in-Q4-More-Than-was-Lost-in-All-of-2007 (archived at https://perma.cc/4T4Q-LDTU)

5   European Central Bank. Monthly bulletin, October 2010, www.ecb.europa.eu/ pub/pdf/mobu/mb201010en.pdf (archived at https://perma.cc/4QYL-UFEH)

6   France 24. EU and IMF agree 750 billion-euro fund for crisis-hit eurozone members, 2010, www.france24.com/en/20100510-rehn-salgado-eurozone-720-billion-bailout-fund-crisis-eu-package (archived at https://perma.cc/ LLQ2-94Y9)

7   Reuters Staff. FACTBOX-What has happened to more than 30 bailed-out European banks, Reuters, 21 August 2015, www.reuters.com/article/europe-banks-bailouts-idUKL5N10W0XJ20150821 (archived at https://perma.cc/ 5JPL-3K56)

8   M Taibbi. Turns out that trillion-dollar bailout was, in fact, real, Rolling Stone, 2019, www.rollingstone.com/politics/politics-features/2008-financial-bailout-809731/ (archived at https://perma.cc/R6K6-TKNA)

9   D Lucas. Measuring the cost of bailouts, Annual Review of Financial Economics, 2019, 11 (1), 85–108, doi:https://doi.org/10.1146/annurev-financial-110217-022532

10 L Story and E Dash. Bankers reaped lavish bonuses during bailouts, The New York Times, 30 July 2009, www.nytimes.com/2009/07/31/business/31pay.html (archived at https://perma.cc/933H-G43T)

11 U Dadush, L Falcao and S Ali. The unequal impact of the economic crisis, Carnegie Endowment for International Peace, 2009, carnegieendowment. org/2009/07/09/unequal-impact-of-economic-crisis-pub-23385 (archived at https://perma.cc/L7JS-2YBN)

12 J Kollewe and A Seager. Sharp rise in unemployment as financial crisis hits jobs market, The Guardian, 2008, www.theguardian.com/business/2008/ oct/15/unemploymentdata-recession (archived at https://perma.cc/QFS4-5ZR3)

13 J Weinberg. The Great Recession and its aftermath, Federal Reserve History, 2013, www.federalreservehistory.org/essays/great-recession-and-its-aftermath (archived at https://perma.cc/V2UM-G3D6)

14 J Gallagher. Recession 'led to 10,000 suicides', BBC News, 12 June 2014, www.bbc.co.uk/news/health-27796628 (archived at https://perma.cc/FGB9-LES8)

15 S Haber and W S Stornetta. How to time-stamp a digital document. Journal of Cryptology, 1991, 3 (2), doi:https://doi.org/10.1007/bf00196791 (archived at https://perma.cc/3F5K-NXU4)

16 V Bharathan. Blockchain was born 20 years before Bitcoin, Forbes, 2020, www.forbes.com/sites/vipinbharathan/2020/06/01/the-blockchain-was-born-20-years-before-bitcoin/?sh=58b0d9ef5d71 (archived at https://perma.cc/BJV2-EDWB)

17 A Back. Hashcash – a denial of service counter-measure, Hashcash, 2002, www.hashcash.org/papers/hashcash.pdf (archived at https://perma.cc/VZT9-KC7G)

18 C Dwork and M Naor. Pricing via processing or combatting junk mail. Advances in Cryptology — CRYPTO' 92, 2019, pp.139–147. doi:https://doi.org/10.1007/3-540-48071-4_10 (archived at https://perma.cc/A4E7-PPJW)

19 Blockchain.com I Charts – average transactions per block, www.blockchain.com/explorer/charts/n-transactions-per-block (archived at https://perma.cc/TBV4-S2QQ)

20 J Frankenfield. 51% attack: definition, who is at risk, example, and cost, Investopedia, 2023, www.investopedia.com/terms/1/51-attack.asp (archived at https://perma.cc/7R4X-49FZ)

21 Blockchain.com I Charts – transaction rate per second, www.blockchain.com/explorer/charts/transactions-per-second (archived at https://perma.cc/6JWM-UZJ2)

22 Visa. Annual report 2022, annualreport.visa.com/financials/default.aspx (archived at https://perma.cc/HPL3-7Z3B)

23 The White House. FACT SHEET: climate and energy implications of crypto-assets in the United States, 2022, The White House, www.whitehouse.gov/ostp/news-updates/2022/09/08/fact-sheet-climate-and-energy-implications-of-crypto-assets-in-the-united-states/ (archived at https://perma.cc/MXE9-QS84)

24 L White. British public don't trust banks 10 years after crisis, survey finds, Reuters, 16 August 2018, www.reuters.com/article/uk-britain-banks-idUKKBN1L11EL (archived at https://perma.cc/838N-FZTS)

25 M Brenan. Americans' confidence in major U.S. institutions dips, gallup.com, 2021, news.gallup.com/poll/352316/americans-confidence-major-institutions-dips.aspx (archived at https://perma.cc/9UTP-3WNA)

26 J Bausch. 9 of the weirdest and most immoral things you can get on the Dark Web, Electronic Products, April 10 2015, www.electronicproducts.com/9-of-the-weirdest-and-most-immoral-things-you-can-get-on-the-dark-web/ (archived at https://perma.cc/4UG7-UUFK)

27 E Cheng. US government misses out on $600 million payday by selling dirty bitcoins too early, CNBC, 2017, www.cnbc.com/2017/10/03/us-government-misses-out-on-600-million-payday-by-selling-dirty-bitcoins-too-early.html (archived at https://perma.cc/HF8W-HKL8)

28 M Kutylowski and J Vaidya. Computer security – ESORICS 2014: 19th European symposium on research in computer security, Wroclaw, Poland, September 7-11, 2014, Proceedings, Part II, Google Books, google.co.uk/books?id=sOhKBAAAQBAJ&pg=PA314&dq=mt.+gox+70&hl=en&sa=X&redir_esc=y#v=onepage&q=mt.%20gox%2070&f=false (archived at https://perma.cc/6PN9-UQBZ)

29 R McMillan. The inside story of Mt. Gox, bitcoin's $460 million disaster, Wired, 2014, www.wired.com/2014/03/bitcoin-exchange/ (archived at https://perma.cc/BZ3V-EHYH)

30 American Bankruptcy Institute. Bankrupt bitcoin exchange Mt. Gox begins to pay back account holders in Bitcoin, n.d., www.abi.org/feed-item/bankrupt-bitcoin-exchange-mt-gox-begins-to-pay-back-account-holders-in-bitcoin (archived at https://perma.cc/52DF-FX3D)

02

Ethereum and DeFi: The creation of crypto's financial ecosystem

The success of the Bitcoin blockchain demonstrated that cryptocurrency was viable in modern finance, and that currency could be transferred reliably from one address to another. It also prompted onlookers, especially programmers, to ask whether the innovation was being fully utilized. Could blockchains be capable of handling more complex transactions, or recreating and restructuring the financial instruments used by professional traders, investors, insurers and more? Vitalik Buterin would take up this challenge in 2013, building out the concept for a new blockchain, Ethereum.

Outlining his vision the following year, along with fellow founders Gavin Wood, Charles Hoskinson, Joseph Lubin and Anthony Di Iorio, Vitalik explained that distributed ledger technology could indeed make use of coding to execute a wide range of financial agreements.[1] Vitalik would comment that his new blockchain might facilitate hedging contracts, derivatives, savings wallets, wills, sub-currencies, and potentially, in time, certain types of employment contracts. Non-financial uses were suggested, too, namely online voting and decentralized governance.

These new applications are made possible through 'smart contracts', an idea conceived in 1994 by computer scientist and legal scholar Nick Szabo, who outlined how computerized protocols could execute the terms of a contract (Szabo is one of many people rumoured to be Satoshi Nakamoto. He has repeatedly denied these claims).[2] These protocols, which are now deemed capable of forming the basis for legally accepted contracts in numerous jurisdictions, allow things like payment terms, ownership rights, confidentiality and enforcement of an agreement to be coded into peer-to-peer agreements.

Why is this not possible on the Bitcoin blockchain? The answer rests with addresses, which are used to identify the sender or receiver of cryptocurrency on the network. With Bitcoin, all addresses are externally-owned accounts (EOAs), consisting of a private–public key pair. The private key, made visible only to the owner, is used to withdraw currency. The public key is derived from the private key (through public key cryptography) and, in contrast, is visible to all so that senders know where to send coins. Users of Ethereum also have EOA addresses but importantly, the network allows for a second type of address, known as a contract account.

A contract account effectively houses smart contracts deployed to the Ethereum network. These accounts are controlled by code and will only send transactions if prompted to by an EOA.[3] Once triggered, the code in the contract account will perform an action or multiple actions, and in doing so, can mimic certain financial instruments that have historically been provided by regulated providers. This makes DeFi possible, though contract accounts need to be created with care. Once a smart contract is deployed on the Ethereum network, it cannot be altered. Bluntly, bad code creates bad contracts.

Being able to code activities, contracts and finance into a blockchain is intriguing. However, a peer-to-peer decentralized platform does nothing to democratize finance if it can only be used by a select few with specialized knowledge. Vitalik pinpointed this problem in his whitepaper, and countered it through the concept of decentralized apps, also known as dApps, which run on top of the blockchain network and add frontend user interfaces to underlying smart contracts. These interfaces make smart contracts accessible and vastly improve the likelihood of widespread adoption, which is crucial for any peer-to-peer network.

In the same year that Vitalik published his Ethereum paper, David Johnston et al produced work detailing the definition of a dApp.[4] They note that dApps should be completely open source and anonymous, with no entity having majority ownership, and that changes should only be made in accordance with the consensus of users. They also state that data and records should be stored in a public and decentralized blockchain, and that dApps should use a cryptographic token, which may be bitcoin, for instance, or a token that is native to the dApp.

How dApps and ICOs changed the game

dApp creators did not wait long to get started. MakerDAO, formed in 2014 (but launched in 2017), would create several key projects, leading to achievements such as the launch of Ethereum's first decentralized exchange, OasisDex (named Oasis.app in 2016), and the issuance of the first collateral-backed and decentralized stablecoin, DAI, in 2017. It also introduced a governance token, MKR, which allows holders to govern DAI protocol and maintain the stability and transparency of the token. Additionally, Maker made it possible for borrowers and lenders to participate in collateralized debt positions (CDPs), providing an example of how DeFi could recreate financial instruments available in centralized markets (in a CDP, borrowers must post sufficient collateral to repay a debt should they become otherwise unable to do so. A common example is home equity release, in which a property is used as collateral against a debt position).

The importance of these tools is amplified by the open nature of the Ethereum blockchain and the interoperability of the protocols within it. Components within DeFi are often referred to as money legos, referring to how they can be slotted together to create new applications. In contrast to centralized innovations, where an entity may intend to singularly profit from a new product or concept, the entire blockchain network notionally benefits when a new money lego is created.

As a side point, it is important to distinguish between CDPs and the CDOs that crashed the economy in 2008 – in a CDP, the full loan amount is staked upfront, meaning that lenders will not be left out of pocket should the borrower lose the ability to repay a debt with other funds. A CDO, meanwhile, is a structured and asset-backed security, including debt of varying types and risk levels. Investors will be out of pocket if debt obligations are not met.

Maker was not alone in seeing the value of dApps and smart contracts, and several other decentralized projects worked on breakthroughs, too. This enthusiasm, or at least curiosity, was shared by numerous institutions and corporations that the disruptors were hoping to displace. International banks, asset managers, big tech and multinational corporations formed groups to explore new opportunities in smart contracts and blockchain, including the R3 Consortium, Digital Asset, the Enterprise Ethereum Alliance, and The Hyperledger Foundation. Many believe that this heavyweight support was the catalyst for a meteoric rise in the value of Ethereum's native token, Ether, from $8.19 per token on 1 January 2017 to $754.84 exactly a year later.

There were several other reasons for heightened interest in Ether. As bitcoin began to take off in value, investors turned to Ether as a means to diversify their portfolios and gain varied exposure to the emergent asset class. We can reasonably deduce that this was largely new money; 83 per cent of Ether purchases had been made in Bitcoin in 2016, but as Ether's price increased the following year, this had dropped to 32 per cent. Investment was flowing more heavily from fiat currencies.[5] Another factor, not without controversy, was the rising prominence of initial coin offerings (ICOs).

INITIAL COIN OFFERINGS (ICOs)

ICOs are crypto's answer to initial public offerings (IPOs) in traditional finance, where a private company 'floats' and sells its first shares on the public market, usually raising substantial sums in the process. ICOs, by contrast, involve a sale of tokens to fund a decentralized project. With the purchase of tokens, buyers access a share in the success of a project and may also be conferred certain utilities such as governance rights.

Throughout 2017 and 2018, there would be a mesmerizing salvo of ICOs owing largely to the fact that anyone, within reason, could raise one thanks to the development of the ERC20 token standard on Ethereum. The standardization given by ERC20, an independently monitored contract, had created a template of sorts for token production. Despite the risk that this introduced to token investment, it also gave cryptocurrencies, protocols and organizations a promising new route towards funding. In ideal scenarios, many of which have occurred, investments can pile into projects that are believed to have serious potential to benefit the ecosystem. Potential, of course, is not always fulfilled.

From here, it is likely that some confusion will be caused by the use of the terms DeFi and crypto. Typically, crypto refers to cryptoassets, and DeFi refers to the financial ecosystem through which cryptoassets flow. As we'll see later, there are also centralized methods (CeFi) for transacting with crypto. There are, however, times when crypto may refer to the entire ecosystem. This is convenient in situations where CeFi is included.

As we can see, smart contracts, finance dApps, institutional interest, rising Bitcoin prices and ICOs sent Ether to new heights. That said, it would be remiss not to offer a passing mention to CryptoKitties, a dApp game involving the trading and breeding of cartoon cats with transactions carried out in Ether. In late December 2017, rampant demand within the CryptoKitties marketplace considerably slowed activity on Ethereum, provoking genuine concern about its scalability and speed.[6] The popularity of the game would fizzle out in the following years and its growth phase did not even span ten days, but for a time CryptoKitties were responsible for over a tenth of Ethereum network traffic and they ultimately instigated tens of millions of dollars in transactions (the most expensive CryptoKitty, named Dragon, sold for $170,000).[7]

This short-lived phenomenon signposted future destinations for crypto. For instance, it demonstrated the first major use case for non-fungible tokens (NFTs), which will be discussed in depth later, and it arguably presented proof of Ether's functionality for frictionless trading. It also, unexpectedly, outlined the need for developers to consider wealth distribution and inequality within an in-game economy – early purchasers of CryptoKitties had access to far greater revenue streams than those who arrived later. In the research paper published by Frontiers in Physics, Xin-Jian Jiang and Xiao Fan Liu would observe that the increasing revenue gaps caused people to lose interest in the game, and eventually leave.

Jiang and Liu may well have been describing a game of Monopoly, and some may consider this a metaphor or warning for decentralized finance. To be clear, traditional finance is not excelling on this front either.

DeFi begins!

In 2018, decentralized finance was clearly in full swing but 'DeFi' as a term was yet to be coined. That changed in August of that year, when a Telegram chat between Ethereum developers and entrepreneurs, including Brendan Forster, Inje Yeo and Blake Henderson, turned to the topic of naming the growing movement and development of open financial applications on the blockchain. After some deliberation, and suggestions including Open Horizon, Lattice Network, and the less than snappy Open Financial Protocols, the group settled on DeFi, with its likeness to the word 'defy' cited as a reason.[8]

DeFi now had a name and had started to find its swagger. A new host of DeFi protocols would emerge, with names such as Compound, Uniswap, Aave, Yam Finance and Synthetix achieving a reasonable degree of brand recognition (several protocols and their DeFi creations will be discussed later). In turn, this proliferation of dApps and money legos would convert the concept of DeFi into a fully-fledged system, albeit one in its infancy, and usher in a new wave of investment and ideation.

This inspired considerable growth in DeFi and to understand this growth we should contemplate the TVL (total value locked), measuring the value of assets locked within DeFi protocols. According to TVL aggregator DeFiLlama (other aggregators are available and figures vary between providers), measurable TVL was just beneath $500 million at the start of 2019. This figure would remain steady, certainly by crypto standards, until 2020. And then things got interesting.

2020 began in a relatively calm and positive manner. TVL crossed the $1 billion mark for the first time, major protocols continued to improve, and the market grew despite the February double-hack of borrowing, lending and margin trading protocol bZx. In March, however, the Covid-19 pandemic would wipe significant value from all markets, centralized and decentralized alike. Economic uncertainty and national lockdowns of varying strictness eventually triggered a 'Black Thursday' for DeFi on 12 March, and between the 12th and 13th many cryptoassets fell in value by 50–60 per cent, with Ether dropping from $193 to $95 in less than 24 hours.[9]

This decline presented DeFi with its first serious stress test and it did not emerge unscathed. Network traffic again caused delays for Ethereum users as they reacted to the unfolding chaos. The frustration caused by this was not insignificant, as users attempted to trade their assets for stablecoins or increase their collateral on lending protocols (to prevent the liquidation of existing collateral). This was yet another reminder of Ethereum's scaling problems, and the rising transaction fees (gas fees) that accompanied the flurry of activity also prompted a moment for reflection. MakerDAO was engulfed in controversy too as its price oracle, designed to supply its protocols with accurate real-time asset valuations, reported an incorrect price for ETH/USD. For a short time, people were able to successfully bid 0 DAI for Ether collateral. More than $4 million of Ether was lost from Maker accounts.

Despite taking a battering, DeFi would emerge stronger from Black Thursday. Just two months later there would be a 'DeFi Summer', brought on by new DeFi improvements and in particular yield farming (often referred to as liquidity mining).

YIELD FARMING / LIQUIDITY MINING

Yield farming is a process whereby asset owners lend their tokens to a DeFi platform such as Compound, Aave and Curve, in return for a passive income. In doing so, they provide liquidity to various DeFi markets, helping to maintain them and improving token availability for borrowers.

This newfound function, promising far superior rates to the dismal ones on offer from bank accounts in many nations at the time, encouraged a serious acceleration in TVL. Other dApps would build upon this and Yearn Finance did so by providing a yield optimization protocol to automatically switch yield farmers to more profitable opportunities.

The DeFi summer also dished up an insight into the possible nature of decentralized competition, as pseudonymous developer Chef Nomi forked the Uniswap code (effectively copying its protocol) to create a clone competitor, SushiSwap. The forking and cloning was not necessarily against the ethos of decentralization, but the 'vampire attack' that SushiSwap launched thereafter perhaps was. A vampire attack, in simple terms, occurs when a DeFi protocol offers incentives to attract investors from another platform to its own. SushiSwap was able to do this by offering rewards in its SUSHI tokens to anyone depositing tokens from UniSwap's liquidity pool into SushiSwap. It also moved to maintain its growing liquidity pool by encouraging people to stake their SUSHI (staking offers interest payments to people who lock up their tokens for a given period), sending a portion of the protocol's fee revenue to those who did so. In sum, SushiSwap copied Uniswap's tool and paid its users to come across to its platform.

At a glance, this incident was bad news for DeFi. Regardless of anyone's views on vampire attacks, protocols rely on deep liquidity pools to fully function, and the fragmentation of liquidity pools across protocols is not typically a good thing. Nonetheless, the vampire attack attracted new investors to both exchanges, and the TVL of both Uniswap and SushiSwap would benefit; SushiSwap's by more than $800 million, and Uniswap's by almost $3 billion. There was another unusual benefit for Uniswap. As people caught on to SushiSwap's offer, many would use Uniswap for the first time in order to get in on the action.

The DeFi Summer had ignited DeFi markets, and $15 billion was locked in by the end of 2020. Again, other factors would drive money into DeFi such as the quadrupling of Bitcoin's price in 2020 and renewed institutional interest. As lockdowns took their toll, it is also possible that boredom or long-term financial anxieties drove people towards new investment opportunities. While this is tricky to prove outright, there are indications that it is true. A Charles Schwab survey of 500 retail investors found that 15 per cent began playing the market in 2020, and to speak more directly to crypto, UK-based crypto app Ziglu claims that transaction values and new customer numbers grew during this period.[10] [11]

DeFi made its mark in 2020, but 2021 saw its success truly explode as TVL reached $180 billion in early December. As ever, the sublime and the ridiculous were hand-in-hand and the biggest crypto story of the year, quite possibly, was the NFT boom. NFTs had already been influential during the CryptoKitties craze but this time the impact was greater by magnitudes, as attention turned towards their value proposition.

WHAT IS AN NFT?

NFTs are unique digital receipts that cannot be altered or copied and can be used as proof of ownership and identity for a wide range of things. They are stored on blockchains, can represent partial or whole ownership of an asset, and through the use of smart contracts can be programmed to carry out a range of functionalities when ownership is transferred. For example, NFTs can be coded to pay resale royalties to an original creator. In this initial boom, their value was largely realized through profile pictures and art.

NFT sales would hit $17.6 billion in 2021, and this occurred despite the fact that images 'owned' by an NFT can be copied and used by anyone, and that many of the most popular markets were for 2D JPEG images.[12] The most popular NFTs of this time, including Bored Apes and CryptoPunks, received celebrity endorsements and received widespread attention. The new trend also shot a small number of artists into the headlines, such as relatively unknown (at the time) artist Mike Winkelmann, AKA Beeple. Beeple would sell the first 'purely digital NFT-based artwork', *The First 5,000 Days*, for $69.3 million at a Christie's auction. A former Christie's auctioneer, Charles Allsopp, was reported as saying that the sale of NFTs made 'no sense'.[13]

2022 – A year of reckoning

After the excitement and hedonism of DeFi's emergence, 2022 would provide a wake-up call for those with a 'line goes up' mentality due to four events. In turn, these would be a fizzling out of the NFT buzz, a hack of the Ronin Network, the collapse of the Luna Network, and the breathtaking demise of the world's second-largest centralized crypto exchange, FTX. By 1 January 2023, the DeFi market was a quarter of the size that it had been a year prior, a development that would concern any investor or indeed any author committed to writing a book on the topic.

The NFT story is relatively straightforward. The initial mania wore off, and trading volumes in September of 2022 would be 97 per cent lower than those in January.[14] Sure, former US President Donald Trump raised over $5 million with an NFT collection released in December, but across the board there was a drop in valuations and activity, coinciding with challenging macroeconomic conditions and the falling value of major cryptocurrencies.[15]

The Ronin hack, involving an exploit of a blockchain 'bridge' that allows users to transfer assets between crypto networks, raised a range of serious issues; not least because it involved the theft of

$615 million worth of Ether and USDC tokens from the Ronin Network, home to popular blockchain game Axie Infinity.[16] DeFi insiders noted that the attack had occurred due to a reliance on a centralized 'proof-of-stake' (PoS) validation system on Ronin. PoS offers benefits in speed, cost and energy efficiency, but in operating a network with only nine validators, hackers had only needed to control five to take control.

While cryptoland bemoaned the lack of decentralization that had encouraged the hack, others were eager to highlight that billions more had been hacked from crypto in 2022, and that regulators should step in.[17] The Ronin hack had also carried potential for a major international incident as it was linked to a North Korean state-backed collective named Lazarus Group. Thankfully, World War Three did not materialize but it was reported that the hackers had successfully laundered $17 million through centralized exchanges before using a 'mixing service', Tornado Cash, to conceal their actions.

2022 had provided its answer to the Tulip Mania of the 1630s and offered up a huge and politically sensitive heist, yet silly season had only just begun. Attention now turns towards the confusing decline of the Luna Network and its algorithmic Terra stablecoin (UST). First, some context. Luna and UST were sister tokens on the Luna blockchain. UST was designed to match the value of the US dollar, and Luna was used for payments on the network, transaction validation, governance and maintaining UST's peg. Luna would be a breakout success, climbing from less than a dollar in early 2021 to a value of $116 in April 2022, making numerous people wealthy almost overnight, and earning notoriety for outspoken co-founder Do Kwon.

Stablecoins are a crucial part of the DeFi ecosystem. They are designed to match the value of a fiat currency and offer a less volatile alternative to making payments with other cryptoassets. They are usually backed by low-risk investments and fiat currency to ensure that they can be redeemed at the same value as the fiat equivalent.

Luna did not gain value for no reason. For a time, those who staked UST on the Anchor platform were offered annual yields of 20 per cent and the only way to create UST was to burn Luna. With this injection of demand, it did not take long for the value of Luna to rise sharply, and so long as UST maintained its dollar peg, $1 worth of Luna could be traded for 1 UST at all times. There is reason to pause here. Algorithmic stablecoins were largely untested, and UST had no USD backstop and instead was dependent on code, market activity and billions in bitcoin reserves; and yes, 20 per cent returns in any scenario warrant close inspection.

An obvious Ponzi scheme then? Many thought otherwise, and the mental gymnastics required to reach this position were not spectacular. Kwon's company, Terraform Labs, had allayed such fears by raising significant capital ($200 million) from investment firms, and in response to the Ponzi accusations, he likened the 20 per cent yield offering to loss-making growth plans deployed by other companies at the time. The initial yield giveaway was no different to amassing debt to fund an expansion, which could be strategically beneficial. Those inclined to agree could readily identify companies such as Uber, WeWork and Airbnb, who had all prioritized growth over profit.[18,19] All was well until May 7, when more than $2 billion of UST was removed from Anchor and large amounts of it sold. This may have simply been cynical (but effective) short selling, or it could have been a malicious attack on Terra or something else entirely. The price of UST dropped to $0.91, causing a significant problem for a stablecoin supposedly pegged to the dollar; 91 cents of UST could now be traded for $1 of Luna, and this created a frenzied selloff of UST and further drops in its value, triggering a 'death spiral' in Luna. By the time the spiral had played out, the Luna token was practically worthless and the network had suffered $40 billion in losses.[20] The rest of the crypto market (not to be confused with the DeFi market here) in turn lost an estimated $300 billion.[21]

CeFi AND THE GROWTH OF CRYPTO

By this point, centralized finance (CeFi) had established itself as part of the crypto universe. CeFi platforms usually resemble TradFi offerings to some extent, are regulated, and allow users to buy cryptoassets with fiat currencies. They also have centralized ownership structures with identifiable leaders.

The contagion from the Terra collapse brought down a number of multi-billion dollar enterprises, causing serious harm to investors and dragging crypto's reputation through the mud. Crypto hedge fund Three Arrows Capital (3AC) was ordered to liquidate, and as it did so people began to question the governance of its co-founders, Su Zhu and Kyle Davies, who had grown increasingly ostentatious as the firm grew. Besides blowing $50 million on a yacht named Much Wow (a Dogecoin reference) and alienating most of their friends, Zhu and Davies had lost sight of compliance and made a string of disastrous investments (in particular their position in the Grayscale Bitcoin Trust) as they tried to counteract losses inflicted by the falling Bitcoin price.[22] This strategy culminated in a $200 million investment in Luna, an act of desperate gamblers doubling down on a bad beat. When Luna blew up and lenders began asking for their money back, 3AC was too far gone. There are several footnotes to this story. Some believe that Zhu and Davies had borrowed money from criminals to pay their debts, which may explain why they eventually went into hiding. Executives at crypto exchanges would also later find that the 3AC hedge fund hadn't hedged any of its investments.

The next big departure was Voyager. Many believed Voyager to be a credible crypto lending platform, yet it quickly became clear it could not retrieve the $650 million that it had loaned to 3AC.[23] Celsius also fell within days, owing $4.7 billion to its users while having a $1.2 billion hole in its balance sheet.[24] To compound the woes of investors, Celsius had written in its terms and conditions that transfers of digital assets to its platform constituted a loan to Celsius.

Given that Celsius had offered no collateral to match the deposits, users had essentially made unsecured loans and found themselves with no obvious legal recourse.

With three major collapses in so little time, had crypto had its Lehman Brothers moment? You'd think so, but 2022 had saved its best until last. Step forward American whizz kid Sam Bankman-Fried, or SBF, CEO of cryptocurrency exchange FTX and for a time the white knight of the industry, whose legend had grown through actions such as playing online game League of Legends during a successful pitch to VC firm Sequoia Capital (Sequoia would become the lead investor in a $1 billion funding round).[25] In August 2022, while crypto firms crashed left, right and centre, FTX had apparently charted a course for success, and SBF would appear on the front cover of *Fortune* magazine alongside an unironic question: 'The Next Warren Buffett?' We were closer to receiving the answer than reporters could have hoped.

It would take ten days for FTX to capitulate, starting with a 2 November report by CoinDesk highlighting an irregularity on the balance sheet of hedge fund Alameda Research, FTX's sister company.[26] The two entities, both led by SBF, were supposed to be sufficiently distinct with FTX operating as an exchange and Alameda as a trading firm. However, the balance sheet showed that one-third of Alameda's assets, reportedly worth $5 billion, were attributed to holdings of the FTT token, the native token of the FTX exchange.

Four days later, Binance, the largest centralized crypto exchange in the market, sold $529 million FTT tokens – the entirety of its FTT holdings – citing risk management as motivation (intriguingly, Binance sold its stake in FTX in 2021 and was partially remunerated in FTT). In a now-familiar turn of events, the value of FTT fell 80 per cent in two days as investors rushed to the exit, requesting withdrawals totalling $6 billion. SBF turned to outside investors for a rescue fund, and when that failed, he turned to Changpeng Zao (CZ), CEO of Binance. This fleeting hope was dashed when CZ pulled out of the deal due to concerns about the handling of client money.

FTX filed for bankruptcy on 11 November, with SBF replaced as CEO by experienced restructuring expert John Ray III. This was not the first high-profile role for court-appointed Ray, who had carried out similar duties when recovering assets for those stung by the scandalous collapse of Enron. Considering the notoriety of Enron's unravelling, Ray's FTX bankruptcy filing was eye-catching, as he declared the extent of FTX's failures to be both unprecedented and the worst failure of corporate controls that he'd seen.[27]

And just like that, the crypto market cap had dropped to its lowest value since the start of 2021. The year was not completely bereft of reasons to be optimistic though. On 6 September, Ethereum successfully completed 'The Merge' and switched from a PoW validation system to PoS, an action that the Ethereum Foundation would liken to hot-swapping the engine on a spaceship mid-flight.[28] Time will tell if this new method is as robust as hoped, but the 99+ per cent drop in Ethereum's energy usage offers hope of a sustainable future for cryptoassets.

Where do we go from here?

This madcap flurry of activity puts crypto at a crossroads. There are significant reasons for concern as crypto, a largely unregulated market (and DeFi in particular is unregulated), is now associated with scams, hacks, major investment losses, grifters and outlandish governance. To those not immersed in the cryptosphere, it may seem as though the momentum has gone or at the very least that someone needs to step in and rid it of its worst excesses. There is also a very understandable outcry that financial experimentations of this scale were allowed to run riot, and this 'crypto winter', as it happens, played out as economies worldwide were digging their way out of recessions caused by a pandemic and international conflict. These losses would sting in any circumstance, but they seemed particularly pronounced in 2022.

Equally, the achievements of Bitcoin, and thereafter Ethereum, dApps, and DeFi, could be described as spectacular. A one-time $3 trillion crypto market has been weaved from thin air in just over a decade, and in the case of DeFi the world briefly had an alternative financial system worth $180 billion, and it appeared to be largely independent of any financial institution.

There are reasons to be excited about the future too, and impetus to make the ecosystem safer, more energy efficient and versatile. We are only beginning to see what blockchain technology is capable of, and where decentralization can add value. This promise will help sustain crypto and DeFi. On an individual level, there are hopes that cryptoassets might be leveraged for financial inclusion, and that their continuation will inspire new innovations. For example, DeFi has spawned new tools for organizational governance, and is working towards solutions that could overhaul the ways in which online verification and identification take place. There are also hopes that it will lead to cheaper international remittances, or that it might provide a fitting financial ecosystem for the inchoate spheres of web3 and the metaverse. As we will see later on, DeFi has already inspired changes in major traditional finance institutions too, and it has influential support as well as detractors.

Despite the craziness associated with crypto and DeFi's early years, there are reasons to stress the importance of a longer-term view. We might observe that the Terra debacle does not negate the point of stablecoins, and that the NFT hype does not equate to the technology being frivolous. Similarly, it was clear that human error, mismanagement and greed brought down a number of firms in the crypto winter. The mistakes and chutzpah of SBF, or 3AC's Zhu and Davies, could be said to support DeFi's argument against centralized power.

So it is not all doom and gloom for DeFi, and in reality far from it. There are countless opportunities to explore but also, it should be added, brazen claims to critique. If the years since Ethereum's launch are anything to go by, we can at least be sure of one thing. That the future promises one hell of a ride.

References

1 V Buterin. Ethereum: a next-generation smart contract and decentralized application platform, Ethereum, 2014, ethereum.org/669c9e2e2027310b6b3c dce6e1c52962/Ethereum_Whitepaper_-_Buterin_2014.pdf (archived at https://perma.cc/8KAF-A55M)

2 N Szabo. Smart contracts, 1994, www.fon.hum.uva.nl/rob/Courses/ InformationInSpeech/CDROM/Literature/LOTwinterschool2006/szabo.best. vwh.net/smart.contracts.html (archived at https://perma.cc/5XVJ-NJHQ)

3 ethereum.org. Ethereum accounts, Ethereum, 2023, ethereum.org/en/ developers/docs/accounts/ (archived at https://perma.cc/S9HB-7VXA)

4 D Johnston et al. The general theory of decentralized applications, Dapps, GitHub, 2015, github.com/DavidJohnstonCEO/DecentralizedApplications (archived at https://perma.cc/5E7F-CVUY)

5 A Kharpal. Bitcoin may have more than doubled this year, but rival Ethereum is up 2,000 percent. Here's why, CNBC, 2017, www.cnbc.com/2017/05/24/ ethereum-price-bitcoin-rally.html (archived at https://perma.cc/YZT9-PQG7)

6 BBC. CryptoKitties craze slows down transactions on Ethereum, BBC News, 5 Dec 2017, www.bbc.co.uk/news/technology-42237162 (archived at https:// perma.cc/9TSM-Y9A7)

7 X-J Jiang and X F Liu. CryptoKitties transaction network analysis: the rise and fall of the first blockchain game mania, Frontiers in Physics, 2021, 9: 631665. doi:10.3389/fphy.2021.631665 (archived at https://perma.cc/ SSA6-PKSC)

8 C Russo. What is decentralized finance?: a deep dive by the defiant, CoinMarketCap, 2022, coinmarketcap.com/alexandria/article/what-is-decentralized-finance (archived at https://perma.cc/2A3A-WJHN)

9 E Frangella. Crypto Black Thursday: the good, the bad, and the ugly, Aave Blog, 2020, medium.com/aave/crypto-black-thursday-the-good-the-bad-and-the-ugly-7f2acebf2b83 (archived at https://perma.cc/8E2D-T275)

10 M Fitzgerald. A large chunk of the retail investing crowd started during the pandemic, Schwab survey shows, CNBC, 2021, www.cnbc.com/2021/04/08/ a-large-chunk-of-the-retail-investing-crowd-got-their-start-during-the-pandemic-schwab-survey-shows.html (archived at https://perma.cc/ MF6H-QKHJ)

11 L Berry. How lockdown changed the crypto market, Ziglu, 2021, www.ziglu. io/blog/how-lockdown-changed-the-crypto-market (archived at https://perma. cc/Q2XD-XW2F)

12 S Kim. How OpenSea cornered the $17 billion market for NFTs, CNBC, 2022, www.cnbc.com/2022/04/15/how-opensea-cornered-the-17-billion-market-for-nfts.html (archived at https://perma.cc/8VU3-RBTQ)

13 BBC. What are NFTs and why are some worth millions?, BBC News, 16 December 2022, www.bbc.co.uk/news/technology-56371912 (archived at https://perma.cc/FVU3-DHKA)

14 S Shukla. NFT trading volumes collapse 97% from January peak, Bloomberg, 2022, www.bloomberg.com/news/articles/2022-09-28/nft-volumes-tumble-97-from-2022-highs-as-frenzy-fades-chart (archived at https://perma.cc/79K4-WJBX)

15 B McGleenon. 2022, the year NFTs fell to earth, 2022, Yahoo, uk.news.yahoo.com/nft-crypto-2022-bitcoin-ethereum-060050452.html (archived at https://perma.cc/4XTB-FQD2)

16 R Browne. U.S. officials link North Korean hackers to $615 million cryptocurrency heist. CNBC, 15 April 2022, www.cnbc.com/2022/04/15/ronin-hack-north-korea-linked-to-615-million-crypto-heist-us-says.html (archived at https://perma.cc/ZUQ6-ZPAG)

17 N Bambysheva. Over $3 billion stolen in crypto heists: here are the eight biggest, Forbes, 2022, www.forbes.com/sites/ninabambysheva/2022/12/28/over-3-billion-stolen-in-crypto-heists-here-are-the-eight-biggest/?sh=78e8a86c699f (archived at https://perma.cc/5WBU-RW6W)

18 N Balu. Uber shares surge on solid profit forecast as rideshare recovery defies inflation, Reuters, 1 November 2022, www.reuters.com/business/autos-transportation/uber-forecasts-operating-profit-above-estimates-rideshare-recovers-2022-11-01/ (archived at https://perma.cc/HXG8-VSL6)

19 E Bavin. Airbnb, Reddit, Deliveroo: huge companies that have never made a profit, 19 April 2022, au.finance.yahoo.com/news/companies-that-have-never-made-a-profit-011104731.html (archived at https://perma.cc/F7BL-VNN9)

20 D Yaffe-Bellany and E Griffith. How a trash-talking crypto founder caused a $40 billion crash, The New York Times, 18 May 2022, www.nytimes.com/2022/05/18/technology/terra-luna-cryptocurrency-do-kwon.html (archived at https://perma.cc/3U5U-TGFV)

21 Q.ai. What really happened to LUNA crypto? Forbes, 2022, www.forbes.com/sites/qai/2022/09/20/what-really-happened-to-luna-crypto/?sh=2d3132654ff1 (archived at https://perma.cc/6HAM-F98V)

22 J Wieczner. The crypto geniuses who vaporized a trillion dollars, Intelligencer, 2022, nymag.com/intelligencer/article/three-arrows-capital-kyle-davies-su-zhu-crash.html (archived at https://perma.cc/ENS6-MKZS)

23 D Nelson and D Z Morris. Behind Voyager's fall: crypto broker acted like a bank, went bankrupt, CoinDesk, 2022, www.coindesk.com/layer2/2022/07/12/behind-voyagers-fall-crypto-broker-acted-like-a-bank-went-bankrupt/ (archived at https://perma.cc/D2SS-9Y8G)

24 K Sandor. Celsius acknowledges $1.2B hole in balance sheet, Yahoo, 2022, finance.yahoo.com/news/celsius-acknowledges-1-2b-hole-192539375.html (archived at https://perma.cc/YV2A-Q376)

25 B Nguyen. Sam Bankman-Fried was once caught playing the video game 'League of Legends' during a pitch meeting for FTX, Business Insider, 11 November 2022, www.businessinsider.in/investment/news/sam-bankman-fried-was-once-caught-playing-the-video-game-league-of-legends-during-a-pitch-meeting-for-ftx/articleshow/95436178.cms (archived at https://perma.cc/33PS-Q6R4)

26 I Allison. Divisions in Sam Bankman-Fried's crypto empire blur on his trading titan Alameda's balance sheet, CoinDesk, 2022, www.coindesk.com/business/2022/11/02/divisions-in-sam-bankman-frieds-crypto-empire-blur-on-his-trading-titan-alamedas-balance-sheet/ (archived at https://perma.cc/A9AJ-4XKK)

27 D Rushe. New FTX boss, who worked on Enron bankruptcy, condemns 'unprecedented failure', The Guardian, 2022, www.theguardian.com/technology/2022/nov/17/ftx-enron-crypto-collapse-john-ray-unprecedented (archived at https://perma.cc/7GPP-DDET)

28 ethereum.org. The Merge, Ethereum, 2023, ethereum.org/en/upgrades/merge/ (archived at https://perma.cc/FR8N-7W2M)

03

Key DeFi terms

So far, the story of cryptoassets and DeFi has been told with key information provided along the way. However, there are several important concepts and terms that did not slot neatly in, so before going any further these will be explained. Once this is done, a range of DeFi's most important protocols will be explored to show how the core tenets of DeFi have manifested as working protocols on blockchains.

Besides introducing the key protocols, there will also be an outline of why they matter. Many of these ideas and protocols are in the early stages of their journey and may increase or decrease in importance as DeFi evolves. Note that there is greater emphasis on Ethereum in this chapter (and several others), as this is by far the most dominant blockchain in DeFi.

Proof-of-stake (PoS)

What is it?

Proof-of-stake is a method for processing and validating transactions on blockchains.

Why it matters

Since The Merge, PoS has made Ethereum more than 99 per cent more energy efficient, and is the most prominent of the many alternatives to

Bitcoin's PoW validation. This method is considered preferable for several reasons, such as its potential to simplify network upgrades and cut fees. Chiefly, however, PoS's advantage is its energy efficiency. On the morning before The Merge, Ethereum was using as much electricity as the entirety of Chile and yet the following day, energy use had dropped over 99 per cent.[1] Ethereum transactions remain more than twice as energy-intensive as Mastercard transactions but Ethereum's viability as a platform for international commerce and finance has increased immeasurably.

For PoS to work, it needs to tackle the same challenges as PoW. The system needs to be, first and foremost, decentralized and secure. In order to tackle decentralization, we need a network of validators (the term validator replaces miners in PoS) who are sufficiently incentivized to accurately process the many transactions that will be made on the blockchain. Ethereum has achieved this by introducing staking, in which validators stake 32 Ether (equal to $51,000 in January 2023) in return for a set of validator keys. The keys activate software that allows users to store data, process transactions and add new blocks to the chain, and in return for doing so, they are paid a sum (in Ether) that varies in relation to deposit sizes and the number of validators on the network.[2] In the sense that validators are paid a percentage of their stake, an interest rate of sorts, staking operates similarly to a perpetual bond. Anyone interested in staking should note that penalties are imposed on validators who are absent (offline) during validation. The costs are equal to the rewards that would have been granted had the validator operated successfully.

There is no benefit to depositing more than 32 Ether within a validator account, though people and groups may activate multiple validator keys. The fee is prohibitive for individual investors, but validation pools and centralized exchanges can help people club together and take part with smaller individual stakes. For anyone lacking confidence to take responsibility for the staking process, there are also staking-as-a-service options that will validate on your behalf (centralized exchanges will also do this).

The 32 Ether limit is designed to prevent any one validator having an overly powerful vote on the state of the chain. In addition to this, there are limits on the number of validators that can leave the system at any given time and the 32 Ether limit reduces the risk of the network being compromised, especially in relation to attacks, by the exit of validators of significant influence.

In terms of security, a block is only finalized if two-thirds of the network agree to it. Those concerned by the risk of a 51 per cent attack, as utilized in the Ronin hack, may be reassured by the size and utility of Ethereum's PoS network. An initial barrier to a 51 per cent attack would be cost, as attaining a sufficient stake in Ether to control the network in 2023 would be astronomically expensive (the sum required could rise or fall sharply as the price of Ether fluctuates).[3]

If hacks do occur, network participants have a new way to counter it. They can create a user-activated soft fork (UASF), which continues the chain, but action can be taken to freeze and drain the attacker's account. The attacker would ultimately be forced out of the network, and their Ether burned before they can utilize it.

The ability to burn the hacker's Ether is introduced by slashing. On Ethereum, slashing is a process that empowers network participants to boot an offending validator from the chain, draining their stake by up to 100 per cent as they do so. For slashing to occur, at least one other validator needs to be a 'whistleblower' and send a message to be validated on the next block (there would need to be consensus in validating this). There are numerous acts that could instigate a slashing, such as a validator acting against the consensus of the network, or behaving in a particularly misleading or unexpected manner. When slashing is confirmed, a 36-day period begins and the validator's stake is gradually burned. At the midway point, there is an additional 'correlation penalty' applied, which grows in size relative to the number of validators involved in the wrongdoing. Naturally, a 51 per cent attack would involve a huge correlation penalty due to the number of nodes required to perform one. Unless the network, for whatever reason, would prefer to proceed with the hacked chain, the attackers are unlikely to benefit.

A largely unrelated but interesting consequence of slashing is that centralized crypto exchanges may need to think twice before censoring transactions if they are facilitating staking. It would be controversial, though not impossible, to slash an exchange's account. Proof-of-stake systems are new and largely untested. They also require a strong and decentralized network to uphold. Nonetheless, Ethereum's Merge could prove to be a development that builds energy efficiency and safety into DeFi, while providing a sound platform from which to scale its operations.

Gas fees

What is it?

Gas fees are transaction fees, which are paid to the Ethereum network and then burned.

Why it matters

Gas fees are the transaction fees paid for Ethereum transactions. By creating a cost for transactions, correlating to network traffic and transaction complexity, gas fees smooth the flow of transactions on Ethereum. This helps negate the issue of Ethereum's processing speed limitations, but can create frustration when costs remain high. Gas fees also offer a method for tipping, and thus incentivizing, validators. They help maintain the value of Ether too, as gas fees are burned post-transaction. This serves a deflationary purpose and keeps a steadier number of Ether in circulation.

At present, gas fees play a crucial role in guaranteeing network security. At a basic level, if all transactions were free of charge the network could be spammed relentlessly, causing congestion that would bring it to a standstill. Therefore transactions are bound by a 'gas limit', a measurement that restricts them to a set number of computational steps. This step limit eliminates the issue of infinite loops, which occur when a smart contract issues a set of instructions with no logical conclusion.

Following the August 2021 London Upgrade, gas fees are formulated as follows:

Total gas fee = Units of gas used × (base fee + priority fee)

The amount of gas used will vary by transaction and, in 2023, the minimum amount of gas that will be used is 21,000 units. The number of units required will increase as transactions become more complicated, generally speaking. Users need to ensure that they set a sufficient gas limit. If they don't, they will still be charged for the gas that is burned (as computing power is still used) and their actions will be unsuccessful.

Base fees are a value set by the protocol and a priority fee is a tip, acting as an incentive for validators to process the transaction. The party that initiates a transaction can also set a maximum fee, which states how much they are willing to pay in order for it to be completed. The difference between the maximum fee and the actual fee will be refunded at the end of the transaction.

Base fees should be given further analysis, and in providing it there should be an acknowledgement of block size. Each block that is added to Ethereum has a target size of 15 million gas, though block size will increase or decrease relative to demand, up to a maximum size of 30 million gas. As the protocol attempts to average out the size of the blocks at 15 million gas, base fees will rise by up to 12.5 per cent per block every time the block target is exceeded. With blocks added roughly every 12 seconds, gas prices can soar during periods of high demand.

The Ethereum network is not currently optimized for intense usage. In early 2023, it was capable of processing 12–24 transactions per second (tps) and therefore has limits as a global network that handles DeFi protocols and NFTs, as well as peer-to-peer transactions. At times of high demand, network users should exercise restraint, as a simple act such as moving Ether from one wallet to another could cost excessive sums, possibly even hundreds of US dollars.[4]

This presents a poor user experience and potentially a painful one. For instance, when Yuga Labs, creators of Bored Ape Yacht Club, launched its Otherside NFT collection in 2022, transaction fees became unmanageable and impacted users regardless of what they wanted to do. Towards the height of this three-hour scramble, Mashable reporter Matt Binder found that the cost to register a $5 .eth domain name, including gas fees, would be $4,661.88.[5] In total over $175 million was spent on gas in just one night and as failed transactions still incur a charge, some people paid as much as $4,500 for purchases that never materialized.[6] This is obviously far from satisfactory, although the rapid rise in gas fees did deter users from increasing network traffic.

Gas fees also serve a deflationary purpose as the base fees of all transactions are burned. This is intended to help Ether maintain or lift its price, reducing the number of Ether in circulation despite its potentially infinite supply. Prior to The Merge, the supply of Ether had been increasing by about 4.5 per cent per year.[7]

As fees are measured in denominations of Ether, network users will also encounter swings in transaction costs in fiat terms as Ether's value changes. Fees are denoted in gwei (gigawei), which is one billionth of one Ether. Gwei is a portmanteau of gigawei, as one gwei is equal to 1,000,000,000 wei, the smallest denomination of the currency. Wei is named after Wei Dai, mentioned in chapter one.

Ethereum is the focus here as it hosts the majority of DeFi transactions. However, DeFi transaction fees on a number of other blockchains are far cheaper, and Layer 2 solutions are being introduced to lower gas fees on Ethereum. Average transactions on Solana and Avalanche are reported to cost less than a hundredth of a cent.[8]

Stablecoins

What is it?

A stablecoin is a cryptocurrency, the value of which is pegged or tied to another store of value, often the US dollar.

Why it matters

The volatility of cryptoassets makes them generally unsuitable for payments. Stablecoins fix this by providing assets that hold a steady fiat value, while also offering a potentially safe harbour from market downturns. Despite the disastrous UST example discussed earlier, stablecoins have a valuable role to play within DeFi. Their ability to bridge on-chain and off-chain assets could prove especially powerful as people find new ways to tokenize assets.

There are three widely recognized types of stablecoin:

- **Fiat-collateralized stablecoins:** These stablecoins are usually backed by a reserve of fiat currency (or currencies) and money market funds (such as US Treasuries, low-risk, short-dated bonds), which can be used to align the coin's value with its peg. A stablecoin of this nature may also be backed by commodities or other off-chain assets. Example: Tether, USDC.

- **Crypto-collateralized stablecoins:** These stablecoins are backed by other cryptocurrencies. Collateral is likely to be set at a high level to combat the volatility of cryptocurrencies. Example: DAI.

- **Algorithmic stablecoins:** As we have seen, these are largely untested and there is no enduring successful example. These stablecoins are engineered to maintain a steady value through an algorithm that controls supply. Algorithmic stablecoins, in some cases, will hold some form of collateral. Example: Terra (UST).

Exchanges: AMMs vs centralized exchanges

What is it?

Exchanges create markets for the trading, lending and borrowing of cryptoassets. They can be run by a company (centralized) or entirely reliant on smart contracts (decentralized).

Why it matters

Most people will use an exchange to make crypto transactions. Different exchanges have different pros and cons and will vary by what they offer, security standards, governance methods and ease of use. It is worthwhile to know your options before using one.

For DeFi to be a credible ecosystem requires exchanges where people can trade their assets. To date, both centralized (CEX) and decentralized exchanges (DEX) have proven popular.

Commonly used CEXs include:

- Binance
- Coinbase
- Kraken
- Gemini

Prominent DEXs include:

- Uniswap
- dYdX
- Curve Finance
- Kine Protocol
- PancakeSwap

CEXs operate in a similar manner to conventional exchange platforms, albeit the assets exchanged are primarily cryptocurrencies and users can deposit their assets in an exchange wallet, which many find preferable. For these exchanges to facilitate instantaneous transactions and ensure enough liquidity exists to achieve this, market makers are deployed. Market makers, which in conventional markets are usually financial institutions or large investors, ensure that it is possible to buy or sell assets quickly, and they are remunerated by the bid-ask spread, the difference between the highest price a buyer is willing to pay for an asset and the lowest price that a seller is willing to accept. As such, there is an incentive for market makers to facilitate the flow of trade within the exchange.

A small number of CEXs have courted controversy due to their use, or alleged use, of unregulated or closely affiliated market makers, and FTX and its market maker, Alameda Research, were both founded by SBF, as discussed earlier.[9] This issue is raised to illustrate that CEXs are not, at least not yet, a neat replica of traditional exchanges. Another concern, especially among DeFi maximalists, is that the centralization of exchanges is not in the spirit of crypto.

CEXs have initially been more popular than DEXs as they offer slicker user interfaces, customer support and the ability to use fiat currency, all while being capable of handling higher volumes of trans-actions across a broader range of assets. Regulation is likely to have a significant impact on the operations of many CEXs, and should, if implemented effectively, improve operational standards while improving transparency and consumer confidence. This is a work in progress but appears to be the direction of travel and is in part a response to major mismanagement issues such as those mentioned earlier. Given that CEXs typically have custody of customer assets, the need for robust management is considerable.

DEXs, which operate by using smart contracts on public block-chains, are somewhat different. Users retain custody of their own assets, can only trade on-chain tokens, and trade in a 'peer-to-pool' manner. Peer-to-pool relates to users trading their assets against assets held by a liquidity pool, rather than an exchange, and in place of market makers we now have Automated Market Makers (AMM). AMMs make a DEX possible by setting the price of assets in relation to a mathematical formula and the number of tokens in the liquidity pool. These formulas help to balance the exchange and ensure that trading opportunities remain close to optimal.

As assets are paired in AMMs, there are instances where high demand for token A can cause token B, which is used to buy it, to trade at a significant discount. This creates arbitrage opportunities across exchange platforms, and as such, the subsequent demand increase for token B will drive its price back towards its recognized market rate. The AMMs used by DEXs do not all use the same formula. DeFi liquidity protocol Balancer, for example, is designed for more complex trading and can form liquidity pools consisting of up to eight different assets.

In the absence of larger entities acting as market makers, and without a bid-ask spread to serve as compensation, protocol users are encouraged to become liquidity providers in several different ways. They might be rewarded with a percentage of the transaction fees paid to a liquidity pool, or be issued governance tokens that grant voting privileges on decisions relating to the AMM protocol.

Accordingly, AMMs and their reward mechanisms have spawned the activity of yield farming, in which liquidity providers engage in various strategies to maximize the yields they receive for staking their assets for a given period. They might switch their assets on a regular basis, seeking out liquidity pools with higher yields (usually accepting greater risk as they do so), and put any earned rewards back to use by staking as they receive them. While yield farming can be risky, and can create the problem of impermanent loss (impermanent loss occurs when the profit attained from staking a token in a liquidity pool would have been exceeded if the asset had simply been held), its existence allows early adopters of a protocol a chance to make serious returns and allows protocols to attract a sufficient liquidity pool without outside funding. There is a hint of Jekyll and Hyde about it. On one hand, it makes rapid scaling of DEXs possible. On the other, it creates liquidity pools that are dominated by mercenary capital, which will likely flock to another protocol, if possible, when yields drop.

DEXs are preferable to some users as they allow you to retain full control of your assets and can be accessed by anyone with a live internet connection. Transactions on the exchange are transparent (this is not always a good thing, as evidenced by front running) and can be fully audited. These protocols, some believe, cannot be fully shut down or banned and are arguably the go-to exchanges for DeFi enthusiasts. Use of DEXs has trailed the centralized alternative, but this could change as protocols become easier to use, as crypto ownership proliferates, and if popular DEXs are able to market their services as effectively as CEXs have.

It is possible to run a DEX without using an AMM. On EtherDelta, the first noteworthy DEX (prior to a SEC investigation and subsequent sale), order matching was peer-to-peer and managed off-chain on an order book. On IDex and Paradex, the exchange itself will match orders for a smart contract to process.

Front running

What is it?

Front running in crypto is an arbitrage process where miners and validators can view upcoming transactions and price mismatches in the market. They can profit, without breaking any law, by placing competing trades.

Why it matters

Front running demonstrates how crypto operates with different rules to TradFi. It highlights the potential implications of transaction transparency, and how sophisticated network users can maximize their advantage over those with less knowledge. In some respects, it's nothing new. In traditional finance, front running involves a broker receiving insider information, such as knowledge of an upcoming trade or analyst's report, before buying or selling shares or an asset. Let's say the broker is aware of a large order coming through that will drive up the price of an asset; they can accordingly delay the trade, buy a portion of the asset themselves, and profit when the brokerage executes the trade. Front running differs from insider trading in that it specifically refers to actions taken by brokers with a brokerage, whereas insider trading involves people with ties to a company acting on privileged information.

Due to the nature of the Ethereum blockchain, where prospective orders are transparently pooled prior to being selected and confirmed as a block (this queue of transactions is called a mempool), traders are presented with a very different front running opportunity or problem. This type of front running involves arbitrage bots, deployed continuously to identify price mismatches. As it is possible to identify when orders are being made, arbitrageurs can front run those orders, jumping the queue by posting a higher reward for validators. A known mechanism here is the 'sandwich manoeuvre', whereby a trader front runs a token purchase, knowing that this will drive up its price on an exchange, and then sells for the higher price to the initial bidder, knowing they will most likely still want to purchase the token.

The authors of the 2019 study *Flash Boys 2.0* identified over 500 bots working across DEXs, making as much as $20,000 per day.[10] One of the authors, Professor Ari Juels, later estimated that this type of front running, if extrapolated to CEXs too, could be a multi-billion dollar arbitrage market. In true crypto fashion, a free, open source tool named 'Flashbots' has since launched, allowing validators to profit without needing their own bot. Although the majority of validators use this in 2023, it is not universally popular among the user base and the proliferation of flashbots has been compared to a city auctioning the right to commit burglaries in order to fund the police, when other options could be available such as encrypting the mempool.[11,12]

Front running puts a spotlight on several other drawbacks in crypto validation. It shows that network congestion and rising fees can be caused by bot activity. It also shows that an entire market exists for siphoning resources from less knowledgeable traders to more sophisticated ones. Front running also presents questions about the prioritization of crypto transactions, which is currently based purely on what is best for validators, rather than what is best for the ecosystem. The current system, while effective, is imperfect.

Flash loans

What is it?

Flash loans are uncollateralized and notionally unlimited loans, whereby the user borrows an asset, makes a transaction, and repays the loan plus interest within the same validated block. It is made possible by the validation methods of blockchain and by price mismatches (arbitrage).

Why it matters

As with front running, flash loans show how those with appropriate knowledge can profit from market inconsistencies. Where they differ, in a sense, is that they allow people to profit on a grand scale without needing to provide collateral.

To explain the workings of a flash loan, imagine there are two exchanges, both selling the same token but for different prices. Exchange A is selling it for $10 and Exchange B is selling it for $11. There is an opportunity here to buy the token from Exchange A and sell it on Exchange B for a $1 profit. A rational actor here might gather as much disposable income as they can and execute this transaction on as large a scale as possible. This involves a degree of risk and the trader is restricted by the limits of their capital.

Flash loans can provide a better deal for the trader. They are bespoke smart contracts that allow loans of significant value to be taken out for arbitrage opportunities, and will only execute if the smart contract is simultaneously able to complete the transaction, deliver the arbitrage opportunity to the trader, and repay the loan plus interest. Should the smart contract be unable to do this, the agreement will not go ahead.

These loans will not be great news for everyone, as you might suspect from the paragraphs above. Bots are again rampant, and those seeking new opportunities will be competing against them, provided they have the knowledge or tools to do so. A more high-profile problem is that they can be used to drain money from protocols. Stablecoin provider Beanstalk was taken for $182 million when an attacker exploited its governance protocol to gain a controlling share and pilfer its funds (the attacker made away with roughly $80million, with the rest of the funds financing the loan; this caused Beanstalk's stablecoin to fall about 75 per cent from its $1 peg).[13] Similarly, lending protocol Cream Finance lost over $260 million of assets to a flash loan attacker.[14]

Altcoins and memecoins

What is it?

Altcoins and memecoins are both Doge and not Doge.

Why it matters

The two are bundled for ease of description but vary considerably. Altcoins usually belong to credible projects and are emerging alternatives to bitcoin and Ether. Shitcoins and memecoins are often minted as a joke, a scam, an experiment, or some degree of all three. It is worth acknowledging that crypto has many currencies, with different traits.

An altcoin, short for alternative coin, is widely considered as any coin other than Bitcoin or Ether. In 2023, notable altcoins include Litecoin, Dogecoin, Bitcoin Cash and Cardano.

Shitcoins, as the disparaging name implies, are cryptocurrencies with no discernible value or purpose. They may also be memecoins, in which case they are created purely as a joke. On very rare occasions a memecoin, such as Dogecoin, may cross the threshold from meme to altcoin, though this typically occurs through a social phenomenon rather than a financial one.

A list of almost every coin, active or dead, can be found at coinopsy.com.

Tokenization

What is it?

Tokenization is the process through which an asset's value or ownership is represented by a token.

Why it matters

If ownership or the value of an on-chain or off-chain asset can be represented by a token, and tokens can be traded on-chain, then DeFi and blockchain can play a huge role in creating new investable assets and stimulating trade.

Tokenization occurs when an asset, or the ownership rights to an asset, are converted into tokens. Tokens can grant ownership of an entire asset, or a portion of one, and can be assigned to virtually anything deemed to have value.

On blockchains, tokens take four main forms:

- **Fungible tokens:** These tokens are identical, divisible and have a defined market value. Cryptocurrencies usually fit this bill.

- **Non-fungible tokens (NFTs):** NFTs do not have a defined value. Instead, they signify the ownership of a unique underlying digital asset.

- **Utility tokens:** Utility tokens are used to access certain products, services or rewards within a blockchain project. They can serve practically any purpose that a developer desires but are not usually considered currency. They have often been used as incentives during initial coin offerings and are often created prior to one.

- **Governance tokens:** These tokens offer voting rights within a blockchain system.

Types of blockchain

What is it?

Blockchains can take different forms and serve various purposes. There are also many blockchains in existence besides Bitcoin and Ethereum.

Why it matters

This is nascent technology, and new chains will emerge, with different utilities and traits. It is also worth knowing the different types of blockchain available, as different types of chain can meet very different needs. The blockchain required to optimize an international supply chain will probably vary greatly from a blockchain designed for a single business, or a blockchain built for open public access.

At the time of writing, the most commonly used blockchains can be categorized as public, private, permissioned and consortium.

PUBLIC BLOCKCHAIN

As the name indicates, anyone can participate, view activity, or become a validator in a public chain. They are permissionless (in the sense that visibility and usage is guaranteed merely by access to the internet) and decentralized. Ethereum and Bitcoin are prime examples.

The size of a public blockchain network can be a great strength. Validations are more effective if more people are incentivized to uphold the system, and likewise, network security is stronger if it is spread across a greater number of nodes. Ethereum's slashing and UASF options demonstrate this; anyone intending to cause harm to members of the network will ostensibly need to convince more than half of the network that it's a good idea. Conversely, smaller networks may be more vulnerable.

Possible drawbacks for users of public blockchains include loss of privacy, and in the case of larger networks, being an attractive target for hacks and scams.

PRIVATE BLOCKCHAIN

These blockchains are permissioned and usually managed by a single entity, which holds the right to decide which users (nodes) can join. Users will not necessarily be granted equal rights to perform functions, and validation will be carried out by the network operator or a smart contract. This allows for higher transaction speeds, relative to public networks that require the participation of a range of nodes (which could be millions in number).

Private blockchains are typically used to execute a specific function or functions. As such, there are limits to their applications and ability to interact with other networks. The narrowed scope of their function and centralized management does, however, simplify regulatory compliance.

Private blockchains are not risk-free. If the security protocols of the organization running the blockchain are compromised, users could be compromised. Similarly, it might be possible to overrun the network by corrupting a small number of validators.

PERMISSIONED BLOCKCHAIN

A permissioned blockchain utilizes features of both public and private blockchains. Like public blockchains, the data on these blockchains are usually publicly available and anyone, theoretically, can become a network member. However, as with a private blockchain, they will need to be granted permission to do so. A centralized entity will control permissioning on a blockchain like this, but the entity will not hold authority over the data that is held on the chain.

CONSORTIUM BLOCKCHAIN

Consortium blockchains are permissioned and operated by multiple organizations rather than just one. This lends a degree of decentralization to the arrangement. Their primary usage, currently, is to create a shared ledger between businesses so that various operations can be simplified and optimized.

Consortium blockchains can potentially benefit entire industries. For example, the Global Shipping Business Network (GSBN), created by CargoSmart, uses a consortium blockchain to improve cooperation between companies and digitize the industry. GSBN intends for its ledger to allow sharing of verified logistics data, a streamlined supply chain, and value creation for each participant.[15] The network includes terminals, carriers, shippers, freight forwarders, truckers, customs and financial institutions.

Another example is R3's Corda blockchain, which uses distributed ledger technology (DLT) to connect a range of banks, insurers, exchanges and infrastructure providers. This approach appears beneficial from a regulatory standpoint, as a permissioned structure can be upheld between trusted and regulated parties, who have completed the relevant know-your-customer (KYC) and anti-money laundering (AML) checks. As (arguably if) interoperability between blockchains improves, there is also potential for integration between public and permissioned blockchains, where transactions might be simultaneously recognized on multiple blockchains.[16]

Beyond the blockchain types mentioned, there are myriad ways that blockchains differ. Blockchains vary in how centralized they are, their validation methods, transaction speeds, scalability, security against hacks, abilities to host smart contracts, coding language used for smart contracts, and the number of protocols built on top of them. Due to the composability of protocols (i.e. their ability to slot together as money legos), blockchains with a longer history may have a head start unless their protocols can be easily replicated.

Notable blockchains include:

- Bitcoin
- Ethereum
- Ripple
- Hyperledger
- Tron
- BNB Chain
- Arbitrum
- Polygon
- Avalanche
- Solana
- Algorand

Forking

What is it?

Forking can introduce a major change to the underlying blockchain code, or updates to its rules and network.

Why it matters

Forks play a vital role in governing and upgrading a blockchain. They are also a useful tool for resolving major disagreements in how a protocol is run, and have instigated important conversations about decentralization.

With blockchain, it is possible for a chain to split in two and this is known as a fork. The chains' histories remain shared up until the point of the fork but from there they diverge, into either a hard fork or a soft fork.

A hard fork involves a complete split between a new and old chain and is not backwards compatible. In that sense it is akin to a road splitting in two directions, never to meet again. In a hard fork, there will be a change to the blockchain's underlying code, meaning nodes will need to be upgraded in order to operate on the new chain.

There are several reasons why a hard fork may be required. Often it will be for significant updates or improvements to the network, to keep pace with developments in technology elsewhere. It may also be the result of significant disagreements within the network community about how a blockchain should evolve. When a split of this nature occurs, asset owners will have a claim to assets on both forks. This may seem like a doubling of assets, though it rarely works out this way. Should the fork be due to a necessary improvement that the community broadly agrees upon, validators and miners will have little interest in maintaining the 'outdated' fork, rendering it practically worthless. If the fork is a result of a disagreement on how a blockchain should proceed, however, it is possible that both forks will receive sufficient support to continue, as was the case when Bitcoin Cash (BCH) forked from Bitcoin. BCH remains just inside the top 30 cryptocurrencies by market cap in April 2023.

Another potential purpose of a hard fork is to reverse transactions. When the Ethereum DAO was hacked in 2016, stolen assets were recovered through a controversial Ethereum hard fork that rolled transaction history back to before the hack. This decision, while effective, offered reason to doubt claims that blockchains are immutable and censorship-resistant. The fallout from the incident led to the creation of Ethereum Classic, a continuation of the original Ethereum blockchain.

A soft fork differs from a hard fork, as it is backwards compatible and can't create a new currency. It will usually be introduced for smaller alterations such as a minor rule change or a network upgrade. While there is a split, of sorts, nodes running in a pre-fork manner will still be able to process transactions and process new blocks, provided that they operate in a manner that doesn't breach new rules or requirements. Any actions that don't meet new requirements will not be processed. While a soft fork doesn't demand that nodes take immediate action, it does create inefficiencies for those that don't upgrade (especially if further changes are made at a later date). This encourages nodes to eventually step in line.

Cryptocurrency mixers

What is it?

A cryptocurrency mixer is a privacy tool used to disguise transactions made by a crypto wallet.

Why it matters

Mixers could be used to facilitate criminal activity, especially money laundering. They could also be a vital tool when anonymity is needed or preferred. Their existence raises valuable questions about legality, regulation, privacy and the ability of DeFi to elude the control of centralized governments and authorities.

Mixers obfuscate the trail of transactions by shuffling pools of assets between multiple addresses and holding them for a randomized duration, before distributing them back to owners at randomized times. Regulators have good reason to watch these protocols closely. Tornado Cash, which some believe has helped launder billions of dollars (US) of assets, was blacklisted by the U.S. Department of the Treasury in 2022.[17]

An alternative to crypto mixers is privacy wallets, which can connect groups of people who want to mix transactions. Privacy wallets and mixers highlight an ongoing issue in DeFi, that is the trade-off between the right to privacy and its benefits, and the ability for bad faith actors to profit by disguising their identity. To be philosophical for a moment, mixers could also be valuable in moments when legality and morality are not aligned. A good use case for a crypto mixer could be found in funding political protest or dissident action, especially as regimes will likely become more effective at tracing flows of crypto.

Sharding

What is it?

Sharding involves splitting a database in a manner that makes it easier to update.

Why it matters

As of 2023, the vast majority of blockchains are not capable of processing transactions at the speeds and volume required for everyday international use. Sharding is being pursued as a potential remedy for this problem.

Sharding involves splitting a database into multiple databases known as shards. If this is effectively performed with a blockchain, nodes only need to maintain data related to their shard rather than the entire chain. This release of burden ensures that nodes can then process transactions at greater speeds, and the integrity of the chain remains uncompromised as nodes continue to share information across the network, with other nodes maintaining other shards.

Sharding works well for PoS networks and may yet prove a valuable tool in the proliferation of DeFi. Nonetheless, sharding is not considered well-suited for PoW protocols and is relatively untested in blockchain technology. It is possible that it could create network vulnerabilities.

Layers of blockchain networks

What is it?

Presently it can be said that there are four recognized layers to blockchain networks, though various sources describe the ecosystem as having fewer or more layers. Layer 0 is the infrastructure on which Layer 1 networks are built. Layer 1 networks are base layer blockchains, and Layer 2 networks are built on top of them to deliver an improvement and help them scale. Layer 3 is for apps (and dApps), wallets and games that users can interact with. Sources differ on the number of layers that exist.

Why it matters

Understanding the relationships between network layers can help explain how DeFi systems are evolving. Improvements to these layers can make DeFi more scalable, user-friendly and useful, which in turn might accelerate its proliferation into everyday life and finance.

Layer 2 integrations have been especially important in the early 2020s, as developers have sought to improve the functionality of blockchains with considerable adoption and network effects. These integrations seek to improve features such as a blockchain's capacity for new services and lower transaction fees, or – as was the case with Ethereum 2.0, which reverted to 'Ethereum' once implemented – alter the network's consensus mechanism (as Ethereum did from PoW to PoS). In terms of scalability, Layer 2 networks can add speed to Layer 1 transactions by bundling multiple off-chain transactions into a Layer 1 that it is compatible with. With the Layer 2 protocol handling the computational heavy lifting, the Layer 1 blockchain can now process far more transactions at lower costs and higher speeds. These benefits are all necessary if the popular blockchains of today are to underpin everyday transactions, commerce, retail and online gaming networks, which by their very nature need to operate seamlessly on a grand scale.

There are numerous Layer 2 solutions being worked on including zero-knowledge rollups, optimistic rollups, validiums and sidechains. In 2023, Layer 2s that have achieved recognition include Optimism, Arbitrum, Polygon, Loopring and the Lightning Network. The improvements offered by Layer 2s may explain why blockchain transaction volume grew in Q4 of 2022, despite the crypto winter.[18]

To go back to Layer 1, there are several blockchains poised to grow in stature, such as Solana, Cardano, Avalanche and Polkadot. Mass adoption and interoperability of these chains, the creation of new chains, and the Layer 0 infrastructure beneath them, will add new depth to what crypto and DeFi can do.

Crypto wallets

What is it?

A crypto wallet stores a user's passkeys and allows them to transact.

Why it matters

Anyone who wants to buy and trade cryptoassets should consider the various wallets available to them. Wallets differ in their levels of security, ease of use, appearance, cost and more. While they do not actually store assets (all cryptocurrencies are held in a database), they often provide a navigable interface through which to make transactions.

Wallets can be custodial or non-custodial. Users of a custodial wallet are trusting a third party to store their keys, and non-custodial wallet users are responsible for their own keys. A point of note on custodial wallets is that users should research these wallets where possible, as their features and security will vary.

Another distinction is that wallets can be 'hot' or 'cold'. A hot wallet is connected to the internet, either directly or via another device. A cold wallet is not connected to the internet. Some wallets can flick between either state, and an exchange may hold some assets in a hot wallet and others in a cold one.

A final distinction is that wallets can be hardware, software or paper-based. A paper wallet is quite literally a piece of paper, which can work perfectly well so long as the written note isn't damaged, lost or stolen.

Hardware wallets connect to an online device, typically through a USB drive, and can allow the user to make transactions without entering their key (the key is stored on the hardware). These wallets require an internet connection and are considered to be cold wallets, except when they are online and plugged in.

Software wallets can take a variety of forms, such as browser extensions and apps for desktop and mobiles. These wallets allow for straightforward interactions with DeFi protocols and are generally the most efficient. As software wallets are permanently online, users should acknowledge an ongoing risk (even if minimal) of being hacked. Similarly, devices used to access the wallet should be protected by a password or multi-factor authentication.

Oracles

What is it?

An oracle connects a blockchain with information that is held off-chain.

Why it matters

Oracles allow data from a wide variety of sources to communicate with blockchains. This opens up countless possibilities for DeFi to filter into finance, and creates a communication channel between blockchains, which are closed systems, and the outside world.

In blockchain, an oracle is a mechanism that sends information between a blockchain and external systems, enabling them to interact and potentially execute smart contracts. This expands the range of smart contracts immensely and allows information on one blockchain to cooperate with data on other chains, or a different type of database entirely.

There are many use cases for oracles and they are growing in number. More obvious ones include using an oracle to peg the value of DeFi assets to traditional assets or using information about an incident such as a flight cancellation to trigger an insurance payout. Oracles are not without flaws, unfortunately. If an off-chain data source is incorrect or does not immediately update, the smart contract could be undermined (and still be carried out).

In time, oracles can help facilitate countless smart contracts where a financial exchange or transaction is actioned when irrefutable conditions are met.

References

1 Digiconomist. Ethereum Energy Consumption Index (beta), Digiconomist, 2021, digiconomist.net/ethereum-energy-consumption (archived at https://perma.cc/5K8H-FZFR)

2 ethereum.org. Staking with Ethereum, Ethereum, 2023, ethereum.org/en/staking/#comparison-of-options (archived at https://perma.cc/A4VX-T99A)

3 S Nover and N DiCamillo. What is the ethereum merge?, Quartz, 2022, qz.com/what-is-the-ethereum-merge-1849419652 (archived at https://perma.cc/NSK9-U36Y)

4 R J Fulton. 3 Things Every Crypto Investor Should Look Out For in 2023, Nasdaq, 2023, www.nasdaq.com/articles/3-things-every-crypto-investor-should-look-out-for-in-2023 (archived at https://perma.cc/W7MK-PM2A)

5 M Binder. Bored Ape Yacht Club caused Ethereum fees to soar to astronomical levels, Mashable, 2022, mashable.com/article/ethereum-gas-fees-skyrocket-bored-ape-yacht-club-otherside-nft-launch (archived at https://perma.cc/P96B-C5KN)

6 daddy_gainz. Just spent $175m on gas [Tweet]. Twitter, 31 October 2022, twitter.com/daddy_gainz/status/1520625186260889601 (archived at https://perma.cc/6AMH-53MU)

7 D Basulto. Why is nobody talking about this new feature of ethereum?, The Motley Fool, 2022, www.fool.com/investing/2022/11/19/why-is-nobody-talking-about-this-new-feature-of-et/ (archived at https://perma.cc/PV7R-T8FC)

8 D Phillips. Sick of high Ethereum gas fees? Do this instead, Alexandria, 2022, coinmarketcap.com/alexandria/article/sick-of-high-ethereum-gas-fees-do-this-instead (archived at https://perma.cc/6RV5-6RQ5)

9 C Ostroff, P Kowsmann and D Michaels. SEC probes trading affiliates of crypto giant Binance's U.S. arm, The Wall Street Journal, n.d., www.wsj.com/articles/sec-probes-trading-affiliates-of-crypto-giant-binances-u-s-arm-11644948162 (archived at https://perma.cc/9NER-E6N2)

10 P Daian, S Goldfeder, T Kell, Y Li, X Zhao, I Bentov, L Breidenbach and A Juels. Flash boys 2.0: frontrunning, transaction reordering, and consensus instability in decentralized exchanges, IEEE S&P, Cornell University, 2019, arxiv.org/abs/1904.05234 (archived at https://perma.cc/A6FJ-FWPP)

11 S Kessler. The money in Ethereum's middleware: can flashbots still call itself a 'public good'? CoinDesk, 2023, www.coindesk.com/tech/2023/01/25/the-money-in-ethereums-middleware-can-flashbots-still-call-itself-a-public-good/ (archived at https://perma.cc/5P73-FF9U)

12 O Kharif. Robot crypto traders are the new flash boys, Bloomberg.com. 23 September 2021, www.bloomberg.com/news/articles/2021-09-23/crypto-trading-how-flashbots-work-to-front-run-ether-and-other-coin-purchases (archived at https://perma.cc/G3CT-9ZV4)

13 S Shukla. DeFi project Beanstalk loses $182 million in flash loan attack. Bloomberg.com, 18 April 2022, www.bloomberg.com/news/articles/2022-04-18/defi-project-beanstalk-loses-182-million-in-flash-loan-attack (archived at https://perma.cc/M9CM-M46V)

14 A Thurman. Cream Finance exploited in flash loan attack netting over $100M, CoinDesk, 27 October 2021, www.coindesk.com/business/2021/10/27/cream-finance-exploited-in-flash-loan-attack-worth-over-100m/ (archived at https://perma.cc/9SDZ-KMRJ)

15 GSBN. Home page, 2023, www.gsbn.trade/ (archived at https://perma.cc/R5T9-ULL6)

16 PYMNTS. R3 blockchain finds a foothold beyond banks, 2022, www.pymnts.com/cryptocurrency/2022/r3-finds-a-niche-helping-financial-firms-work-together/ (archived at https://perma.cc/26JM-5FNG)

17 U.S. Department of the Treasury. U.S. Treasury sanctions notorious virtual currency mixer Tornado Cash, 2022, home.treasury.gov/news/press-releases/jy0916 (archived at https://perma.cc/LDQ9-G7PT)

18 S Haig. Optimism activity hits new highs as Layer 2s close in on Ethereum, 2023, thedefiant.io/optimism-transactions-ath (archived at https://perma.cc/ESU5-SH8M)

04

What does DeFi do?

Having explored some of the history, core principles, technologies and terminology of DeFi, it's time to look more closely at what it really does. In taking this analysis forward, there are two ways to look at developments in DeFi. One is to look at the growth of DeFi as an independent ecosystem that can operate independently of the traditional system. The other is to look at how DeFi, and the innovations it inspires, are transforming the financial ecosystem at large. This chapter primarily looks at DeFi, to the extent that it can be one, as a standalone concept.

DeFi protocols: A starting point for mass financialization

DeFi protocols have come a long way in a short time. Vast sums of money, and no shortage of endeavour, have been devoted to DeFi as people look to fulfil the promise provided of blockchain, smart contracts and dApps. This has led to the emergence of a range of protocols that meet various financial needs. Some allow DeFi to mimic tools that have existed in the traditional system for years (such as derivatives), others allow us to buy and exchange a range of cryptoassets more easily (DEXs and NFT marketplaces), and others allow us to use crypto in ways fiat currency cannot be used (yield farming). New protocols have also emerged to help strengthen and widen the DeFi ecosystem, and of course, promote further use by offering advancements such as bridges between blockchains (so that assets can be swapped between them) and indexes for categories of cryptoassets (replicas of these indexes can be tokenized and exchanged). This digital marketplace is evolving at breakneck speed, largely unfettered by regulation or access issues, and turbocharged by open sourcing and composability, which allows anyone, anywhere, to innovate and upgrade protocols if they have the skills to. The markets do not close at 5pm or the weekends, and the ethos of being always on extends to the architects of the ecosystem.

Users of DeFi protocols have new types of risk and opportunity to navigate. The opportunity is to participate in a new and growing financial ecosystem, with pseudonymity and no real financial or verification barrier to entry to speak of, in which a handful of coins and tokens have delivered hefty investment returns. The risks include smart contract risk, as users need to be sure that the code will execute the transaction correctly. There is also a risk that protocols are hacked. While DeFi lacks formal regulation, there is also regulatory risk as governments may decide to zero in on DeFi activities, or individuals and protocols that they've identified as suspicious. Users also face considerable volatility risk. Those same assets that can make people rich overnight might make someone not so rich overnight. There is also an element of market risk. If the prices of major coins fall, there is usually a corresponding drop in the rest of the market.

Considering the unregulated nature of DeFi, other writers have neatly conceptualized it as a Wild West Wall Street, a moniker that does a reasonable job of depicting this particular intersection of genius, opportunity, chaos and risk. In time, as protocols and networks strengthen, perhaps the emphasis can shift further towards the first two of these words.

Let's look at the types of protocol being built. Rather than list every protocol, instead we will examine different use cases for DeFi and what they add to the environment. This will not be an exhaustive overview of every type of protocol, and could quickly become outdated, but gives a snapshot of where DeFi is in 2023 relative to where it began. There are also examples of each type of protocol on offer. These are neither endorsements nor necessarily the best protocols, but have been mostly selected due to their TVL and categorization with DeFi Llama, as of February 2023.[1]

Types of protocol

Decentralized exchanges

WHAT IT DOES

DEXs were mentioned in the previous chapter, but should be mentioned again as they provide an ecosystem for protocols that enable the exchange of cryptoassets without the need for intermediaries. They are made possible by AMMs, liquidity pools and smart contracts, and are designed to allow the flow of assets with lower costs and faster settlement, especially when settling complex transactions. In the trading of non-blockchain native assets, these same protocols may also become important. DEXs are already being configured to trade tokenized real estate, and it is highly probable that DEXs will be used to transfer a wide range of off-chain assets, in time.[2]

Examples:

- Curve
- Uniswap
- PancakeSwap
- Balancer
- Sushi

Lending platforms

WHAT IT DOES

Lending protocols allow users to borrow and lend DeFi assets. Most of these protocols offer collateralized lending, whereby lenders earn interest by adding their assets to a liquidity pool, and borrowers are required to provide collateral to ensure that the liquidity pool cannot be short-changed.

There is also an emerging market for uncollateralized loans. These often have high minimum borrowing limits and are chiefly targeted at DeFi institutions. The options for everyday investors are also limited, but there are protocols in existence that verify borrowers and provide on-chain credit ratings. This could inspire a profitable and valuable DeFi lending market, but will, of course, introduce new risks for lenders.

Examples:

- Aave
- JustLend
- Compound Finance
- Venus
- Euler

Example (uncollateralized):

- TrueFi

Bridge

WHAT IT DOES

A bridge protocol transfers tokens between networks. This is useful where assets are not recognized on the same chain and builds interoperability into DeFi. As of February 15, 2023, roughly 90 per cent of DeFi trading takes place on eight chains, with 59.2 per cent on Ethereum, 10.7 per cent on Tron and 10.1 per cent on Binance Smart Chain.

These figures do not account for Bitcoin, which is often disregarded in DeFi measurements due to its lack of smart contract compatibility. It follows that Wrapped Bitcoin, a protocol that allows users to represent their bitcoin holdings on other chains, which brings the liquidity and trading of bitcoin to DeFi, is a popular bridge.

Examples:

- WBTC (Wrapped Bitcoin)
- JustCryptos
- Multichain
- Poly Network
- Portal

Collateralized Debt Positions (CDPs)

WHAT IT DOES

As mentioned earlier, the CDP was one of DeFi's first breakthroughs. It allows users to take out loans by posting cryptoassets they already own as collateral. The key difference between this and a lending protocol is that borrowers are not receiving funds taken from a liquidity pool. The loan value they receive is instead in the form of an asset-backed (usually Ether) stablecoin, minted by the CDP protocol. The issuance of DAI from MakerDAO is an example DeFi natives will be familiar with.

CDPs and lending protocols are especially useful for people who want to use their cryptoassets as collateral to make further investments, without needing to sell them to do so. This allows users to borrow without forfeiting upcoming gains from asset appreciation (users do, of course, remain exposed to losses in the asset that they have used as collateral).

Examples:

- MakerDAO
- JustStables
- Liquity
- Abracadabra
- Kava Mint

Yield farming and yield aggregators

WHAT IT DOES

DeFi protocols often need liquidity pools to facilitate trading and leverage network effects, and they can meet this need by encouraging users to stake assets on their platform in return for interest and other rewards, such as governance rights. This process is called yield farming and attracts users who are looking to make returns on their holdings.

A yield aggregator, or yield optimizer, will scan the market for staking opportunities and move the user's assets into the highest-yielding liquidity pools or a portfolio of them (which spreads risk and allows exposure to more opportunities). These mechanisms have enabled protocols to rapidly scale their operations and provide the liquidity required for a range of DeFi operations. In the best-case scenario, the growth of platforms will lead to a price increase of any native token that it has.

There are risks for platforms to navigate too. Liquidity could drain rapidly if interest rates drop or users flock to platforms with higher rates. Rates also need to be sustainable.

Yield examples:

- Convex Finance
- Aura
- Arrakis Finance
- Alpaca Finance
- Coinwind

Yield aggregator examples:

- Yearn Finance
- Beefy
- Idle
- Flamincome
- Origin Dollar

Derivatives

WHAT IT DOES

Protocols have been built to allow the trading of crypto derivatives, such as futures, perpetual futures and options relating to cryptoassets. Perpetual futures, a crypto-only derivative with no defined expiry date and no assets changing hands, have been by far the most commonly used.

Crypto derivatives may also have leverage built in, which is to say that gains and losses can be amplified by an agreed rate. Therefore, investors can profit or lose at steeper rates than would have been experienced by simply taking a position on the asset that is the subject of the agreement. Crypto derivatives can potentially help sophisticated traders hedge against market crashes, for example by reserving the future right to sell a token at a price not dissimilar to its current market value, but due to their complexity and risk, the average investor would do well to approach them with caution or avoid them entirely.

On a different tangent, but still within derivatives, there are DeFi protocols that create 'synthetic' assets that mimic and tokenize the value of a range of off-chain and on-chain assets (at this point, this is mostly limited to a handful of cryptocurrencies and fiat currencies). Traders can take investment positions relating to the price fluctuations of these assets, without ever needing to buy the underlying asset.

Centralized examples:

- Bybit
- Huobi
- Bitmex
- Binance

Decentralized examples:

- GMX
- dYdX

Synthetic asset example:

- Synthetix

Indexes and copycat investing

WHAT IT DOES

Indexing protocols bundle assets together into an investable strategy. As is the case with TradFi indexing, these protocols are used to make investments that track a particular market, sector or type of asset. This means that investors spread their risk and invest in strategic positions, so they are investing in their belief in a market or idea, rather than an individual asset.

Copycat investing, sometimes called coattail investing, allows DeFi investors to purchase assets in the same allocations as those bought by successful investors. This could be likened to investing in an investment fund manager but there are several key differences. A DeFi copycat investor is copying the investment strategies of pseudonymous investors who have achieved success in DeFi, rather than investing in regulated funds created by teams of professionals who have risen through the ranks of established asset and wealth management companies.

A word of caution is perhaps needed here, as there will be unregulated investors who outperform. This is not unlike having millions of punters placing bets on horse races over the course of a day. There is a significant likelihood that the gambler with the best returns achieves them through luck rather than judgement or knowledge. So too with DeFi investing, though this is not to say that there will not be prominent, capable and credible DeFi investors. It should be noted that investors can participate in copycat investing via regulated assets on apps like eToro.

Index examples:

- Set Protocol
- Index Coop
- Toros

Copycat investor examples:

- dHedge
- Enzyme

Insurance

WHAT IT DOES

Considering the risks present in DeFi, the potential benefits of introducing crypto insurance are abundant. While there are ongoing projects devoted to applying DeFi protocols and blockchain to familiar insurance products, DeFi insurance protocols have so far been focused on DeFi-specific risks.

It is possible to acquire insurance for a range of risks including smart contract failure, governance errors, stablecoin depegging, oracle malfunctions, custody problems (most likely with an exchange), wallet exploits or specific losses incurred while staking or yield farming. Insurance also exists for slashing risk, in case the validator you use to stake your assets is slashed for wrongdoing.

Should a payable event occur, the insured will be compensated via a pooled fund. In crypto insurance, those who pool their funds may also have a say in how the contract is governed and who receives a payout.

Separately, off-chain insurance for DeFi assets is available, and may take on a prominent role as regulation develops and if crypto adoption grows.

Examples:

- Nexus Mutual
- Unslashed
- InsurAce
- Risk Harbour
- Guard Helmet

Payments

WHAT IT DOES

Cryptocurrencies have not yet achieved widespread use in everyday finance, and even in El Salvador, where Bitcoin is legal tender, initial regular usage has been low and concentrated within educated and banked young men.[3] There are several hurdles to jump, including transaction speed and volume, chain interoperability and fluctuations in asset value.

These challenges are actively being attacked. In terms of speed, payment protocols now exist to pool transactions off-chain, bundling them together to lighten the load on networks. Protocols are also being used to facilitate immediate exchanges between different currencies, including fiat, digital and crypto. Should this reach maximum potential, users will be able to safely and securely buy products using any asset they want, and the seller will be remunerated in their own currency of choice. If widespread adoption occurs, this could remove layers of costs for merchants, and resolve a longstanding drawback from digital payments. Equally, as crypto is not widely accepted as payment off-chain, do not overlook the need for fiat conversions, which can reduce or eradicate the benefit of using crypto for payments.

Another innovation of note is payment streaming. This involves incremental payments, such as a salary, rent, mortgage or debt repayment, being made continuously in real time rather than recurring weekly, monthly or annual chunks (or any agreed timeframe). This service also exists outside of crypto.

Examples:

- Lightning Network (Bitcoin only)
- Flexa
- Sablier Finance
- Llama Pay
- Sushi Furo

Gaming

WHAT IT DOES

Professional services giant PwC has estimated that the worldwide video gaming industry (as opposed to the gambling industry, which sometimes goes by the tag of 'gaming') will be worth over $300 billion by 2026.[4] Naturally, efforts are now being made to grow DeFi in this market.

This is being achieved in various ways. Some DeFi protocols have built interfaces, such as Aavegotchi and AstarFarm, to gamify interactions and make staking or NFT collecting more enjoyable. Elsewhere, games have incorporated NFTs and cryptocurrencies to create marketplaces or even paid jobs for players; 'play to earn' models, as used by Axie Infinity, show how players can be rewarded for their engagement.

Some games allow players to purchase virtual land or an NFT (this is occasionally a prerequisite for participation), and some have their own native currency. In time, it is expected that games will also start to utilize virtual (VR) and augmented reality (AR), opening up countless opportunities for engagements, and in the case of AR, turning the real world into a playground.

Virtual economies are not new and have existed in games like *World of Warcraft*, *Eve Online*, *Entropia Universe* and *Second Life*. There is also history for non-DeFi items selling for significant sums in fiat currency. A *Second Life* user bought a virtual Amsterdam for $50,000 in 2007, and a virtual property sale in *Entropia Universe* netted $635,000 in 2010.[5, 6] Nonetheless, NFTs provide a new way to demonstrate ownership of 'land' or items on-chain, and games could prove to be a valuable platform for decentralized microeconomies.

'Real-World Assets'

WHAT IT DOES

These protocols allow physical, non-cryptoassets to be traded via DeFi protocols. This is achieved through tokenization, where a token represents ownership of an entire asset or a fractional share in one. So far, this has mostly been used to facilitate investments in luxury goods and real estate. In real estate, people can invest in fractionalized ownership of a property, which can be rented to generate ongoing revenue. Luxury goods are monetized in a different manner and can be tokenized (and usually fractionalized) before being stored and sold at a later date, or if the whole asset is owned, simply stored and received at a later date.

In sum, real-world asset protocols add value by tokenizing assets and bringing them to blockchains, and through fractionalization they can offer access to asset classes that have historically been out of reach of most investors. They also illustrate a blurring of the boundaries between 'real-world' and DeFi trading and ownership.

Examples:

- RealT Tokens
- Lofty
- CACHE.gold
- Tangible
- Landshare

Esoteric protocols

WHAT IT DOES

This is not a formal category, but rather a handful of creative DeFi protocols. Examples include:

- **Bounties Network and Gitcoin:** allows people to offer crypto rewards for the fulfilment of a task or job. These protocols are designed with freelancing and grassroots social action in mind.

- **Augur:** a blockchain-based predictions market for people to gamble on sports or world events.

- **PoolTogether:** a DeFi protocol that operates in a very similar manner to premium bonds. Essentially, users pool their money and the combined interest is paid out to a winner every day. Users do not pay to enter the system but do need to trust the protocol with their assets.

What is the impact of DeFi protocols?

In a mere five years since its coining as a term, DeFi protocols have started to form a sprawling ecosystem. We're maybe looking at shoots more than blossoms, but in crypto exchanges, bridges to TradFi, and protocols for lending, borrowing, investing, gaming and more, there are the beginnings of an exciting and valuable digital economy. This in itself is interesting to finance professionals and hobbyists but does not convey why DeFi has provoked such strong emotional responses from those in financial services and beyond. This part of the narrative needs expanding beyond the loss of faith in institutions described earlier. We need to consider why DeFi materially changes anything about finance.

The answer to this can be found in the introduction of blockchain and cryptography, which is not something that people would typically be passionate about. After all, cryptography is the exchange of encrypted messaging, and blockchain is an accounting tool, an internet-based distributed ledger the core purpose of which is to add utility to how messages are exchanged and records are kept. None of this is particularly glamorous. However, this method of record keeping and messaging is interesting for its potential to reduce centralized activities to lines of code that anyone could access.

In a fully decentralized economy reliant on shared blockchain databases, all exchanges are made between people and the network, or are peer-to-peer, and there is no government, corporate or institutional processing involved. There is no need for verifications, bookkeeping, translations, foreign exchange or regulatory procedures. Everything is coded into transactions and in optimal cases, transactions of varying complexity can be made and completed with relative ease. With DeFi protocols, we now have a self-sustaining, uncensored, borderless system that mimics some of the financial operations that form the backbone of TradFi, adds new functions to finance, and in theory allows for greater scrutiny (through blockchain analytics) and personal control over assets (through self-custody). These characteristics may be novel or preferable for some. For others, who are underserved or excluded by TradFi, or who find themselves in situations of political or national economic turmoil, the existence of an accessible and international financial system could be a vital lifeline.

More exciting, yes; but a sense check is needed here. While we can comfortably say that DeFi and blockchain 'might', 'can' or 'could' overhaul our financial lives, it is a new system and remains a niche area. DeFi TVLs show us that the bulk of activity taking place in DeFi is either speculative trading or lending of varying complexity, and that usage is skewed towards certain demographics, and towards individuals and organizations with investment expertise. In a 2022 paper, the OECD notes the relatively high knowledge barrier to entry in DeFi, surmising that many existing users will have a strong comprehension of crypto, other asset classes, and smart contracts.[7] Also, the influence of institutional investors on crypto could become far more significant as time passes. The PwC Crypto Hedge Fund Report 2022 found that the market for crypto hedge funds is growing in terms of assets under management, supported by significant investment from high-net-worth individuals and family offices. It also found that 41 per cent of crypto hedge funds surveyed were using decentralized exchanges (this report was written while Terra unpegged. Institutional interest appeared to recover in 2023).[8] Despite DeFi's potential, it should still be considered a niche market. It also remains a smaller market than CeFi, which hints at public opinion relating to user interfaces, accessibility and regulatory oversight.

DeFi is not without controversy, either. As DeFi largely exists outside of regulation, asset owners typically have limited or no recourse if their assets rapidly fall in value or are lost or stolen. Let's note that private keys can easily be lost and many DeFi tools have been hacked. An increasing reliance on cryptocurrencies could also hamper efforts made by governments and central banks, many of which are put in place through legitimate and democratic processes, to use monetary policy to stabilize their economies.

> Users who lose their passwords have probably lost their assets. Programmer Stefan Thomas famously lost the password to an account holding 7,002 bitcoins, equivalent to hundreds of millions of dollars. His USB device allows 10 password guesses before locking him out indefinitely. He's made eight incorrect attempts so far (at the time of writing).

We should go back to the issue of cryptocurrency valuations, as the success or failure of DeFi activity is dependent upon them. In contrast to the programmable nature of DeFi, valuations often fluctuate due to hype, fear of missing out (FOMO) and sizable money movements made by the largest accounts, known as crypto whales.

The factors that determine the value of a cryptoasset can therefore be very slippery. In an exceptionally written Bloomberg piece, 'The Only Crypto Story You Need', Matt Levine elaborates on this by providing two simplifications for understanding bitcoin's valuation. The first is that if you can create a token that trades electronically, and there's a chance people will pay some amount of money for it, then why not?[9]

This mentality gets to the heart of a critical point in crypto valuation. A token project might represent an intriguing economic philosophy or economic innovation, or it might be a joke, scam or pastiche. Regardless, if people agree that the token or the project has value, or at least believe or speculate that its value will rise, the token's price will correspond gradually or quickly.

The second simplification involves an argument that was made about bitcoin in its infancy. Prior to this theory being debunked, some believed that bitcoin's value would be capped as people could replicate its software (which is open-sourced), create a copy of bitcoin with a new name, and sell the new token at a discount. This would dilute inflows to bitcoin, prove that bitcoin's supply was limitless, and prevent bitcoin's price from rising beyond a certain point. This scenario simply didn't play out. Instead, the crypto market wanted the original bitcoin. As Levine notes, the social acceptance of bitcoin gave it value, rather than the elegance of its code.

So DeFi protocols and assets offer a new economic environment, where regulation is sparse or non-existent, and the assets being traded can plummet or climb on a whim. 'So what?' you might ask. The transparency of public blockchains is a reasonable platform for trust and confidence, and the validation and mining networks of larger cryptocurrencies show how social backing can add substantial value, and how a longstanding and reliable network can appear robust. It can also be pointed out that the value of most major fiat currencies is governed by social forces, to a point. The US dollar, for instance, hasn't been backed by a physical commodity since 1971 when it dropped the gold standard. Its market value derives from supply and demand, which isn't a million miles removed from social acceptance.

Fiat and crypto currencies are very different though. The value of national currencies, or regional ones such as the Euro, are linked to a government or central bank's ability to repay its debts and manage the stability of the currency. For readers in many nations, it seems there is little to fear on this front. This could be a bad thing, though, if you're in a nation like Sri Lanka, Lebanon, Zambia or Ghana, which defaulted on debt in 2022, or if you're from Zimbabwe, Argentina, Sudan, Venezuela or Iran, which have endured high and sustained inflation rates in the early 2020s. Defaults and low credit ratings create enduring problems as nations, and corporations within them, need to pay higher interest rates when borrowing funds. This stifles growth as nations with lower credit ratings receive less favourable terms when borrowing money and are deemed less attractive and riskier to foreign investors. High inflation, on the other hand, will sharply erode the purchasing power of a national currency over time, leading to soaring prices and cutbacks in the consumption of many goods and services.

From this, we might conclude that the long-term utility people find in DeFi will correlate with their perception and experiences of their domestic financial system. The concept of using a new, unregulated and somewhat controversial system might be more tempting if you don't consider your own economy to be reliable and trustworthy. If the financial system works well for you, then DeFi's value is more likely to be for speculation rather than the basis for your entire financial life.

That said, it is also true that strong national or central bank economies do not ensure that all citizens or entities are treated equally. You may be less bought into your national economy if you were among the 11 per cent of UK households who used a food bank in October 2021 [the UK's food banks are designed to support the UK's poorest households; users usually need to be referred by Citizens Advice, a GP, social worker or housing association], or based in the United States, where the 1 per cent of wealthiest people own more wealth than the poorest 90 per cent combined.[10] There is intersectionality to consider too. In the United States, the average black, Latino or Hispanic household earns roughly half as much as the average white household and possesses about 15–20 per cent as much net wealth.[11] To take a more global perspective, we could highlight that the wealthiest 1 per cent captured 63 per cent of all new wealth creation between 2020 and the start of 2023, years in which the pandemic took a major toll on economies and people's living standards.[12] Whether this translates into crypto adoption is another issue, however. Crypto and DeFi are far more accessible to those with assets to invest, reliable internet access and financial education. DeFi is not necessarily, and to date hasn't been, much of a market for financial inclusion.

There are many reasons why the prospect of DeFi could be appealing. Regardless of whether it will actually shift us to a better economy, whatever that is, and regardless of who is currently using it or for what reason, the concept of a new and improved financial system is relatively easy to market. Simultaneously, crypto is an easy sell to those who believe in a libertarian society with an unrestricted free market and no government intervention. This is yet another reason why crypto and DeFi have proven so divisive in such a short time. A lot of people are willing to claim that the technology possesses certain traits de facto, and a large proportion of them are projecting a narrative or trying to sell you something.

There is no need to be wedded to an all-or-nothing mentality here, as DeFi may even be complementary to existing markets. It is also sensible to abandon the idea that DeFi is monolithic. It can be a varied universe of ecosystems, working towards the achievement of differing objectives.

IS IT ALL A BIG PONZI SCHEME?

An accusation often levelled at cryptocurrencies and DeFi is that the whole thing is a massive Ponzi scheme, where investment returns are paid to existing investors from sums deposited by new investors. In typical Ponzi schemes, early investors make attractive sums of money, spread the word to new investors, and start a cycle that perpetuates so long as the scheme can satisfy client redemptions. Once the cycle becomes unsustainable, the scheme crumbles, a lot of people lose their money, and a handful of people end up in jail, generally speaking. Ponzi schemes are named after Charles Ponzi, whose pyramid-style investment scam cost investors $20 million in the 1920s.

DeFi involves a lot of projects that are Ponzi adjacent at best. This can be evidenced in projects that offer high yields to early adopters, such as Terra, which offered lenders up to 20 per cent returns for adding to its liquidity pool. While high yields do not immediately equate to a Ponzi, and while there is logic to growing the liquidity pool quickly, there is also a risk that liquidity dries up when yields reduce, and also that tokens will not maintain their value. There eventually comes a point where a high-yielding project needs to justify its value, and because DeFi projects need to achieve scale, and will be best served by achieving it quickly, a lot of projects overreach. Also, it cannot be denied that many supposed DeFi projects have simply been Ponzi schemes.

A credible crypto project differs from a Ponzi scheme in that there will be underlying value to it that extends beyond yield alone. However, this value is contingent on people perceiving that it exists (a rather non-trivial issue), as well as rival protocols, external economic factors and confidence in the crypto markets. We can use currencies such as bitcoin and Ether to show that crypto is not a Ponzi scheme. While the valuation of these currencies fluctuates, both have endured multiple downturns and neither relies on money from new investors to pay existing ones.

References

1 DefiLlama. DefiLlama, 2023, defillama.com/categories (archived at https://perma.cc/3LAZ-N7UR)

2 digishares.io. DigiShares to trade real-world assets with Balancer, 2023, digishares.io/real-estate-exchange (archived at https://perma.cc/LH2Y-KHFC)

3 F Alvarez, D Argente and D Van Patten. Are cryptocurrencies currencies? Bitcoin as legal tender in El Salvador, Becker Friedman Institute, 2022, bfi.uchicago.edu/insight/finding/are-cryptocurrencies-currencies-bitcoin-as-legal-tender-in-el-salvador/ (archived at https://perma.cc/57J5-4MR2)

4 W Ballhaus, W Chow and E Rivet. Perspectives from the Global Entertainment & Media Outlook 2023–2027, 2022

5 R Dotinga. Second Life's Amsterdam snapped up on eBay, Wired, 2007, www.wired.com/2007/03/second-lifes-am/ (archived at https://perma.cc/799E-Y24S)

6 O Chiang. Meet the man who just made a half million from the sale of virtual property, Forbes, 2010, www.forbes.com/sites/oliverchiang/2010/11/13/meet-the-man-who-just-made-a-cool-half-million-from-the-sale-of-virtual-property/?sh=1e7ca5cd21cd (archived at https://perma.cc/FMM4-ZTJE)

7 OECD. Why Decentralised Finance (DeFi) matters and the policy implications, OECD Paris, 2022, www.oecd.org/daf/fin/financial-markets/Why-Decentralised-Finance-DeFi-Matters-and-the-Policy-Implications.pdf (archived at https://perma.cc/QDQ4-68A8)

8 M Willems. Aggressive institutional investors pushing into digital assets set to replace retail players, CityA.M., 2023, www.cityam.com/unstoppable-institutional-investors-pushing-into-digital-set-to-replace-retail-players-in-2023/ (archived at https://perma.cc/6CJW-6MQJ)

9 M Levine. The only crypto story you need, Bloomberg.com, 2022, www. bloomberg.com/features/2022-the-crypto-story/#xj4y7vzkg (archived at https://perma.cc/LBA5-8EWF)

10 B Francis-Devine, S Irvine and A Gorb. Food banks in the UK, commonslibrary.parliament.uk, 2021, commonslibrary.parliament.uk/ research-briefings/cbp-8585/ (archived at https://perma.cc/2P3S-QP4Y)

11 A Aladangady and A Forde. Wealth inequality and the racial wealth gap, 2021, www.federalreserve.gov/econres/notes/feds-notes/wealth-inequality-and-the-racial-wealth-gap-20211022.html (archived at https://perma.cc/J79E-5333)

12 Oxfam International. Richest 1% bag nearly twice as much wealth as the rest of the world put together over the past two years, Oxfam International, 2023, www.oxfam.org/en/press-releases/richest-1-bag-nearly-twice-much-wealth-rest-world-put-together-over-past-two-years (archived at https://perma.cc/ FTQ8-6FVL)

05

DAOs: The organizational framework for DeFi

Blockchain, smart contracts and DeFi raise pertinent questions about the nature of organizational structure and governance, both in finance and beyond. Let's consider the growing range of protocols mentioned in the previous chapter. If smart contracts are to replace financial institutions and intermediaries, and protocols become the vessels through which financial activity flows, then who or what exactly is governing the protocols? The answer to this question, usually, is a decentralized autonomous organization (DAO).

Centralization and the introduction of DAOs

Before diving into DAOs, let's first consider centralization. Centralization, like decentralization, can exist to varying degrees, though a 'perfect' model of centralization occurs if authority and control over an activity or organization are held by a singular entity. If we apply this rationale to financial services, there is no singular entity running the show, but the industry is centralized in the sense that a relatively small number of organizations and individuals wield enormous influence over the direction of our economies. This has implications for financial stability, and some institutions are recognized by the Financial Stability Board (FSB) as being 'too big to fail' and classified as 'systemically important financial institutions'. In banking, the FSB's 2022 list of

G-SIBs – global systematically important banks – includes 30 banks whose demise would cause considerable financial harm, and therefore they are required to meet stricter regulatory standards such as higher capital requirements, or more stringent stress tests.

This centralization has numerous pros and cons. To speak in favour of it, we can say that it offers efficiencies, allows for clear and hierarchical structures of command and facilitates straightforward divisions of labour. If problems arise, centralized structures can respond quickly, typically through actions chosen by a leader or board members. Due to their size, they are also more able to absorb the impact of fraud, hacks, investment losses and economic slumps. They are also manageable (in a sense) for regulators and governing bodies, and the G-SIBs mentioned above provides an example of how scrutiny can be applied to larger organizations to protect the system against vulnerabilities. To discuss the downsides of centralization, we can turn to the concentration of power in the hands of a few, a lack of transparency, a general absence of stakeholder control, and, for many reasons, the existence of organizations that are 'too big to fail' makes the system more vulnerable. Despite its shortcomings, which is not to say that any paradigm offers perfection, centralization has been a consistent and effective feature of international finance for generations and has taken on new dimensions as technology has opened the door to globalization. Finance aside, the centralization of power is deeply socially embedded in many respects.

Decentralized finance, by definition, seeks to avoid this approach, and this is where DAOs come in. DAOs are blockchain-based and decentralized ownership structures designed to help members of a community or group reach decisions, manage treasuries, decide on project roadmaps, and govern more equitably. In contrast to decisions being made behind closed doors, or being unilaterally made by powerful individuals or boards, most DAO activity takes place on public permissionless blockchains for transparency, and a community can reject unpopular proposals. Decisions are typically made using voting mechanisms with outcomes based on the weighted support of DAO token holders. Ostensibly, DAOs are the de facto governance model of

DeFi, offering flattened hierarchies and democratizing the power to shape and contribute to governance among members.

There is already a wide range of DAOs, serving multiple purposes. They exist for protocol governance, the funding of public goods, charitable work, community building, investments and much more. They possess differing governance frameworks, tokens and voting mechanisms, and also differ in how decentralized they are. The World Economic Forum's 2023 DAO Toolkit offers three useful points for assessing if an organization qualifies as a DAO. To paraphrase slightly:

1 Does it leverage blockchains, digital assets and related technologies?

2 Does it coordinate activities and/or allocate resources?

3 Is it governed primarily on a decentralized basis?[1]

If an organization meets all three criteria, it can be considered a DAO.

How DAOs work

Decision-making, voting and tokens

The leadership structure of a DAO is different to a centralized organization, but there is a similarity in the sense that some DAO members will hold elevated status and influence. Founders, for example, are responsible for creating an overarching mission or purpose for a group, and this responsibility may be ongoing even if their control over governance diminishes. Some DAO members may also be granted access, rights or permissions based on expertise, especially for roles such as treasury management and smart contract deployment.

MULTISIG WALLET

Treasurers and developers often deploy a multisig (multiple signature) wallet, whereby a combination of separate keys is required to authorize a change or activity.

Some DAOs will also create panels or councils to deliberate on important or specialized activities, which can offer valuable structure in instances where a vote would be impractical or ill-advised. Token holders who are not founders, developers, treasurers or council members may also receive governance-related incentives based on their participation levels. In relation to this, governance tokens may be awarded to community members whose behaviour matches the ethos of the group, or be apportioned based on contributions to the DAO, competence or trustworthiness.

DAO activity and governance are not exclusively on-chain. In fact, voting usually occurs off-chain (this is for practical reasons, such as the accessibility, functionality and availability of voting platforms) and many DAOs routinely use communications platforms such as Discord and Telegram to manage their communities and propose votes. The projects or work that DAOs create may also be at a distance from blockchain. DAOs might be formed by collectives of artists or content creators, or they might exist to support communities in physical locations. Some DAOs will issue bounties for tasks to be carried out by a group of people with relevant skills and expertise, usually referred to as a workstream, and in such instances a workstream leader is appointed to manage the allocated resources and ensure that a task is carried out, organizing recruitment and remuneration where necessary.

HOW WORKSTREAMS SHOWCASE THE FUNCTIONING OF A DAO

Workstreams are useful in illustrating the decentralized structure of a DAO. Resources are unlikely to be allocated unless the community agrees to the plan of action, and this community will probably include the expected participants in the workstream. This differs from conventional workplace arrangements where a manager's directive may be final, regardless of the opinions of those who report to them. It instead allows a negotiation of terms, including timeframe, pay, workstream size and more, which continues until both parties are satisfied. This is illustrated excellently here: www.agileleadershipjourney.com/blog/decentralized-autonomous-organization-impact-collaboration.[2]

While hierarchy is not entirely absent from the governance of DAOs, leadership figures do not impose strategy or decisions upon the community, and if they do, they are likely serving a failsafe function. Instead, decisions within a DAO are usually prompted by proposals made within the community, which are later put to a vote. Votes are usually weighted in relation to governance tokens, regular tokens or NFTs, and might be decided by a simple 'most tokens wins' format, or alternatively might be measured by a 'one-person, one-vote' system, insofar as it is possible.

There are many voting mechanisms available to DAOs, each with benefits and drawbacks. DAOs ultimately need to select a voting system that is suitable for their activities, which offers a suitable balance between effective decision-making and speed of consensus. Mixed in with these challenges is the desire to create voting processes that don't usher in plutocracy, with a handful of people holding a majority of voting power, and also to avoid voter apathy, where people feel little incentive to participate.

DAO voting mechanisms

Token-based quorum voting

This is a simple but popular voting process. In token-based quorum voting, a certain percentage or number of tokens need to be committed for a proposal to be submitted and passed. To pick random figures, a proposal might be considered for a vote if 100 tokens or 1 per cent of the token supply is committed to it. If approved, the proposal might then be acted upon if owners of 1000 tokens or 10 per cent of the overall supply commit to the vote and a majority is achieved. When selecting a threshold, DAOs should ensure that they are low enough for decisions to pass, but high enough that major decisions are not approved with minimal support.

In situations where token supply is heavily concentrated among several members, DAOs can quickly become undemocratic, as the votes of one account might outweigh the votes of hundreds. In token-based quorum voting, we might also consider tactical voting. If token holders disagree with a new proposal that is expected to have majority support, they might choose to abstain rather than vote 'no' in an attempt to prevent the quorum from being achieved. In other instances, a sensible decision might fail to pass if it simply doesn't garner enough interest.

WHALE HUNTING

Token-based quorum voting can run into difficulty when voting thresholds are not being met. To counter this, there are instances where members of a DAO attempt to flag the attention of a major token holder in order to reach the voting quorum for an important vote. This is known as 'whale hunting' and may become crucial if a decision needs to be made with urgency.[3]

Permissioned relative majority

If the rules of token-based quorum voting apply but we remove the quorum, we have relative majority voting. This method is especially prone to attacks, whereby multiple unpopular or obscure proposals could be proposed with one or few votes, and these proposals will pass unless DAO members are vigilant. Permissioned relative majority voting adds a layer of security to this, by ensuring that proposals can only be valid if sponsored by DAO members.

Continuous approval voting

This process, utilized by MakerDAO, insists that voters lock their tokens within a voting contract and allocate them to either the status quo or a newly proposed state for the protocol. For a new proposal to pass, it must achieve a majority of voting weight.

As tokens are continuously staked, this ensures that the current state of the DAO is adequately represented in a voting process, lessening the chance of a proposal being passed on the basis of being new and exciting. Nonetheless, this can serve as a barrier to change, especially where an update is beneficial but not critical. As with a number of other weighted voting mechanisms, it can also keep DAOs aligned with the views of a small number of whale accounts.

Optimistic governance

Optimistic governance flips the quorum threshold on its head, replacing the minimum token commitment with a minimum rejection threshold. Using this model, proposals will pass unless there is strong resistance to them. Optimistic governance operates on the principle that all proposals put forward are improvements, unless proven otherwise.

Quadratic voting

Quadratic voting provides a method for diluting the voting power of the largest account holders, while still recognizing their influence. It does this by counting votes according to their square root, so the vote of one account with 100 tokens will carry less weight than the votes of two accounts with 50 tokens each. To explain, any single account will need 1 token to make 1 vote, 4 tokens to make 2 votes, 9 tokens to make 3 votes, and so on.

This method might lessen the imbalance of power in DAOs, but is also subject to Sybil attacks, whereby one person spreads their assets across multiple accounts. This issue might be lessened if it becomes possible to safely link pseudonymous accounts with personal identities without making identities public.

Identity-based voting

Rather than rely on coin staking or weighting, DAOs may opt for voting systems based upon personal identification. This is an emerging technique and is likely to make use of NFTs. Another version of this, using Proof of Attendance Protocols (POAPs), could confer voting rights to those who have participated in certain activities, such as votes or community events. In principle, this might weigh votes in relation to member enthusiasm and community engagement, rather than token ownership.

Skin-in-the-game

It is possible that voting will follow a more honest path if members are rewarded or punished in relation to the outcome of their votes. In this type of system, voters are effectively betting for or against the success of a proposal, and a proposal might be put in place if voters, on balance, expect it to be good. A prominent concern with such a method is deciding a metric for a 'good' decision. Token price seems an obvious choice but may be impacted by factors that are not connected to the vote.

Conviction voting

Conviction voting requires members to stake their tokens on proposals, and if proposals eventually accrue enough support they will pass. Multiple proposals can coexist and this means members are likely to devote their voting power to proposals of greater importance. While this voting method does not remove voting inequality, it does potentially offer minority voters a better chance of making an impact.

Councils/Committees

Some DAOs adopt a council or committee of representatives, elected via a decentralized voting process. The tenures of these representatives will vary, but generally there are regular procedures where DAO members can vote in favour or against them, and those who do not uphold community interests will likely be removed. In some instances, the council or committee operates a little like a board, albeit one that needs community approval to take action. DAO councils and committees might oversee basic and non-contentious decisions or be brought in on issues where action is required but voting processes do not deliver an outcome.

Delegation

In some DAOs, token holders are able to delegate their voting power to a third party within the DAO, which may be another person or group. This can ensure that voting thresholds are met while removing the burden of voting from token holders. This practice is somewhat similar to allowing an asset manager to vote at AGMs on your behalf. Nonetheless, asset managers are publicly visible and will suffer significant reputational damage if they vote in a controversial fashion, whereas a DAO member may be pseudonymous, and even if publicly known, is unlikely to be exposed to the same level of accountability.

The voting systems available to DAOs extend beyond this list, and theoretically there are near-endless variations to how voting might be structured. As the examples suggest, the extent to which DAOs are decentralized or democratized will vary, and their structure is likely to be tailored to the purpose and community of the DAO, rather than a puritanical adherence to decentralization. It is also possible for DAOs to deploy hybrid or mixed voting systems, or to transition from one system to another as the group matures. Many DAOs begin life in a relatively centralized fashion, with the openly stated intention of decentralizing as they grow.

Are DAOs legally recognized?

The philosophy of decentralized ownership does not always mesh well with the need to register a DAO with a government agency. Even so, founders may find that a legal wrapper offers them and their community protection and stability if legal issues arise. Furthermore, and regardless of a lack of DAO-specific legal frameworks, a DAO in any jurisdiction is likely to find that it does not simply operate outside of the law, as much as the idea may or may not appeal.

While DAOs are a recognizable type of organization, their legal and regulatory standing remains hazy. This is partly because they are new and partly because of how customizable they are (despite the customizable nature of DAOs, it is true that many are built with the same tools. For example, platforms such as SuperDAO and DAOhaus exist for creating and managing DAOs, and Snapshot might be used to implement governance and voting). Accordingly,

DAO founders need to weigh up their options when choosing a legal wrapper for their DAO, if they choose one at all, and they need to also consider the regulatory framework of the jurisdiction in which they incorporate.

> If a DAO has no legal wrapper, courts may still find a way to classify it. Some nations have not yet set precedent for the treatment of a DAO in court.

There are several legal wrappers available, including corporations, partnerships, trusts, limited liability companies (LLCs), foundations, charities, associations and cooperatives. In selecting one of these wrappers, a DAO should consider whether the wrapper is fit for a decentralized organization, and whether it accurately reflects the operations of the DAO. Further to this, founders should consider whether the DAO is recognized as a distinct and separate legal entity. If not, they may be subject to limited or unlimited liabilities should the DAO run into severe financial or legal difficulty. Other considerations include the ease with which a legal wrapper can be established, and the possibility of avoiding formal registration. After all, pseudonymity is often desirable for DAO leaders, but if DogeLord420 tries to register an organization it probably won't go down too well.

A handful of specific and national legal wrappers have proven popular in the early years of DAOs. For example, in Switzerland, a hub for DeFi ever since the Ethereum Foundation planted roots there, the relatively flexible structure of an ownerless foundation has proven popular. An ownerless foundation company will have a separate legal status, can be designed to have no shareholders, and include directors who will act according to the votes or best interests of token holders.[4] A supervisory authority of some sort will hold power over such an organization but have no claim to ownership of the foundation or its assets. Besides Switzerland, ownerless foundations are also available in Panama and the Cayman Islands.

Special purpose trusts, such as those available in the Cayman Islands or Guernsey, have also been used by DAOs. In a trust of this nature there are no beneficiaries, and a DAO's founders or token holders can transfer assets to trustees, who themselves are obligated to manage the assets in line with the conditions set out by the trust agreement. Not only do trustees need to act in accordance with the agreement, but they also have a general fiduciary duty to act in the best interests of the trust. A failure to do so can result in their removal as trustees. Special purpose trust agreements can be written carefully to ensure that the will of the DAO is upheld, and they also require minimal, if any, ongoing filing or reporting obligations.

With the United States being a hotbed for crypto, a handful of states have attempted to provide a welcoming regulatory environment, too. In 2018, Vermont established Blockchain-based limited liability companies (LLCs), for businesses that rely heavily on blockchains for business activity. In 2021, Wyoming began allowing DAOs to register as DAO LLCs, with limited liability and no single commanding decision-maker. Additionally, the Marshall Islands amended its Non-Profit Entities Act in 2022 to allow DAOs to register as non-profit LLCs.

Legal wrappers can be highly influential in deciding the locality of a DAO's registration. Besides legal wrappers, DAOs are more likely to flock to regions with favourable tax regimes, welcoming governments, crypto-friendly banks and available professional support. El Salvador, for example, has introduced Bitcoin as legal tender, with the consequence that income tax or capital gains tax will not be due if the price of Bitcoin rises. Germany treats cryptocurrencies as private money rather than a capital asset, meaning no tax will be paid when selling, swapping and spending cryptoassets, provided they have been held for longer than a year. Singapore, meanwhile, does not have capital gains tax at all, and in Malta, sometimes described as a crypto tax haven (it is not alone in this), there is no requirement to pay capital gains tax on long-term gains from crypto provided it is regarded as 'a store of value'.[5] We can also highlight Switzerland again, where selling and trading crypto is tax free for retail (non-professional) investors, and there is greater availability of banks that will work with crypto and DAOs. These nations contrast with the likes of China, Qatar, Oman, Morocco, Algeria, Bangladesh, Tunisia, Egypt and Iraq, which have banned crypto transactions, and 42 other countries that have implicitly banned digital assets by stifling crypto exchanges and preventing banks from handling crypto.

The range of legal and organizational considerations for a DAO will vary by jurisdiction and may be as demanding as those enforced upon centralized and registered organizations. DAOs may be subjected to employment and labour law requirements, and in nations where welfare benefits are limited or absent, or where employers are known to offer a wide range of benefits, DAOs might also consider offering employee benefits such as healthcare, income protection and life insurance. As DAOs can be created by anyone, it is also possible that employees or workstreams might form their own, for the formation and governance of sub-groups or a union.

There are compliance factors to consider, too. A DAO might be well advised to adopt practices and appoint representatives to comply with anti-money laundering (AML), know your customer (KYC) or counter-terrorism laws. In time, this could provide conflict in situations where DAO treasurers and developers are pseudonymous, and where regulators require names to be provided for accountability purposes. Those in charge of handling assets, or those responsible for the legal wrapper of a DAO, could also add insurance and banking to their to-do list. In doing so, their choice of legal wrapper, and especially a choice not to use one, could limit the availability of policies and accounts.

Tax positions, as touched upon earlier, will correspond to the legal wrapper of the DAO, as well as to its location, which may encapsulate areas of operation and trading as well as where it is headquartered. Income and capital gains taxes are a chief concern, and perhaps more so the latter as cryptoassets are usually volatile investments that might accrue significant value. The methods and remuneration allocated to token mining and validation may also trigger a taxable event or raise questions about a miner's legal relationship to the DAO. Mining, as an activity, may even become highly taxed in some countries. The U.S. Department of the Treasury proposed in March 2023 that crypto mining be subjected to a 30 per cent excise tax on the cost of powering mining facilities, a policy purportedly designed to limit environmental impact, to be accompanied by mandatory reports on energy usage and sourcing.[6]

DAOs should also understand the tax position of their chosen legal wrapper, and may elect to use one as protection against being defined as something else should an issue arise, or as a safeguard against double-taxation whereby its income is taxed by two different countries. At the time of writing, there is no internationally-agreed tax position relating to DAOs but initiatives are developing. For example, the Crypto-Asset Reporting Framework (CARF), published by the OECD in response to a G20 mandate, requires exchanges and other virtual-asset service providers (VASPs) to report crypto transactions to their relevant tax body.[7] It remains to be seen if DAOs will qualify as a VASP – they are not mentioned by name in the CARF despite their popularity. Nonetheless, initiatives such as CARF have been established in response to the fact that cryptoassets have fogged the visibility of tax-relevant activities, and in principle we can assume that most jurisdictions are seeking to address this.

Securities laws are also an important factor, and become highly relevant when focusing on token issuance because many, if not most, tokens might be classified as investments. In the US, for example, any asset deemed a security receives similar treatment to a share in a company. This famously became an issue when 'The DAO', the first DAO in existence, was shut down by the U.S. Securities and Exchange Commission (SEC). The SEC judged The DAO's tokens to be securities, so had it continued operating, the members responsible for operations and token issuance may have been fined or sanctioned. This decision was reached according to the Howey Test, used in the US to determine whether transactions constitute an 'investment contract'; the test considers an investment contract to be:

1 an investment of money

2 in a common enterprise

3 with the expectation of profit

4 to be derived from the efforts of others.

As an aside, the Howey Test is derived from the 1946 Supreme Court case of SEC v W.J. Howey Co., which relates to the sales of tracts of citrus groves to buyers in Florida. This unusual case provides a neat example of how existing case law holds influence over crypto innovation, but also of how many aspects of DeFi are not as new as they seem.

In the US, any security will need to be registered with the SEC, and if cryptoassets are to be considered securities, then exchanges that handle them will need to register as broker-dealers and DAOs may be categorized as 'reporting companies'. For DAOs, this would require ongoing reporting and transparency in relation to its operations and financial health. This may simply be unfeasible for a DAO, or at least antithetical with its underlying principles and governance. Similarly, the European Union's Markets in Financial Instruments Directive (MiFID II) outlines the scope for what can be defined as a security, and the Markets in Crypto Assets (MiCA) Regulation, expected to roll out in 2024, helps identify requirements for tokens to avoid classification as securities. MiCA sets out to standardize the legal treatment of crypto throughout the EU and seeks to create crypto-specific rules regarding e-money tokens, 'asset referenced' tokens and stablecoins. There are also proposals in MiCA for energy usage in crypto mining to be reported.

In relation to securities, governance and utility tokens remain a confusing area for lawmakers and regulators. It remains possible that some jurisdictions will consider neither to be securities and likewise the opposite. The bespoke or varied nature of these tokens, combined with the nuances of international law and regulation, could make this a persistent challenge.

MIMICKING TRADFI

To speak more directly to DAOs engaged in DeFi protocols, founders are well advised to compare their operations with those in traditional finance, as highlighted by the charges brought against Ooki DAO by the Commodities Futures Trading Commission (CFTC).[8] Ooki DAO, which governs a crypto margin trading protocol, was charged with illegally offering leveraged and margined retail commodity transactions in digital assets; transactions which are required to take place on designated contract markets. Ooki DAO was also charged with participating in activities reserved for registered futures commission merchants (FCMs), and in turn failing to achieve the customer identification requirements that FCMs are subjected to.

There are other reasons why the Ooki DAO case is a point of interest. Firstly, when announcing the charges, the CFTC also declared charges and a simultaneous $250,000 settlement from Tom Bean and Kyle Kistner, the co-founders of bZeroX, LLC (and accordingly the bZeroX protocol used by Ooki DAO). However, the act of serving a lawsuit to a DAO might be far from simple. The CFTC's initial approach, a novel one to say the least, was to serve Ooki DAO via a chatbox on its website and a post on its online discussion forum.[9] Moving beyond the topic of identifying founders, receiving a settlement from a DAO could be complicated. If token holders are judged collectively responsible for a payout, the act of initiating the payout could be impractical where members, developers and treasurers are pseudonymous. A DAO's ability to elude governments and regulators may even add to its popularity and membership. Let's also not forget that DAOs might participate in market manipulation activities, such as front running. The MiCA regulation is intended to ban such activities and bring DeFi more in line with traditional finance.

In summation, the legal status and wrappers attributed to DAOs and their functions are hugely important. Some economies may welcome DAOs with open arms, others have already shut the gates and this variance in facilitation could add further complexity in circumstances where a DAO's activity is best understood as international. We might also consider the level of decentralization that truly occurs within a DAO. Reporting standards and liabilities can be assigned to senior figures within a legal wrapper, yet a fully decentralized system, with an international and community-based governance structure, may have no leaders or even figureheads. Considering the unknown identity of Satoshi Nakamoto, it is reasonable to assume that founders might be untraceable. When conducting any DAO-related activity, members might consider their personal liabilities as well as any professional obligations that are acquired. They should be mindful of the legal classification of any DAO-linked assets they own, and key members and issuers within a DAO should acknowledge this, too.

Why DAO governance can be a murky issue

The central premise of DAOs is that they offer member-owned communities with relatively flat hierarchies. Without denying that some organizations may have achieved this, more or less, it is clear that the premise is hard to achieve. In 2022, SEC Commissioner Hester Peirce, known by some as 'Crypto Mom' due to her support of digital assets, issued a warning against 'shadow decentralization' in DeFi, whereby opaque governance had helped protocols advertise as decentralized despite being far from it.[10] This is more than just sentiment; a 2022 Chainalysis report, which studied 10 major DAO projects, found that on average less than 1 per cent of token holders have 90 per cent of the voting power. Within these DAOs, it estimates that somewhere between 1 in 1,000 and 1 in 10,000 voters hold enough tokens to single-handedly create a proposal, and somewhere between 1 in 10,000 and 1 in 30,000 token holders have enough influence to, theoretically, single-handedly pass a proposal.[11]

We might also consider the roles of developers, treasurers and founders in relation to decentralization, especially when emergencies arise. An obvious incident to reflect this is the hack of The DAO, whereby Ethereum's leadership team stepped in to propose a hard fork (see Chapter 3) when it was hacked. This, in a sense, reflects the potential of DAOs to empower the community during pivotal moments – the hard fork proposal passed with a 97 per cent majority – but the vote also enforced an action that some considered antithetical to DeFi (the original Ethereum blockchain lives on in the form of Ethereum Classic).

WHEN DAOs NEED URGENCY

In 2022, the issue was drawn into sharper focus by a multimillion-dollar margin call on Solend, at the time the second largest DeFi protocol on the Solana blockchain. The incident arose as Solend's largest account, a $107 million (in USDC) wallet borrowed against $170 million in SOL collateral, was approaching the point of automatic liquidation. Experts were in agreement that such a liquidation would reduce the price of SOL between 60–80 per cent, allowing $21 million of the SOL token to be bought at bargain prices. The result would likely be widespread losses, a huge reputational blow to Solana and crypto markets, and an influx of transactions that would crash the Solana blockchain. Nonetheless, the account holder, who may have been able to add collateral to the loan, appeared to be unreachable despite appeals on social media to identify them (this appeal also made token holders aware of the incident, instigating negative publicity and mass withdrawals).

Solend accordingly held its first DAO vote, SLND1, proposing emergency action to enable Solend to take temporary control of the whale account and liquidate it in a manner that would prevent a larger automatic liquidation and mitigate risk to all token holders. The vote passed with 97.5 per cent approval, with the 1 per cent voting quorum met 14 seconds before the closure of the 6-hour voting window (for clarity, barely over 1% of potential voting tokens were committed, which was enough to meet the voting threshold, and 97.5% of the votes made were in favour of the emergency action). It transpired that the involvement of a single wallet, with 1.01 per cent of the committed turnout tokens, proved decisive.[12] While the proposal passed, it was controversial enough to be overturned the following day by SLND2, which increased governance voting time while invalidating SLND1 and Solend's right to take over a whale account. SLND2 passed with a majority of 99.8 per cent, with one wallet paying $700,000 to increase its voting power and therefore being responsible for 90 per cent of votes.[13] Intriguingly, pseudonymous Solend founder 'Rooter' would later observe that the loudest opposition to taking action came from DeFi enthusiasts with no assets at stake.[14] The whale account later moved a large portion of its loan to another lending protocol, reducing the risk to Solend.

The takeaway from this is not that DAOs are a scam or a fraud, but instead that certain organizations that identify as DAOs are not decentralized, and that there are consequences to this, especially when activities are large enough to impact the health of DeFi markets (comparisons could be made with the 'too big to fail' organizations mentioned earlier). This may be explicit, as in the case above, or it may be more subtle; for instance, in situations where the same person holds multiple accounts, or where off-chain connections hold influence over on-chain votes. Another issue is that voter participation in DAOs is widely reported as being low (this was a factor in the Beanstalk flash loan attack mentioned earlier).[15]

On a different tangent, the distinction between legal wrappers and the DAO itself can present further challenges, as seen when Brantly Millegan, a senior figure at the Ethereum Name Service, was removed from directorial posts at the ENS Protocol and the ENS Foundation (which represents the ENS DAO), following the surfacing of homophobic and transphobic tweets. Despite being removed from posts within legally recognized organizations, domiciled in Singapore and the Cayman Islands respectively, a vote on his position within the ENS DAO concluded in his favour, ensuring that he retained his position within the DAO. Assessing the situation, Millegan would insist that ENS is a protocol, rather than a company or product.[16] Much can be read into this turn of events, including the potential awkwardness when DAOs intertwine with legal structures, and the ability of DAOs to enforce the will of the community in a manner that a centralized organization would not allow.

To speak of the will of the community, one of the purported benefits of DAOs is that they are democratic. As we see from the imbalance of token ownership within many DAOs, it is clear that this should not be assumed. Instead, DAOs operate with wildly varying levels of decentralization and democratization, and a relatively small number of addresses may possess the majority of voting power. Research from Swiss academic institution ETH Zurich (not to be confused with the Ethereum Foundation) concluded that this is the case within Compound and Uniswap.[17]

DELEGATED VOTING

It is commonplace for DAO members to delegate their voting rights to members whose views align with their own, which is a practical method for countering low voter turnout while adding convenience for DAO members. This is not to say that vote delegation is an entirely virtuous process. Yearn Finance offers a service called yBribe, which allows people to buy and sell voting power. 'It's like DC lobbying, but without the long lunches', its website declares.[18]

It is worth noting that the majority of DAO participants are advanced users of cryptocurrency services, and also that there are demographic trends within this cohort. This is likely to influence the voting patterns within a range of DAOs and may be frustrating for those with under-represented interests.

Moving forward with DAOs

There's a train of thought that says DAOs often fall short of being decentralized and autonomous. Irrespectively, another way to look at it is that blockchain enables new forms of organization to be built, funded and scaled at speed; organizations that contrast with those that govern our financial lives at present. DAOs might not be perfectly decentralized, but they can be more decentralized than TradFi organizations. They're not autonomous, but they might be more autonomous than TradFi institutions. And yes, their classifications and correspondence with legal wrappers are hazy, but they do represent a new model for governance that might better represent the interests of stakeholders. Even opinion leaders are cognizant of the barriers to full decentralization. Vitalik Buterin would remark in 2022 that removing hierarchies of information and decision-making, and so on, is practically impossible, but also stated an optimism about what it might mean to decentralize things by as much as 30 per cent.[19] We should consider DAOs in terms of being 'more democratic' rather than perfectly democratic.

Already there have been countless use cases of DAOs being put to use and many of these, such as Aave, are openly pushing towards greater decentralization.

How DAOs are being used

Protocol governance

As discussed, DAOs can facilitate the governance of protocols.

Examples:

- MakerDAO
- Aave
- Uniswap

Philanthropy and community funding

DAOs can be especially useful for community fundraising and charitable or humanitarian causes. The Big Green DAO, for instance, is a registered US non-profit organization that provides funding rounds for projects that are attempting to advance food and gardening for communities, schools and more. UkraineDAO has been used, meanwhile, to raise over $7 million in cryptoassets to fund the Ukrainian government and related efforts during its invasion by Russia, and similarly, EnDAOment facilitated relief payments following the Turkey and Syria earthquakes, albeit at a smaller scale. In relation to Ukraine, and indeed any instance of conflict or danger, the pseudonymous nature of crypto can be advantageous to those making and receiving donations.

Examples:

- Big Green DAO
- UkraineDAO
- EnDAOment
- PleasrDAO
- Giveth

Investment and venture capital

Investment communities can take the form of a DAO, which might be akin to a venture capital or angel investment fund, or created for the acquisition of a specific asset or type of asset. Current examples include Meta Cartel Ventures, which encapsulates the insurgent spirit of DeFi while investing in projects that will accelerate the rise of web3, and Steel DAO, a community founded by Bessemer Venture

Partners, which has dedicated $250 million to early-stage investments across web3, DeFi and crypto infrastructure.[20]

To give a quirkier perspective, Krause House is a DAO that intends to invest its way towards governing the first DAO-owned basketball franchise to play in the NBA. While this Everest is yet to be scaled, Krause House did make reasonable, albeit fruitless inroads towards being minority owners of the Phoenix Suns in 2023.[21] They may yet achieve their goal of owning 'the internet's home team'.

Examples:

- BitDAO
- Krause House
- Meta Cartel Ventures
- SyndicateDAO
- Bessemer Venture Partners (SteelDAO)

Grants

DAOs may also form to issue grants towards projects, protocols and developers. Notionally, grants could be issued for anything, but they are typically used to support the development of the web3 ecosystem. MetaCartel performs this role, offering grants towards the development of dApps built in Ethereum, new DAOs, community initiatives and more. Aave Grants DAO, similarly, allocates regular funding rounds to projects that strengthen the Aave protocol, and Gitcoin entered existence to provide funding for open source projects, and now uses quadratic funding to allocate resources.

Examples:

- MetaCartel
- Aave Grants DAO
- Gitcoin

Collecting

Collections can be invested in and curated by DAOs such as FlamingoDAO, a Delaware limited liability company. FlamingoDAO's primary business is growing its NFT collection and allowing members to vote on proposals for what it should buy or sell next, with the intention that members will profit from trades and rentals of the NFTs. Members can opt in or out of each transaction, and asset fractionalization is used to allow members to invest in NFTs of varying values.

ConstitutionDAO is now defunct but holds a memorable place in the pantheon of early DeFi protocols. It involved a plucky attempt to purchase an original copy of the United States Constitution, raising $47 million in Ether but ultimately losing out to a $43.2 million (fiat) bid at a Sotheby's auction. It is claimed the DAO did not raise its bid beyond $43.2 million due to fears that it held insufficient additional funds to store and insure the Constitution.[22] There were also significant gas fees involved with the raise; some investors paid more for gas than they were able to contribute to the bid. ConstitutionDAO, in its own quirky way, signalled the incredible potential and unwieldy inefficiencies of the DAO and DeFi all at once.

Examples:

- ConstitutionDAO
- FlamingoDAO
- PleasrDAO

Media

DAOs can be created for media and content distribution. BanklessDAO helps govern the direction and output of Bankless' various news-based and educational content streams and also oversees the guilds through which people can participate in its projects. Guilds are available for video and audio content, project management, writers, lawyers, developers and more. PubDAO, meanwhile, intends to gather a wide range of contributors and encourage the proliferation of higher-quality content relating to web3, crypto and DeFi.

Examples:

- Bankless
- PubDAO

Social groups and networking

Some DAOs operate as communities to support a core interest, theme or hobby. The Friends With Benefits (FWB) DAO is designed to be 'a new kind of social network', operating as a decentralized creative space and club, where people can share ideas and launch new projects.[23] It operates both online and in-person, has chapters in New York, Los Angeles and London, has attracted celebrity members such as musicians Erykah Badu and Azealia Banks, and has been described as being akin to a decentralized version of Soho House.[24]

The ApeCoin DAO has been established for the development of art, entertainment and gaming projects for the popular Bored Ape Yacht Club, and also to arrange online and offline events.

Examples:

- Friends with Benefits
- ApeCoin DAO

Community DAOs

A different angle is provided by Cabin and CityDAO, which are using DAOs to create entire living spaces. Cabin uses its network to provide a 'network city' for online creators, dispersed geographically across a number of coliving spaces, but governed by the same DAO. Just like how nodes operate within a network, Cabin's living spaces connect to form a settlement. In a similar vein, CityDAO has bought land in Wyoming and is building a blockchain-based and community-governed crypto city.

DAOs are also expected to play a role in metaverse governance, and the well-known platform Decentraland already operates with one. The Decentraland DAO helps elect community members for key roles and determines the evolution of certain aspects of the experience. If decentralization is fully realized, metaverses may be entirely shaped and governed by their users. Similarly, to apply this to gaming, communities of players may decide the future of games rather than companies. There are instances where this might eradicate decisions that prioritize profitability over user experience, and games may move in the direction of the modifications and developers that players like the most.

Examples:

- Cabin
- CityDAO
- Decentraland DAO

DECENTRALIZATION AND REIMAGINED CAPITALISM

Many businesses and organizations have attempted to embrace the innovations that stem from decentralization. Blockchain, web3 and metaverse expert Anthony Day, who has helped many of them with this journey, explains the cultural challenge this involves:

'A lot of the time you spend is tailoring the message to the industry, the organization, the geography that you're talking to, because decentralization can apply in every single industry in every single geography around the world. And so, a lot of [the work] is applying context to the business problems that are there.

Inherently, centralized capitalist organizations do not necessarily go hand-in-hand with the idea of decentralization, where listed companies' profit models and growth models are based around consolidation of resources, around centralization and capturing of data, around creating proprietary, intellectual property, and winning where others lose.

Those principles of capitalism don't really lend themselves well to open source, open networks, community development – win-win-win, shared economic models. Part of the learning process, or part of the hard work, in implementing digital transformation through blockchain and decentralized technology, is trying to find both a narrative and a business case behind reimagining capitalism.

It's easier to do when you talk about municipalities, or governments, or philanthropic organizations, because their motives or their purpose is less driven by capital and so on. It's the same in certain geographies too; some of the countries that have made the most progress with their blockchain ecosystems also have decentralized governance inherently embedded in their society. If you look at Switzerland or the Netherlands, for example.'

DAOs and DeFi

DAOs are an exciting addition to organizational structure, and by providing a radical alternative to institutional governance they offer a new direction for finance. If paired with a cultural moment, influential leader or captivating philosophy – or maybe even viral content or a meme – DAOs offer a route towards rapid funding and scalability of an idea, and if they achieve the financial buy-in of participants they sow the seeds for longer-term engagement. What is more substantial as an opportunity, however, and far harder to realize, is a shift in governance from individual interests towards communities. Modern capitalism has myriad benefits, and yet it creates an environment where community interests, especially if misaligned with profit-generating activity, often become secondary or tertiary factors.

Skipping over the fact that DAOs could be used to perpetuate trends that we see in traditional markets, let's consider this idea of community-centric fundraising, grants, governance and accountability. DAOs are already proving effective in raising funds for local and niche interests, and may yet provide spectacular public ownership arrangements, as was almost evidenced with Krause House and ConstitutionDAO. Given that governance is attached, investments of this nature take crowdfunding a step further and bolt on a more tangible sense of asset ownership. This sort of activity is far from dominant though. DAO communities are still, chiefly, a hub for crypto enthusiasts.

DAOs also present interesting questions about democracy as a means of running financial protocols. Is the wisdom of the crowd the best option? Could it introduce an element of populism to finance? We can expect these questions to play out in real life if DAOs become commonplace.

References

1   B Llyr A Slavin and K Werbach. Decentralized Autonomous Organization Toolkit, World Economic Forum, 2023, www.weforum.org/reports/ decentralized-autonomous-organization-toolkit/ (archived at https://perma.cc/ FTW6-KN7H)

2 J Forman. What is a decentralized autonomous organization (DAO) and how might this new organizational structure impact collaboration?, Agile Leadership Journey, 2021, www.agileleadershipjourney.com/blog/decentralized-autonomous-organization-impact-collaboration (archived at https://perma.cc/SM4N-CB4U)

3 E Arsenault. Voting options in DAOs, DAOstack, 2020, medium.com/daostack/voting-options-in-daos-b86e5c69a3e3 (archived at https://perma.cc/BZJ9-GL6A)

4 Law Commission. Decentralised autonomous organisations (DAOs): Call for evidence, 2022, www.lawcom.gov.uk/project/decentralised-autonomous-organisations-daos/ (archived at https://perma.cc/3MNC-3697)

5 OECD. Crypto-asset reporting framework and amendments to the common reporting standard, oecd.org, 2022, www.oecd.org/tax/exchange-of-tax-information/crypto-asset-reporting-framework-and-amendments-to-the-common-reporting-standard.htm (archived at https://perma.cc/8GDK-VGZD)

6 U.S. Department of the Treasury. General explanations of the administration's fiscal year 2024 revenue proposals, Department of the Treasury, 2023, home.treasury.gov/system/files/131/General-Explanations-FY2024.pdf (archived at https://perma.cc/P6XP-A9JL)

7, 8 CFTC. CFTC imposes $250,000 penalty against bZeroX, LLC and its founders and charges successor Ooki DAO for offering illegal, off-exchange digital-asset trading, registration violations, and failing to comply with Bank Secrecy Act, CFTC, 2022, www.cftc.gov/PressRoom/PressReleases/8590-22 (archived at https://perma.cc/9WHK-RX9F)

9 I A Sandoval and S V Riddell. Court OKs CFTC's service of process through online forum, chat box in Ooki DAO action, Morgan Lewis, 2022, www.morganlewis.com/blogs/finreg/2022/12/court-oks-cftcs-service-of-process-through-online-forum-chat-box-in-ooki-dao-action (archived at https://perma.cc/B8DX-GKTN)

10 A S Yin. Why DAO governance is riddled with problems and voting is a farce, forkast, 2023, forkast.news/why-dao-voting-is-problematic/ (archived at https://perma.cc/RH9K-X956)

11 K Grauer, W Kueshner, E McMahon and H Updegrave. The chainalysis state of Web3 report, chainalysis.com, June 2022, go.chainalysis.com/rs/503-FAP-074/images/state-of-web3.pdf (archived at https://perma.cc/LUM4-VP9N)

12 D Nelson and CoinDesk. Binance saves Solana's second-biggest DeFi lender from liquidation, 2022, fortune.com/2022/06/28/binance-solana-defi-whale-account-liquidation/ (archived at https://perma.cc/GB2Y-DPGN)

13 O Knight. DeFi Protocol Solend passes governance vote to reverse 'emergency powers', CoinDesk, 2022, www.coindesk.com/business/2022/06/20/defi-protocol-solend-passes-governance-vote-to-reverse-emergency-powers/ (archived at https://perma.cc/7AKJ-LPN4)

14 L Wright. Solend founder reveals what happened behind the scenes during its whale liquidation event. CryptoSlate, 2022, cryptoslate.com/solend-founder-reveals-what-happened-behind-the-scenes-during-its-whale-liquidation-event/ (archived at https://perma.cc/EX9P-UBRR)

15 Red. The problem with voting in DAOs, The Defiant, 2021, thedefiant.io/the-problem-with-voting-in-daos (archived at https://perma.cc/L6RF-BJ8G)

16 D Kuhn. Fired, but not canceled, CoinDesk, 2022, www.coindesk.com/consensus-magazine/2022/12/05/brantly-millegan-most-influential-2022/ (archived at https://perma.cc/GL54-LBLW)

17 R Fritsch, M Müller and R Wattenhofer. Analyzing voting power in decentralized governance: who controls DAOs? arxiv.org, n.d., arxiv.org/pdf/2204.01176.pdf (archived at https://perma.cc/AD5X-JCVT)

18 yBribe. 2023, yearn.finance/ybribe (archived at https://perma.cc/R3WW-K99N)

19 V Buterin. DAOs are not corporations: where decentralization in autonomous organizations matters, vitalik.ca, 2022, vitalik.ca/general/2022/09/20/daos.html (archived at https://perma.cc/8YXQ-RNXE)

20 E Kurzweil, L Li, C Küng and D Punjabi. Building the web3 ecosystem of the future, Bessemer Venture Partners, 2022, www.bvp.com/news/building-the-web3-ecosystem-of-the-future (archived at https://perma.cc/QT4K-NYX6)

21 Krause House. How Krause House nearly became a minority owner of the Phoenix Suns, 2023, krausehouse.mirror.xyz/JUKeloohXfbbbFKad8nKw717sRYlylHwVrpncLFaiSE (archived at https://perma.cc/U5CF-N666)

22 M Sigalos. The crypto investors who raised $47 million to buy a copy of the Constitution lost their bid — here's where the money goes now, CNBC, 2021, www.cnbc.com/2021/11/18/constitutiondao-crypto-investors-lose-bid-to-buy-constitution-copy.html (archived at https://perma.cc/CA7L-GC52)

23 FWB. About, 2023, www.fwb.help/about (archived at https://perma.cc/MAG4-WQYP)

24 E Woo and K Roose. This social club runs on crypto tokens and vibes, The New York Times, 2 March 2022, www.nytimes.com/2022/03/02/technology/friends-with-benefits-crypto-dao.html (archived at https://perma.cc/DD8D-F398)

06

NFTs: Beyond the hype

NFTs are non-fungible tokens. They are non-fungible because, unlike cryptocurrencies such as bitcoin or Ether, every token is unique and a trade of two NFTs on the same blockchain will not be like-for-like. This sounds somewhat confusing, so instead, NFTs are perhaps better understood as a new form of digital receipt, made possible by blockchain, that can be used to verify or demonstrate ownership of a unique asset. By utilizing cryptography and blockchains, they take identification to a new level. If you want to irrefutably claim that an asset is original, belongs to a collection and is yours, you may now be able to display this on a shared and unchangeable public ledger. An NFT may also be used as a means of verification insofar as an online avatar, for example, can be linked to an offline and/or online identity, be it publicly shared or pseudonymous. NFTs have become one of the most hyped and debated assets in crypto, provoking conversations about what ownership really means, and how we attribute value to digital assets.

As mentioned earlier, NFTs forced their way into the public consciousness in 2021 when soaring valuations of NFT art collections, including several multimillion-dollar sales, inspired rampant investment and media coverage. The subsequent 2022 crash led many to declare NFTs a flash in the pan, though there are a plethora of emerging projects, and the technology has swathes of applications that have yet to be explored. It is not unreasonable to think that the attention directed at NFTs is excessive, at least right now. In late 2022, market adoption and penetration for them equalled less than 1 per cent of the entire crypto market.[1]

They are, nonetheless, ripe for debate and exploration. Yes, there will be gasps when large sums of money change hands for a JPEG, but besides this, the early uses of NFTs have provoked intriguing questions about ownership rights relating to digital assets. To begin, let's look at the assertion that the owner of an NFT has ownership of an underlying asset. This assertion is not necessarily correct, and purchasers of NFTs have learnt on some occasions that they had not bought the intellectual property (IP) of an asset, and therefore had no right to monetize the artwork. In these instances, an NFT merely confers the right to use the asset. This confusion is not solely caused by buyers failing to carry out their due diligence; instead, it transpires that many NFT sellers do not take action to clearly define who owns the IP. In a March 2022 blog, James Grimmelmann, Yan Ji and Tyler Kell, of the IC3 blockchain research initiative at Cornell, noted that many NFT projects did not take the necessary steps to ensure that NFT copyrights behaved in the manner that community members would expect. Nonetheless, this particular issue is primarily the result of early missteps rather than anything fundamentally wrong with NFTs. The authors also state that ownership of an NFT can give owners substantial control over the desired creative work but warn that buyers should take steps to ensure that they will be conferred such rights.[2]

So ownership of IP might be enforceable but should not be assumed. If you successfully purchase the IP, you may expect to at least own something on a blockchain. This, too, is a shaky assumption. NFTs are usually a digital receipt for whatever is found at the end of a weblink, rather than a receipt for data held on-chain.[3] This occurs because it is costly to store underlying content on a blockchain due to the amount of data involved. The NFT will instead be found behind a weblink on a cloud-based web address or an NFT seller's website. This may seem underwhelming, and the use of cloud computing giants such as Amazon, Google and Microsoft looks a lot like a centralized point of reliance (which jars with the ethos of DeFi). Even so, weblinks possess a very wide range of uses. NFTs might therefore grant access to exclusive events, loyalty schemes, digital land or new in-game items or levels for gamers. The important thing here is that NFTs allow you to prove the identity of your account, or maybe even yourself when doing these things.

Regardless, by having data stored behind a weblink, significant power is handed to the owner of the web address and the NFT owner could be exposed to link rot if the domain name is not renewed. The NFT owner is also at the mercy of other inclinations of the web address owner. Moxie Marlinspike, the creator of the encrypted messaging service Signal, illustrated this in a pointed fashion by creating an NFT that changed based on who was viewing it. When viewed in a marketplace, this NFT displayed as an artistic image, but once bought and viewed in a crypto wallet, it would display as a smiling poo emoji (we will set aside the debate about 'what constitutes art' here).[4] The 'piece' was removed from the OpenSea NFT marketplace within days, but the point had been made. You are usually buying a unique link to a web address.

NFTs have also been subjected to mockery from 'right clickers'. Right clicking refers to the simple fact that the JPEGs, GIFs or videos owned (or permissioned, and/or linked to) through lucrative NFT purchases can simply be copied, saved, and used by other people for free. The associated trolling has been notable, and some social media accounts were able to touch a nerve by changing their profile picture to images of expensive NFTs. To make matters worse, there have also been multiple instances in which NFTs have been copies of existing artwork, minted without the artist's permission.

From all of this, we can deduce that NFTs could become very useful and hold legal authority as an identifier of ownership, originality or provenance. We can also see that the market is new, unclear, ripe for scams and mis-selling, and misunderstood by many who observe it or trade within it.

Why are we discussing them?

There is no shortage of farce within the world of NFTs, but this does not invalidate the concept. Potential buyers, and existing ones, should note that legal guarantees could be sought to protect their NFT and ownership rights, and for lucrative purchases they may choose to engage the services of crypto law experts. Buyers may also want to make sure that they are purchasing 'frozen' NFTs, held in a decentralized storage system such as IPFS (the Interplanetary File System), which can never be altered. Savvy users may also use a block explorer such as Etherscan to ensure that the smart contract for the NFT contains an IPFS URL (which will start with: ipfs.io/ipfs/). These solutions do not entirely de-risk an NFT purchase but make the process far safer.

Moreover, and independently of present-day uncertainties over legal rights and the delivery of NFTs, the principle of immutable receipts for digital ownership remains a powerful one. A global and irrefutable (within reason) ledger of ownership for all digital goods could foreseeably have a major impact on gaming, music, video and much more. Even at a less decentralized level, where nations use private and public blockchain ledgers to demonstrate asset ownership, NFTs could be an effective identifier. This might be used for property ownership, or a plethora of uses where a unique token confers rights to the owner.

Like everything else in the world of crypto and DeFi, we should also be mindful of the recency of NFTs. The first NFT in existence was 'Quantum', minted on Namecoin in 2014 by digital artist Kevin McCoy, and it is asking a lot to go from this to an international and multifaceted marketplace in less than a decade. There has also been a shroud of hype and disappointment upon the NFT market following the 2021 and early 2022 boom. As such, some analysts point to the Gartner Hype Cycle when explaining the NFT market in 2023.[5] The cycle shows how technological innovations lead to inflated expectations, followed by a trough of disillusionment, followed by a steadier upward slope of enlightenment. Those who believe NFTs have an exciting long-term future tend to believe that we are in the early stages of this slope of enlightenment.

The next phase for NFTs

While there are countless potential use cases for NFTs, it makes sense to focus on the ones that are currently attracting investment. To provide an overview of where the market is currently at, we can turn to the 10 sales categories defined by NFTGo's 2023 annual report.[6]

1 **Games:** NFT games launched on blockchain using the NFT standard. Users can acquire in-game assets such as property, characters or weapons through ownership of a corresponding NFT.

2 **Collectibles:** A project based around the issuance and collection of tokens, where token collection is the primary objective.

3 **PFP:** PFP is a truncation of 'profile pic'. An NFT PFP is an algorithmically created character displayed in a profile picture format, which can be used in apps and games.

4 **Art:** This simply refers to art, created by people or artificial intelligence, that can be bought, sold or generated as an NFT.

5 **Metaverse:** This relates to the emerging market for virtual and augmented realities, in which people can own assets and identities in the form of an NFT.

6 **DeFi:** Here, this relates specifically to blockchain-based finance using smart contracts, and bypassing centralized financial intermediaries.

7 **IP:** These NFTs are issued by brands and celebrities and involve the monetization of existing and recognized intellectual property.

8 **Social:** Social NFTs are digital collectables, usually representing the likeness of a social media personality.

9 **Music:** These are NFTs issued to support a musician. They can include tickets, songs, albums and other collectables.

10 **Utilities:** These NFTs serve a different sort of utility or application that does not have a gaming or artistic function. Domain names, in particular the .eth domain, are an example of this.

As we can see, these sales categories are limited and the early use cases for NFTs are chiefly found in gaming, collections, art, music and brand engagement. With respect to marketing, several major brands from a diverse range of markets have already launched NFT projects of their own. By offering unique tokens to customers, these brands are using NFTs to raise brand awareness, strengthen customer loyalty, and on some level, ride the wave of the latest trend.

THE MAKING OF A SUCCESSFUL NFT

It's not enough to just thoughtlessly launch an NFT. Max Mersch, co-founder and partner at Fabric Ventures, explains why he chose to invest in Sorare, a popular crypto-based fantasy sports game where unique NFT player cards can be purchased. Sorare has gone on to achieve valuations in excess of $4 billion. Mersch says:

'It's hard to find a bigger community than the football community. You have this trend of people playing FIFA Ultimate Team, where it's quite a similar product, except that every year you have to buy your players again, and every year you have to put in a bunch of cash into the economy again, and get nothing out of it at the end of the day. And you have the fantasy league, which is a very well accepted and commonly played type of game.

The moment where the investment clicked was that – at the time when we invested – when I started playing, all they had was the Jupiler League, Belgian football. Nobody really cared about Belgian football, or at least nobody at that time. And yet you have this community of thousands of people who are logging in every single day, every week, and setting their team, buying and selling these cards, players, that they probably hadn't heard of. And the leagues themselves were very interested to jump on board because it was a new revenue stream for them. Because they were selling TV rights, they were selling merch, they were selling tickets. They might have been selling image rights for Panini stickers and for a few other types of IP, but they never were selling on-chain IP for fantasy leagues that existed as NFTs and so for them it was a very simple yes to give.

There's a lot of clubs that have tried to do their own NFT production, with Liverpool being the biggest failure recently. There's no interest from their fans because there's nothing they can do with it, whereas with Sorare you compete against each other, buy your club's NFTs and get other players across all divisions, all leagues, all clubs in the world. You have a really clear skin in the game type relationship with the sports that you love and the club that you love.'

Examples of brands using NFTs

STARBUCKS

Starbucks' foray into NFTs shows how brands can use NFTs to reach a broad market.[7] Through its 'Participate to Earn' scheme, Starbucks customers take part in 'Journeys', where games, challenges and online Starbucks visits can be used to unlock 'stamps', which grant access to a range of rewards and experiences. By using NFTs in this manner, and by referring to them as stamps, Starbucks is creating a user journey that non-crypto natives can understand. The Journeys also help spread knowledge of the brand and gamify customer loyalty rewards.

CLINIQUE

Clinique's 'Metaverse More Like Us' campaign allowed the cosmetics company to generate press activity while leveraging a positive message around diversity and inclusion.[8] The campaign featured the work of internationally acclaimed make-up artists, who created avatars for the 'Non-Fungible People (NFP)' PFP collection. The avatars were subsequently airdropped to a randomized number of NFP account holders.

MCDONALD'S

McDonald's announced the return of the McRib with the launch of its first NFT promotion. The brand announced that the 10 NFTs would be given out to Twitter users who retweeted their invitation to participate. The promotion achieved more than 80,000 retweets.[9]

NORWEGIAN CRUISE LINE

Norwegian Cruise Line auctioned six NFTs to coincide with the launch of its Prima Class liners. In doing so, and by donating the proceeds to American non-profit Teach for America, it was able to generate publicity and lay a claim to being the first company of its ilk to create NFTs.[10]

NIKE

Of all the brands to launch NFTs, Nike has been the most successful and had reportedly generated more than $185 million in revenue from them by Q3 of 2022.[11] This revenue is a mixture of primary sales and royalties from secondary sales and has been achieved through initiatives including the CloneX avatar collection and the NIKELAND metaverse on Roblox.

The partnership with Roblox, a virtual universe that allows people to build and play games, seems savvy considering that Roblox had 65 million active daily users in January 2023.[12] Figures for NIKELAND, made at a similar time, had put its traffic at over 26 million visits in total.[13]

Intriguingly, Nike's NFT revenues equate to roughly 0.3 per cent of its total annual revenues.[14] It is likely that Nike's core objective through this project is to spread and sustain brand awareness, and to build customer loyalty and engagement.

ADIDAS

Adidas has been an active player in NFTs and the metaverse, partnering with centralized crypto exchange Coinbase, and pairing with brands such as Prada and crypto native collectives such as Bored Ape Yacht Club (BAYC). This has likely been motivated by Nike's NFT success.

In working with BAYC, Adidas purchased one of its highly sought-after ape NFTs (#8774, 'Indigo Herz'), and designed a collection of virtual wearables named 'Into the Metaverse' for blockchain-based metaverse, The Sandbox. Those who bought the NFTs also received access to physical merchandise, such as the tracksuit and hoodie worn by Indigo Herz. The first iteration of this project attracted 21,000 buyers, with 30,000 NFTs minted in total. There were some snags in this project as some prospective buyers were unable to mint the NFTs, and one account apparently minted many of the NFTs. Nonetheless, the collection appears to have sold out in minutes, and while Adidas offered to reimburse those who had lost gas fees through minting issues, it earned over $22 million in revenue from the sale.[15]

In the collaboration with Prada, the two brands invited 3,000 contributors to submit artwork that would be minted as part of the Adidas for Prada re-source NFT project.[16]

PORSCHE

Porsche's first NFT mint divided opinion. The auto brand initially sparked derision from crypto-focused social media accounts for offering 7,500 NFTs at a price close to $1,500 each (0.911 ETH, a play on the famous Porsche 911 model featured in the collection). The NFTs were designed as collectibles, and to give owners some creative input into Porsche's future in virtual reality.[17] Demand did not meet supply so Porsche reduced the size of the mint, but not before buyers had already sold the NFTs on the secondary market at prices beneath the initial purchase cost.

Despite the furore, those who held their asset may have realized a significant gain. The floor price for the 911 NFTs would rise to 3 ETH in less than a month (which is to say nothing of future price movements. Prices move fast in crypto).

With these NFT projects and future ones, there is a wide range of opportunities. NFTs might be JPEGs, GIFs or videos, and they might be membership passes and exclusive content, leveraging community engagement and FOMO as they do so. To a degree, they solidify the connection of their owners with the groups, communities and brands that they participate in. Where owners are granted the licence to commercialize their assets, they may even allow creators to further the reach of a brand, develop new offshoots for it and gain profit from doing so (although this would engender some degree of reputational risk). Additionally, NFTs can take on a life of their own, and might be repurposed as physical toys, merchandise, clothing, accessories and so on. Readers with young children may therefore take note that toy brand Mattel, the makers of Hot Wheels and Barbie, partnered with an NFT firm to add a new dimension to its IP.[18] The success of physical products may spawn new NFTs, and vice versa.

The blurring of the offline and online worlds is also evidenced by Starbucks' participate-to-earn scheme. This example brings gamification of NFTs into the picture and the rich rewards that it might bring. If Axie Infinity and CryptoKitties showed how users can capitalize on in-game activity, then Starbucks has outlined how this applies to marketing. In teaching users new facts about the brand, and by encouraging ongoing engagement, NFT rewards may also turn users into brand ambassadors to varying degrees. Brands might now value their customers in terms of their marketing reach as well as their ability to purchase goods and services, and NFT gamification may blur the lines between influencer and customer.

A final, not necessarily branded, point to raise is that the 'X-to-earn' model, where X might be participation, play or something else, continues to inspire new projects. One of 2022's successes, despite tailing off considerably at the end of the year, was 'move-to-earn' game STEPN on the Solana blockchain, which offered token rewards on NFT shoes corresponding to times that owners had gone for a walk or run (not online). Another emerging project in this respect is Fight Out, which plans to offer a game environment and metaverse experience that takes account of users' real-world training activity and performance, and maps this back onto an avatar that can be used to play the game. These mechanisms might engage users with a community or gaming universe but, as ever, the financialization of these games should be scrutinized. The value of NFT game tokens can fall or rise sharply.

It's all about identity

NFTs are unique identifiers so it seems fitting that PFPs, the NFTs used by enthusiasts as their online avatars, are the largest sector in the NFT market by far (there is some cross-categorization here as PFPs might also be categorized as art). As of early 2023, the market cap of PFPs exceeded 5.6 million ETH. Bearing in mind that crypto is pseudonymous, and that users might have multiple accounts and belong to several communities, it is plausible that PFP growth will not stagnate if crypto and DeFi usage reach a saturation point. PFPs are not just valuable for their ability to offer an extension or abstraction of a user's identity; their ability to denote membership of a community, and the exclusive rights, access and clout that might come with that, is possibly the most valuable asset that NFTs can confer.

There is also a considerable market for domain names, like Ethereum domain names that finish with .eth. At the time of writing, the Ethereum Name Service has registered more than 2.8 million domain names, with over 650,000 unique owners.[19] These names can serve as a crypto wallet address, a simple alternative to the complicated public keys usually shared by users. As well as serving this function, demand for domain names soared on the suggestion that they might serve as an identity card, of sorts, in web3. Opportunism has also played its part and popular brand names have been bought as domain names and either purchased and held or purchased and sold for high prices on the secondary market. This practice is known as cybersquatting.

NFTs are not just about proving who you are or where you belong. They can also be used to show where you have been. This is being achieved through Proof of Attendance Protocols (POAPs), tokens stored in crypto wallets to provide evidence that an owner has attended an event, or belonged to an institution, course or class. There have been many novel and interesting purposes for POAPs already. In crypto, they can be distributed to conference attendees, audiences of podcasts and videos, and gamers who have reached milestones. Outside of crypto, they could commemorate attendance of a wedding or civil partnership, or a show featuring a band or performer, and once again we should remember that the offline and online worlds are not mutually exclusive. POAPs could also hold value as proof of expertise, should universities, schools and training courses issue them to those who successfully complete a qualification. These tokens can link the owner to a serious or frivolous event or achievement and are usually images or GIFs, acquired by scanning a QR code or entering a URL. It is entirely possible that POAPs will become valuable assets, especially where the gatekeeping capabilities and credentials of the issuer are highly regarded. Therefore, they might be important identifiers for proving credentials, or simple collectables, or even a means to demonstrate social status and access. At the time of writing, over 6.4 million POAPs have been minted by more than 28,000 issuers.

On a slightly different note, NFTs can help establish ownership of real-world assets or the provenance of physical artworks. They have also been used as a new form of ticketing, for example when centralized crypto exchange Binance partnered with Primavera Sound, a European music festival with over 460,000 attendees, in 2022.[20] The ticketing scheme allowed for exclusive airdrops, POAPs and personalized experiences. Besides being more dynamic than a typical paper ticket, an NFT ticket is very hard to forge and can produce ongoing revenue opportunities for the artist, through the issuance of royalties. To elaborate on this, an NFT could be programmed to allow or prevent resales, and if they are allowed, the artists or event organizers may recoup a percentage of the value of secondary sales. This could have numerous implications, such as the introduction of new pricing strategies for events, and it may also be used to deter or stop ticket scalpers.

On identity, we should also acknowledge efforts to create 'decentralized identities' that could tie online actors to their 'real-world' identities, adding a layer of reliability to DeFi and crypto participation. It has been theorized that this might be achieved through zero-knowledge proofs, which allow people to prove the truth of a statement without revealing the details of it. If this is achieved, then notionally people can retain their pseudonymity while leveraging their real-world credentials. Personal identities, here, may be represented in 'Soulbound Tokens' (SBTs), as suggested by Vitalik Buterin, E. Glen Weyl and Puja Ohlhaver in their 2022 paper, *Decentralized Society: Finding Web3's Soul*.[21] An SBT, to put it concisely, is a non-transferable NFT that is permanently linked to an individual or wallet.

This clearly takes us into more conceptual territory but consider the benefits that could be attained by tying identity to our activity without needing to disclose sensitive information. This could help creators and public figures establish ownership of their work and protect against deepfakes of photos, videos and artworks. It could also add a verification layer to online marketplaces. Would a seller deliberately sell damaged, mis-sold, unlicensed or counterfeit goods if doing so caused reputational damage to their irreplaceable and hard-earned individual credentials? And if you were buying an expensive item or service, would you not have more trust for someone willing to stake their own reputation on the deal? Such an idea, to give it a relatable angle, might change the way that traders operate on Amazon, Facebook or eBay. This is not to say, however, that SBTs could not be exploited somehow. The key point is that NFTs offer a unique development in receipts, and how we prove the unique identity of people and things. The potential is considerable.

Who owns NFTs and why

Despite the highfalutin concepts and myriad future use cases mentioned above, NFTs remain an investment play for most owners. Respondents to the NFTGo.io user survey, as fate would have it, prioritized profit and loss as the main reason for their interest in NFTs.[22] In terms of how users identify a money-making opportunity, 'community' was mentioned more than anything else (59 per cent of respondents), followed by Twitter (52 per cent), data/news platforms (43 per cent) and marketplaces (16 per cent). Here, we see that communities are both providers and distributors of value to members, and that membership and belonging can be readily monetized as NFT owners may be granted access or association to high-profile clubs and people.

In light of the 2022 NFT crash and the NFT market's close correlation to crypto markets, it is tempting to suggest that NFTs are not a reliable asset class. This is pretty much true at present, yet the market does not respond uniformly to market fluctuations. A handful of projects, often termed 'blue chip' or 'high quality' by NFT buyers, may prove less susceptible to a downturn. The term blue chip mimics its usage in the stock market, where it denotes companies of high value and dependability.

NFTs evidently do not have the track record to be considered 'blue chip' by any stock market standard. The usage of this term reflects the complex relationship between DeFi and traditional finance, as 'blue chip' might be said with varying degrees of sincerity or sarcasm.

NFTs considered as blue chip include BAYC, Azuki, Clone X and Doodles, and these four projects alone accounted for 15 per cent of the entire market volume for 2022. It is worthwhile to note that the value of a 'blue chip' is usually connected to celebrity endorsements, community, the team behind the project, future plans and price history – most of which have value that can largely be considered 'off-chain'. If projects continue to utilize the reputation of designers and members, and if long-term ambitions are recognised by NFT holders, it is possible for the prices of high-profile NFTs to deviate considerably from the direction of the overall market.

Blue chip NFTs, like most forms of expression, have formed the basis for mimicry. Accordingly, there are NFT collections that resemble popular ones, and these may be marketed as satire, mockery, homages or variations on a theme. There are also questions to be asked about what makes a collection valuable. The Goblintown collection, an original series, exemplified this question by briefly achieving a floor price of 6.85 ETH despite being crudely drawn and initially offering no future plans or high-profile community. The ability to know what will 'go viral', or what constitutes a transformative marketing strategy, could be the most valuable competence for an NFT investor.

NFTs, clearly, are not one and the same, and neither are market participants. In this regard, there is a class of 488 NFT whales that hold 12 per cent of the value of the market (whales usually spread their assets across multiple wallets, and the figures here are estimates based on wallet activity). Whales have significant market influence, and any project attracting one or several whales is likely to receive considerable hype. This leads to a scenario where whales become trendsetters, as other investors intend to copy or at least closely follow their investment strategy and activity. Trackers of whale accounts have identified several strategies that are commonly adopted, such as 'bottom-fishing', a form of averaging down where investors intend to invest at the bottom of the market before reaping the rewards on an upswing. It has also been observed that whales buy and sell assets quickly, often within the same day, most likely selling to another whale. In this sense, it is highly likely that the biggest sales and headlines are driven by a small group of wealthy traders.

Another factor to consider in market activity, and one that could be carried out by any number of NFT owners, is wash trading. Wash trading occurs when related accounts buy and sell from each other, creating an illusion of demand to drive up an NFT's value. While this incurs gas fees, meaning that some wash trading accounts are unprofitable, Chainalysis research in early 2022 reported that 110 addresses had earned almost $9 million between them; a drop in the ocean, perhaps, if compared to claims that over $577 million of wash trading took place on the Blur platform within 10 days [24], or NFTGo's report claiming that 35 per cent of all NFT trading volume in 2022 was wash trading.[23, 24]

There is also a notable wealth gap between owners of different NFT projects. The average CryptoPunks holder will have assets per capita of $414,000, and for BAYC this is $254,516, which is likely in stark contrast to owners of projects with a floor price (minimum price per asset) beneath 0.1 ETH. This may seem like a low number chosen to prove a point but in early 2023, 74 per cent of projects have a minimum floor price beneath 0.1 ETH.

So who owns NFTs? The Statista Digital Economy Compass 2022 put Thailand as the global leader in ownership, followed by Brazil, the United States, China and Vietnam.[25] Meanwhile traffic on OpenSea, considered by many to be the world's largest NFT marketplace throughout 2022, recorded one-fifth of its traffic between September–November 2022 from its home nation the United States, with Japan, Turkey, India and Canada much further back but next in line. Google Trends may provide some understanding of where interest is coming from, though this data only indicates search interest relative to population, and doesn't factor in population size, internet access or affluence. In 2022, the nations registering the most fervent interest in NFTs on Google were China, Hong Kong, Singapore, Nigeria and Taiwan.[26]

In terms of demographics, NFTGo's Google Analytics data may offer insight. The NFT aggregation platform's user personas showed that 66 per cent of users are under the age of 34 and 73.4 per cent are male. Data from Similarweb indicated that the most commonly observed interests of OpenSea and NFTGo users were finance, investing, technology, gaming and programming. If we take all of this at face value, we can assume that NFT ownership skews heavily towards young men with an interest in tech and finance.

ARE NFTs THE FUTURE OF SOCIAL MEDIA?

Unique identifiers can disrupt ownership structures in many ways. Lens Protocol, founded by Aave creator Stani Kulechov, does so by creating a new web3 model for social media. Lens allows users to create their own profile, as an NFT, that can be transported between applications. This allows users to easily take their credentials from one platform to another and makes platforms more accountable for their actions, such as algorithm changes, censorship or governance decisions more generally. Kulechov remarks:

> 'With Lens, we're extending the concept of user ownership so that you can own your online profile and digital presence. In traditional social media, it may seem like we're making connections on a daily basis across the internet; we're sharing content and creating content and growing our audience but we don't own the network, our digital identity, content or followers. In many cases, our followers or audiences are just numbers in a database. You can't do a digital exit and take your followers with you, let's say, to another social media platform, which could be more aligned with your experience and audience.
>
> We want to extend the concept of ownership to social media users themselves. So, when users create their profile on Lens it's secured by the blockchain, and when they follow people across the network, that's

also secured by the blockchain. With Lens, users own their online presence and this is valuable social capital that can be monetized. With ownership, users own their audience, share their content directly with them and monetize – tokenizing their content as NFTs, if they wish.

When you own your profile, content and that relationship, there's this big dynamic change. It means users have more power than the social networks. It means applications that are built on top of the Lens Protocol must listen to their users and address the kind of needs they have from these applications.'

NFTfi

As a decentralized and blockchain-based asset, NFTs fit neatly into the DeFi ecosystem. There is now an emerging market for NFTfi, which makes the connection more explicit. NFTfi allows users to financialize their NFTs in several ways, such as fractionalization, renting, lending and borrowing, and derivative trading. While this market is new, the type of activity it facilitates will be recognizable to DeFi enthusiasts.

Fractionalization

This involves splitting an NFT's ownership and tokenizing it. It can increase access to in-demand NFTs, but may be problematic if debate arises over how to utilize or sell the NFT (some of which may be negated by an active secondary market for the fractionalized tokens).

Renting

An NFT owner can rent their asset; this could provoke challenging conversations relating to ownership rights, as discussed earlier. Nonetheless, renting can have straightforward use cases, such as allowing an asset to be used as part of an exhibit, show or display. Any utility conferred by an NFT might be rented too. If an NFT grants access to an event, a willing potential attendee may be willing to rent the NFT for the duration of it.

Lending and borrowing

There are various ways that an NFT can be lent or borrowed. An NFT might be used as collateral for a peer-to-peer loan, or within a CDP or lending pool. This utility allows NFTs to add liquidity within the market, and users to benefit by receiving yields from their assets. A potential problem with lending and borrowing NFTs is that they are not necessarily easy to price, and like other DeFi assets, are subject to considerable price volatility.

Derivatives

These are derivatives based on NFT prices. This market barely exists at the time of writing, but in time could allow futures, options, hedging, leveraging and more, in relation to NFTs.

What does it all mean?

NFTs are a fascinating addition to DeFi and to finance full stop. They are an evolution of record-keeping and ownership made possible by blockchain, and simultaneously a volatile asset class fuelled partly by frivolity, FOMO and greed. Their financialization has proven something of a double-edged sword; the initial influx of investment helped NFTs to infiltrate pop culture and finance, but also subjected many investors to significant losses while diverting attention from what the technology actually does.

In terms of the capacity of NFTs to prove ownership and identity, we have barely scratched the surface. We can look, for instance, at the emerging market for music NFTs, which could provide new avenues for the monetization of compositions, events, ticketing or merchandise. In essence, if we are considering monetization, any moment where a unique identifier for a person or thing holds value could be up for grabs, provided that sufficient attention is paid to IP and copyright. This is highly relevant for people, brands and communities.

To issue a word of caution, we should not brush over the considerable market influence held by a small number of accounts. With crypto being pseudonymous, the concentration of influential accounts may even be higher than described here. The NFT market is dwarfed by crypto markets, and crypto markets themselves are dwarfed by TradFi markets, so it is not unreasonable to believe that NFT investment markets are heavily manipulated and geared in favour of larger investors. If market demographics genuinely correspond with most estimates, we should also be mindful that DeFi markets are subject to gender imbalances, regional imbalances and potentially racial imbalances, just like traditional finance markets.

In a financial sense, NFTs allow us to ascribe a monetary value to things that people and societies have always held dear. Having exclusive access, belonging to a club and owning something that is limited in circulation – these are attributes that generations of people have leveraged for social clout, access and status. NFTs bring this into the modern age, or possibly the web3 age, and allow us to easily and readily demonstrate who we are and what we belong to. You may think this is patently absurd and you may well be justified, but this is unlikely to hinder the enjoyment of others to any great extent, nor will it make NFTs any less of a potential community-building tool.

When setting out to write this, I admittedly intended to show that NFTs were not all about JPEGs of monkeys, by which I am referring to BAYC. This premise was both true and false. It was true in the sense that NFTs are an important identity and ownership tool with the potential to infiltrate our lives in countless ways not utilised by BAYC. The premise was false, however, as BAYC offers a magnificent example of how identity and community hold incredible sway and value. If you think NFTs are just about JPEGs or GIFs, you are probably missing the point.

References

1, 6, 22   NFTGo Team. NFT Annual Report 2023, NFTGo, 2023, NFTGo.io (archived at https://perma.cc/6Y4S-NRHJ)

2   J Grimmelmann, Y Ji and T Kell. Copyright vulnerabilities in NFTs, The Initiative for CryptoCurrencies and Contracts (IC3), 2022, medium.com/initc3org/copyright-vulnerabilities-in-nfts-317e02d8ae26 (archived at https://perma.cc/QEW5-X8GB)

3   B Hitchens, C Kerrigan and J Rigelsford. Where's my 'NFT' gone? Potential pitfalls of NFT ownership, CMS Law-Now, 2022, cms-lawnow.com/en/ealerts/2022/03/where-s-my-nft-gone-potential-pitfalls-of-nft-ownership (archived at https://perma.cc/KEW8-82QA)

4   M Marlinspike. My first impressions of web3, Moxie, 2022, moxie.org/2022/01/07/web3-first-impressions.html (archived at https://perma.cc/37VF-66CH)

5   Gartner. Gartner Hype Cycle, Gartner, 2023, https://www.gartner.co.uk/en/methodologies/gartner-hype-cycle (archived at https://perma.cc/7EM8-DDCM)

7   Starbucks Stories. The Starbucks odyssey begins, Starbucks, 2022, stories.starbucks.com/stories/2022/the-starbucks-odyssey-begins/ (archived at https://perma.cc/48LS-B6CN)

8   Clinique. A Metaverse more like us, Clinique, 2022, www.clinique.co.uk/metaverselikeus (archived at https://perma.cc/H9PT-4QZ6)

9   Twitter. McDonald's, 2021, twitter.com/McDonalds/status/1455174998264586243

10   Norwegian Cruise Line Holdings Ltd. Norwegian cruise line announces cruise industry's first NFT collection, 2022, www.nclhltd.com/news-media/press-releases/detail/480/norwegian-cruise-line-announces-cruise-industrys-first-nft (archived at https://perma.cc/H93B-PDWN)

11   M Schulz. Nike leads NFT success by revenue as fashion shines over Pepsi, Time magazine, Vogue Business, 2022, www.voguebusiness.com/technology/nike-leads-nft-success-by-revenue-as-fashion-shines-over-pepsi-time-magazine (archived at https://perma.cc/7XJY-EBAE)

12   Reuters. Breakingviews – Silly Meta, Roblox isn't just for kids, *Reuters*, 16 February 2023, www.reuters.com/breakingviews/silly-meta-roblox-isnt-just-kids-2023-02-15/ (archived at https://perma.cc/PQL2-6BJL)

13   P Kapoor. Why CEOs shouldn't miss the metaverse bus, Entrepreneur, 2023, www.entrepreneur.com/en-in/technology/why-ceos-shouldnt-miss-the-metaverse-bus/443848 (archived at https://perma.cc/7ZW9-FZ4K)

14   E Malachosky. Nike's NFT sales make it one of the most profitable fashion brands in the digital world, Gear Patrol, 2022, www.gearpatrol.com/style/a40968155/nike-tiffany-gucci-nft-earnings/ (archived at https://perma.cc/WAB7-43SZ)

15 J Peters. Adidas sold more than $22 million in NFTs, but it hit a few snags along the way, The Verge, 2021, www.theverge.com/2021/12/17/22843104/adidas-nfts-metaverse-sold-bored-ape (archived at https://perma.cc/GJ2V-EY6A)

16 Adidas. Adidas Originals and Prada announce a first-of-its-kind open-metaverse & user-generated NFT project, Adidas, 2022, news.adidas.com/originals/adidas-originals-and-prada-announce-a-first-of-its-kind-open-metaverse---user-generated-nft-project/s/30a29dad-6ded-4302-ae40-f9f2338e7298 (archived at https://perma.cc/PS5C-EKR4)

17 A Hayward. How the Porsche NFT drop crashed and burned, Decrypt, 2023, decrypt.co/119912/porsche-nft-drop-crashed-burned (archived at https://perma.cc/6ENK-XRP5)

18 Ledger Insights. Mattel, Nickelodeon to launch new NFT projects, explore future of toys, Ledger Insights – blockchain for business, 2022, www.ledgerinsights.com/mattel-nickelodeon-nft-toys/ (archived at https://perma.cc/2RRF-V5TX)

19 Ens.domains. ENS, 2023, ens.domains/ (archived at https://perma.cc/5DTB-9J59)

20 Binance Blog. What is NFT ticketing and how does it work?, Binance, 2022, www.binance.com/en/blog/nft/what-is-nft-ticketing-and-how-does-it-work-421499824684904022 (archived at https://perma.cc/UD34-U6TU)

21 E G Weyl, P Ohlhaver and V Buterin. Decentralized society: finding web3's soul, SSRN, 2022, https://papers.ssrn.com/sol3/papers.cfm?abstract_id=4105763 (archived at https://perma.cc/VAH8-RTB2)

23 Chainalysis. Crime and NFTs: chainalysis detects significant wash trading and some NFT money laundering in this emerging asset class, Chainalysis, 2022, blog.chainalysis.com/reports/2022-crypto-crime-report-preview-nft-wash-trading-money-laundering/ (archived at https://perma.cc/WML9-3A8C)

24 Z Vardai. At least US$577 million of Blur-linked NFT sales are wash trades, CryptoSlam says, Yahoo Finance, 2023, finance.yahoo.com/news/least-us-577-million-blur-195024607.html (archived at https://perma.cc/64CC-LDYL)

25 A Fleck. Where most NFT users live, Statista, 2022, www.statista.com/chart/27571/where-nft-users-live/ (archived at https://perma.cc/AFC4-BEKU)

26 Google Trends. *Google Trends*, Google, 2023, https://trends.google.com/trends/explore?date=2022-01-01%202022-12-31&q=NFT&hl=en-GB (archived at https://perma.cc/4WGM-NKJQ)

07

Virtually financial: The metaverse, web3 and the gamification of DeFi

DeFi and NFTs are not the only developments to turn heads in the early 2020s. Another, and arguably *the* other, is the metaverse. One of the wonderful things about the metaverse is that even in 2023, 31 years since the term was first written by Neal Stephenson in his novel *Snow Crash*, nobody quite seems to agree on what it means exactly and how it will eventually manifest itself. At its minimum, the metaverse is a marketing gimmick being used to overhype the next wave of online gaming and digital media, and to take the opposite stance, it is the new digital universe where many of us will eventually spend a significant part, or maybe even the majority, of our working and social lives.

Ambiguity about the metaverse has done little to stymie investment. McKinsey's *Value Creation in the Metaverse* paper reported that corporations, venture capital and private equity firms invested $57 billion into metaverse projects in 2021, and a further $120 billion in the first five months of 2022 ($69 billion of the higher figure was locked into Microsoft's agreed takeover of Activision, which has proven complicated and at the time of writing remains pending.[1] We can also question the extent to which this is a play for control of the metaverse). One of the biggest investors has been Mark Zuckerberg, who not only changed Facebook's name to Meta, but also ploughed $36 billion into its VR and AR business unit, Reality Labs. Zuckerberg's unabashed embracement of the metaverse has fuelled both the hype and the sceptics. You might ask why one of the internet's most successful entrepreneurs, following savvy and wildly profitable acquisitions of Instagram and WhatsApp, would invest this amount without good reason. Conversely, detractors have found schadenfreude in the heavy losses that Meta has made so far, and the ill-advised social media and marketing efforts that featured primitive graphics and avatars with no legs (Zuckerberg has since explained, and reasonably so, that tracking where a user's legs and elbows should be in VR is challenging, but for those familiar with modern gaming graphics there was still fun to be had).[2]

Finance has been in on the act too. J.P. Morgan's blockchain innovation unit, Onyx, launched the Onyx Lounge in Decentraland to coincide with the launch of its *Opportunities in the Metaverse* paper. Likewise, HSBC bought virtual real estate in The Sandbox metaverse and designed a space to attract sports, esports and gaming enthusiasts. It went a step further for ultra-high and high net-worth clients in Singapore, launching an investment fund called the Metaverse Discretionary Strategy Portfolio, offering exposure to opportunities in infrastructure, interface, computing, virtualisation, experience and discovery.[3] As an aside, HSBC later prohibited UK card users from crypto purchases, while their Sandbox plot can only be accessed if users buy a pass with cryptocurrency.[4] As for the big players in payments, Mastercard filed 15 trademarks relating to the metaverse and NFTs in 2022, and Visa has filed several trademark applications relating to the metaverse, NFTs and digital wallets.[5] In both cases, these filings were made with the United States Patent and Trademark Office.

The metaverse story is not just about the tech titans and financiers. There is also a prominent role for content creators, who now have a new canvas, theatre, arena and more in which to showcase their talents. From a standpoint of democratization, this is also a platform that might have minimal overheads and great potential for audience engagement, and for now, it is an opportunity for established brands and artists to make their mark in a venue with no capacity limits and new opportunities for expression. The most impactful early example of this is the nine-minute concert held on Fortnite by US rapper Travis

Scott, which grossed $20 million including merchandise sales, and is one of several events said to have attracted tens of millions of attendees, alongside performances by Lil Nas X, Ariana Grande and 24kGoldn.[6]

We can also point to prominent brand partnerships in the metaverse, such as the Gucci Garden and NIKELAND in Roblox, Coca-Cola's NFT collectables in Decentraland and Balenciaga's fashion tie-in with Fortnite. The metaverse has also hosted festivals, shows and conferences, including the Metaverse Fashion Week, also hosted in Decentraland. The 2022 event attracted 108,000 unique attendees, with participation from luxury brands such as Dolce & Gabbana, Estee Lauder, Dundas and Etro. The experience made effective use of blockchain, too, with digital goods, wearable for avatars, sold as NFTs, and the same being true of digital land for the show.[7] In time, we might expect the metaverse to provide a platform for new artists and brands, and NFT collectives such as BAYC and CryptoPunks may even be regarded as prototypes for this.

2023 METAVERSE FASHION WEEK

Following 2022's six-figure attendance, Metaverse Fashion Week wasn't so popular in 2023. Decentraland claimed that 26,000 unique visitors attended, while a third-party analytics firm put the number at 9,000.[8]

Projections for the potential of the metaverse have been eye-catching. Technology research and consultancy firm Gartner has claimed that by 2027, 'over 40 per cent of large organizations worldwide will be using a combination of web3, spatial computing and digital twins in metaverse-based projects aimed at increasing revenue', and also predicts that 25 per cent of people will spend at least one hour per day in the metaverse by 2026.[9, 10] McKinsey, meanwhile, reported that the metaverse will generate up to $5 trillion in impact by 2030, and to look more closely at the high fashion examples provided earlier, Morgan Stanley analysts have hinted that NFTs could provide 10 per cent of revenues for the luxury goods market by 2030.[11]

These are numbers that will straighten the posture of most investors, institutions, disruptors and creators. But can they be trusted? A lot of people have placed enormous wagers on the success of the metaverse, and in some circles, there is hesitancy to criticize it. Vogue Business' report of the first Metaverse Fashion Week states that several industry experts refused to speak on the record about the negative aspects of the experience, citing concerns about losing future business. Potential gaps between hype and reality might also be evidenced by data aggregator DappRadar saying that Decentraland, valued at $1.2 billion in October 2022, had only 38 active users per day.[12] The response of Decentraland creative director Sam Hamilton, countering that the platform averages 8,000 users per day, does little to dissuade the idea that its valuation is heavily weighted towards its potential rather than current activity.[13] Nonetheless, the notion that the metaverse is a generational opportunity remains tantalizing.

Defining the metaverse

Defining this new digital landscape is no small task. Many have tried (Epyllion CEO Matthew Ball offers a comprehensive and viable option in his book, *The Metaverse and How it Will Revolutionize Everything*), but for the sake of this analysis, we'll consider it as an interoperable and interactive network of virtual world experiences that allow people to communicate and interact synchronously, and at scale.[14] There are variances in how these worlds are described. Some believe that the metaverse requires digital identities to be continuous, with identities, history, asset ownership and communications persisting between platforms rather than being limited to them. Others describe gaming platforms such as *Grand Theft Auto V* as forms of metaverse.

To start with the obvious, the metaverse is expected to become a huge, global and interactive online virtual multiverse, in which people can participate with their own unique sense of identity, most likely represented as an avatar. People will be able to exist as an extension of their offline identity, or perhaps lead pseudonymous second lives, and they will be able to do this via virtual reality (VR) and augmented reality (AR) devices (the term extended reality (XR) is often used to encapsulate both), or even just through web browsers or smartphones albeit without the full immersiveness of experience. The metaverse can include spaces for gaming, socializing, working, networking, entertainment and more; it serves as a virtual living environment. It can play host to pretty much anything you can imagine: virtual shopping centres, theme parks, theatres, expos, high streets and sporting arenas. These might be designed to replicate the real world or be thematically rich fantasy lands that push the boundaries of creativity and imagination.

Interoperability is also an important consideration in the metaverse. While it seems that tech giants might want to monopolize or at least earn significant revenue from this market, a fully realized metaverse will likely consist of multiple, and probably many, coexisting virtual worlds that users can engage with, each with their own features and designs, with many such features being compatible with counterparts in other worlds. This means identities, reputations, items and achievements can cross over from one environment to the next. It does not, however, mean that every accessory or facet of identity needs to be transferable, as the designs and purposes for these worlds could be largely disconnected. We might expect, nonetheless, that compatibility of assets will be desirable for users, and virtual environments that achieve greater interaction with other popular platforms will attract more attention, revenue and designers.

The metaverse, in whichever forms it takes, should uncover a plethora of financial and commercial opportunities. These might be found in gamified and beautifully designed worlds that prompt us to spend money, or occur in situations where the metaverse serves as a bridge between the physical and virtual worlds; for example, 3D visuals could allow us to 'try on' items of clothing without entering a store, or could allow designers and architects to produce more accurate and flexible plans for what they will build or create.

Where's the blockchain?

From the description so far, it's not clear where DeFi comes in, and there has not even been a mention of blockchain. This is where another of the zeitgeist's most notorious buzzwords, web3, enters the fray. Web3, originally coined by Ethereum co-founder Gavin Wood in 2014, is widely considered to be the next evolutionary step for the internet and follows on from Web 1.0 and Web 2.0. Let's tackle those chronologically. Loosely defined, Web 1.0 represented the dawn of mass internet adoption in the 1990s, where web browsers delivered static web pages to readers, with minimal capacity for interaction. Web 2.0, ushered in around the early 2000s, marked a change in how the internet is used, with abundant opportunity for social interaction and content generation, and the rise of major online platforms. This is the version of the internet that centralized the internet, taking us from the notion that maybe we'd all have our own website, to instead using shared marketplaces and hubs. These platforms have become huge. Alphabet, Meta and Amazon alone claimed over half of global advertising revenue (outside of China) in 2021, and content creators have become reliant upon a number of other sites including YouTube, Twitch, TikTok and Spotify, which host content and claim a share of revenues.[15] These sites, to varying degrees, can also remove content, change their algorithms and guide the user experience, giving them significant influence over everyday online life.

THE CONNECTION BETWEEN WEB3 AND THE METAVERSE

The link between web3 and the metaverse should not be assumed, but there are reasons to believe that the two are complementary. Industry expert Anthony Day explains:

'There's a strong argument that decentralized principles play well in the metaverse because you can create programmable economies. The environments can be perpetual, they can't be censored and switched off. They're for the community, they're open, they're interoperable, and these are all positive things in terms of the ability to innovate, the ability to progress and advance the technology and the platforms, and the applications that exist there, as opposed to a centralized organization, building a digital environment in which there's not much room to grow.'

Web3, however, hinges on the notion of a decentralized internet, designed in a public and open-sourced fashion that gives users full ownership of the content they create. In this iteration of the internet, networks are run by communities through DAOs and there is intent to democratize the internet experience and give content creators more control over their content and revenues. This is where blockchain comes in – almost every description of web3 depicts it as a blockchain-based internet.

In some corners, there has been an assumption that blockchain platforms require blockchain finance and that crypto and DeFi will grow as web3 grows. This is a neat idea but makes light of the immense change needed for it to occur.

DO WE ACTUALLY WANT A WEB3 BLOCKCHAIN INTERNET?

Despite the upsides relating to DLT, the concept of a blockchain-based internet is not to everyone's taste. With blockchain being immutable, it introduces the possibility that everything posted online can never be deleted. Where open sourcing is involved, it is likely that any individual creations can simply be copied by others. Blockchain, however, does not need to be used for everything, and not everything needs to be openly shareable.

What's happening right now?

In its current state, the metaverse is a melting pot for Web 2.0 and web3. Moreover, many web3 solutions are heavily reliant on Web 2.0 infrastructure for interfaces, apps, community building, governance and more. Still, it is helpful to distinguish between the two competing models for virtual worlds.

Virtual worlds in Web 2.0

In this context, virtual worlds include historically relevant examples like Second Life, but more recent cultural touch points include

Roblox, World of Warcraft and Fortnite. These incredibly popular games are centrally owned by private companies and use centralized data storage systems. They can be run on PCs, laptops, VR/AR headsets and mobile phones (many virtual worlds do not yet have VR/AR compatibility), and allow for live streaming, competitions, multiplayer gaming and social activities. Payments for in-game items are made by credit or debit cards, and games often have their own in-game currencies, such as Robux for Roblox, V-Bucks for Fortnite, and WoW Tokens for World of Warcraft. Anything bought or sold in the game remains in the game, and assets are leased rather than owned outright. This means that if a game or virtual world is shut down, asset owners will have nothing to show for it (equally, if in-game and real-world economies can co-exist, this can imbalance and sour the gaming experience, as wealthier players have an immediate advantage wherever they participate. There is a logic to keeping currencies in-game).

'IN-GAME ITEMS ARE WORTHLESS'

Chinese tech giant Tencent argued that in-game assets are worthless when brought to court in 2021 for allowing gamers to trade virtual coins and merchandise when playing *Dungeon Fighter Online*.[16] Understandably, this did not chime well with people who had bought them.

Virtual worlds in web3

Virtual worlds in web3 are governed by communities and usually have their own DAOs and native tokens. Notable early 2020s metaverses include Decentraland, The Sandbox, Cryptovoxels and Somnium Space. Digital assets are likely to take the form of NFTs and are notionally fully owned by the purchaser. Furthermore, while recognized studios and developers still have a major role to play, web3 metaverses are more likely to leverage open sourcing to allow the community to have a hands-on role in the design and direction of the environment or game. This web3 ethos and its corresponding business models may cause friction where centralized third parties provide hardware such as headsets.

A longer-term ambition for web3, some say, is to provide a new paradigm for self-sovereign cross-platform identities, which would mean that your identity and to some extent your items could travel between metaverses. To date, there is no major example of this.

METAVERSE ECONOMIES

The native tokens of metaverses have not been among the top-performing cryptoassets, but they have accrued plenty of value regardless. MANA, the native token of Decentraland, and SAND, the token of The Sandbox, both had a $1 billion market cap in May 2023. Somnium Space Cubes, meanwhile, had a total value of $15.8m. These tokens can be traded for other crypto and fiat currencies.

Metaverse asset ownership extends beyond currency. The Sandbox's end of 2022 blog reveals that 114,835 plots of its land have been bought, with more than 23,000 owners. The platform now has 4.5 million registered wallets, although, for context, only 1 million unique users played the game. It also achieved brand partnerships with Gucci, Steve Aoki, Kun Aguero, Paris Hilton and Care Bears.

Decentraland's end-of-2022 blog also reported 1 million unique users, with 755 creators receiving royalties, 144,000 wearables sold, 2,800 unique events created and 29 land rental agreements reached (this feature launched in December).[17]

The costs of using tech platforms

Most Web 2.0 platform users will be unaware that app and game developers hand over a hefty chunk of their revenues, usually 30 per cent of revenue from every purchase made, to the providers of app stores and games platforms. This standard is upheld by Apple, Google, Sony, Samsung, Valve, Microsoft, Nintendo and more.

The fee is arguably a straightforward way to reimburse providers for their services, and yet, the percentage taken is arbitrary. It stems from a deal made between Namco and Nintendo in 1983 when Namco approached Nintendo to publish games on the Nintendo Entertainment System (NES). Namco agreed to a 10 per cent licensing fee for all titles appearing on the NES, and an additional 20 per cent for Nintendo to manufacture its game cartridges. The 30 per cent rule, despite dating back to Pac-Man, has since become an industry standard, or a platform 'tax' as some say.[18] The fact that cartridges became pretty much defunct did nothing to curtail this.

Will these fees reduce? Epic Games, creators of Fortnite and Rocket League, have attempted to lead the way by charging 12 per cent on games sold in their marketplace. They also fought a legal battle against Apple and Google's use of the 30 per cent fee. They lost, and paid out $3.6 million accordingly, but did at least attract publicity to the issue.[19] On the flipside, Meta, which is hoping to lead the way in immersive metaverse experiences, has imposed an even higher charge at 47.5 per cent. The fee comprises 30 per cent for sales made on its Meta Quest headgear, plus a 25 per cent sales fee on the remainder.[20]

MAKING SENSE OF META'S PRICING STRATEGY

Meta's 47.5 per cent may be more warranted than some people think. It is often reported that the Meta Quest headsets are sold at a loss, and the $13.7 billion operating losses of Meta's AR and VR division in 2022 may reflect this.[21]

INFRASTRUCTURE DOESN'T COME FOR FREE

To throw another spanner in the works, European telecommunications providers have lobbied regional lawmakers to introduce an additional network fee, to be paid by major content providers, to fund the infrastructure upgrades that they consider necessary for running the metaverse at scale.[22] This would likely pass further cost to the end consumer.

Platform fees touch other forms of media too. Note that YouTube takes 45 per cent of advertising revenue from each channel, and that Twitch takes a 50 per cent cut from streamers. To look at writing, Substack takes 10 per cent of paid subscription revenues, and to glance at marketplaces, eBay takes up to 13.25 per cent of revenue from sold items and Etsy charges a 6.5 per cent transaction fee for every sale.

To be clear, these percentages are not listed because they are bad or wrong. The fees represent varying levels and complexities of service, and access to audiences and advertisers that might not otherwise be achievable. By providing such services, which come at a cost to providers too, a whole raft of businesses, artists and personalities have achieved major success. The model has a lot going for it. However, in a web3 environment, it's projected that such fees will become a relic as content creation becomes community-led and creators earn fees directly from purchases in a peer-to-peer manner. Users of an experience or game may also earn revenue for achievements, contributions to governance, or even merely participating. Further, item resales, facilitated by smart contracts, will allow for royalties to be paid to creators for sales on secondary markets.

How decentralized is the web3 metaverse?

Are we anywhere close to a fully decentralized metaverse? The answer seems to be 'no'. The reality is that blockchain is still heavily reliant on Web 2.0 infrastructure and there is no reason to believe that this will change soon. For example, in April 2023, 63 per cent of Ethereum mainnet nodes were being run on hosting services such as AWS, Hetzner Online and Google Cloud.[23]

There is also a high geographical concentration of nodes, with potentially about 60 per cent of them in the United States and Germany alone.

There are, nonetheless, attempts to decentralize data storage. Filecoin, for example, which raised over $200 million in a 2017 ICO, offers decentralized storage, and in 2023 launched a stack of services that provide an alternative to centralized cloud offerings.[24] Another project of note is Internet Computer, which has bold ambitions of replacing cloud computing with a blockchain-based world computer, connecting all blockchains with no need for bridges. This project achieved a $54 billion ICO before promptly dropping 90 per cent from this valuation.[25] Despite the ICO frenzy, Internet Computer remains a considerable project, and if it achieves its stated ambitions, the idea of a web3 metaverse should be more tangible.

For now, there are limits to what can be placed on-chain. While nobody expects a fully on-chain metaverse at this point, it's true that running one would require immense computing power and energy consumption. To look at the computational aspect of this, compare the needs of the metaverse with Ethereum's crashes when CryptoKitties was popular (CryptoKitties, despite its basic graphics, is also hosted largely off-chain), or when Otherside sales spiked in 2022. If purchases of NFTs for two-dimensional images can have this impact, then the prospect of a metaverse with hundreds of millions of people moving and interacting fluidly, in engaging and real-time rendered worlds, with few if any glitches, seems miles off.

As things stand, there is no popular metaverse running entirely on blockchain, and blockchain gaming, the closest comparison, is considered rudimentary even by enthusiasts. Fully on-chain games are mostly turn-based, have very poor graphics and exist largely as a proof of concept. They have all sorts of hurdles to overcome, such as blocking exploitative bots and being able to quickly patch errors made by developers.[26] Layer 2 and sidechain solutions are likely to improve this situation over time.

DeFi: Chasing the multi-trillion dollar dream

There is a mismatch between what the metaverse is and what it could be, and multiple ways DeFi could prosper as the gap closes. Still, there are several paths towards DeFi and crypto adoption that the metaverse might introduce. These include, but are not limited to the following.

A better user experience and user interface (UX and UI)

The metaverse may provide user experiences and interfaces that introduce more people to crypto and DeFi. To date, most DeFi participants have been enthusiasts, relatively undeterred by low-quality UX and UI. The metaverse could offer the visuals, environment and assistance (likely through AI chatbots) to broaden its appeal. Some experiences may want or need users to provide cryptoassets to participate in experiences.

Marketplaces

With the development of virtual worlds comes the creation of new marketplaces, where digital goods and services are bundled together. This is far from DeFi-specific, but we should observe Morgan Stanley's estimate that the global e-commerce market will be $5.4 trillion by 2026, and that the metaverse adds a new dimension to it.[27] In terms of crypto and DeFi, the opportunity is initially that crypto becomes commonly accepted for online payments (theoretically, low transaction costs and high speeds give it merit). There may also be opportunities for merchants to customize payment experiences with tokens, introducing rewards or new features for customers. Similarly, the deployment of smart contracts could allow royalties to be sent to creators when items are traded on secondary markets.

Beyond this, there could be opportunities if XR headsets bring digital assets to life. We might see a greater role for NFTs in digital galleries, digital real estate design and access to exclusive or popular places, or access to music, books and other media. Another important element of this is digital identity. If our digital lives become more central to our perception of self, we might foresee a huge market for NFTs that allow us to customize and add features to our online appearance.

Events and venues

The metaverse can play host to online shows, performances, e-sports, education and more. It is easy to envision that tokens may become part of this experience, especially Proof of Attendance Protocols that might be linked to loyalty schemes, access or memberships. Events and hosting can, of course, take place without crypto, but again it is worthwhile to consider this as a future avenue for growth.

Employment and the gig economy

An international jobs market and gig economy, initially led by artists, designers and programmers, could stem from virtual worlds. Work carried out could be entirely online, or an extension of roles held in the physical world. In creating a more immersive online experience, the metaverse could also be a valuable platform for services that are historically face-to-face, such as consultancy, therapy, coaching and teaching. Speaking to finance, we can include financial advice and the interpersonal elements of wealth management and investment due diligence. As we saw earlier, workstreams might even be coordinated by a DAO.

Virtual real estate

Despite an absence of mass metaverse adoption, plots of digital land have already sold for million-dollar price tags. It may be tempting to scoff at this, but several attributes might influence the value of virtual real estate, such as plot size, design, utility within the metaverse, and the supply of land (it is both economically and computationally sensible for virtual worlds to be finite). Location is also significant. For a celebrity-infused illustration, note that an investor stumped up $450,000 for the right to be Snoop Dogg's neighbour in the Snoopverse, a virtual neighbourhood built in The Sandbox. If the metaverse does scale up as some expect, land ownership in certain areas could become a major status symbol.

Gambling and betting

A handful of metaverse casinos have sprung up to accommodate gambling and betting using cryptocurrencies. By adding rich visuals to the experience, it is possible that metaverse casinos will become lucrative and the events being wagered on could also be accessible via VR/AR headsets. The legal ramifications of wagering cryptoassets in virtual and possibly decentralized casinos are far from obvious, and user safeguarding is another essential aspect to consider.

Gaming

Gaming is regarded as the obvious route towards DeFi adoption, though the connection is not without friction. Following Steam's dabble with Bitcoin as a payment method from April 2016 and December 2017, the games platform's president Gabe Newell claimed that roughly half of transactions attempted were fraudulent, also decrying issues with pricing relating to Bitcoin's volatility.[28] To date, most major gaming companies do not accept direct payments in crypto for games or in-game items, though workarounds are possible via gift cards. Major platform, console and games providers might change tack if they can be sure of crypto payments being legal and practical.

The NFT market is a more straightforward winner. Games provide new incentives and designs for buyers to latch onto, and the purchase of NFTs, either through fiat or in-game currencies, presents fewer legal issues than trading in crypto. In March 2023, Sony filed a patent to make NFTs transferable between games, headsets and consoles. The patent will potentially provide a connection between Sony and other major companies' platforms, such as Microsoft's Xbox, and also has cross-generational potential, meaning that it might be integrated with older games.[29] The NFT market, if this plays out, could breathe life back into retro gaming experiences.

Real-world assets

There is ample opportunity to blend metaverse assets and services with those existing in the physical world, either through investments, memberships or something else. Here we might note the role of NFTs that represent ownership of 'real-world' assets, either as a whole or a fraction. Ownership of these NFTs might grant rights to an exclusive group of people in relation to both the physical asset and a corresponding metaverse representation. The metaverse may also prove an effective location for crowdfunding.

The future for DeFi in the metaverse

We need a bucketload of disclaimers when depicting the future of crypto and DeFi within a metaverse, whether it's Web 2.0 or web3 (I can only apologize for the amount of jargon in this sentence). First, there are assumptions surrounding how much the metaverse will seep into everyday life, and when. There are also conversations over whether the metaverse will predominantly follow Web 2.0 models or web3 ones, and whether crypto and DeFi will find a home here. We are very much guessing at the future.

To isolate the metaverse, most would likely agree that there is a very profitable long-term opportunity for XR experiences, and their reduced equivalents on tablets and smartphones, too. In fact, Web 2.0 metaverses, to use that categorization, can already be described as very popular and successful. Roblox alone made $2.2 billion in revenue in 2022 and has seen its daily active user numbers reach 66 million.[30,31] While Meta's more ambitious plans to bring the metaverse into everyday life through its Horizon Worlds platform have been less successful, with fewer than 200,000 monthly users, its arrival, and the involvement of Meta and Zuckerberg, have helped to popularize the term and to a degree the idea behind it.[32] It has also raised awareness of the capabilities of VR/AR, which have yet to be widely implemented across metaverse experiences.

Should metaverses grow as some anticipate, it is only natural that they will host thriving marketplaces, provide jobs and host content, events, artwork and far more. There is a chance that crypto will be exchanged here, and also that DeFi protocols will prosper. Thinking longer term, these protocols might facilitate experiences to the point where many people won't know or care that a protocol is being used. The financialization of the metaverse will not go unnoticed, however, and the European Commission is already exploring its options for regulating the metaverse. Unlike the finance and tech subculture found in DeFi, the metaverse is likely to have greater appeal to younger children and accordingly requires careful handling. Roblox's 2020 reports showed that more than half of its users were under 13 years of age, and while this game is marketed towards children, regulators will be wary of any potential risks to vulnerable users and reminded of controversies regarding children being targeted with loot boxes and microtransactions within their favourite games.[33] To look at this another way, though, the regulatory concern does insinuate that the metaverse is likely to remain relevant.

The web3 part of this seems much further off. Investment in the metaverse has chiefly originated from institutional investors, and this even stretches to web3-themed initiatives, which may seem a little contradictory. Whichever way you look at it, the idea of a dominant web3 metaverse, as initially outlined, should not be considered an inevitability. A successful web3 metaverse is also likely to be built on and supported by technology and infrastructure that hasn't been launched or built yet, and in being swept up by the crypto hype machine, outsiders have plenty of ammo for describing it as an empty promise.

Even so, a closer inspection reveals a few elements of decentralization and web3 brought to life. Initiatives like The Sandbox's Game Maker Fund, which raised $12 million in funding for 130 independent game studios in 2022, look a lot like the web3 ideal brought to life.[34] Likewise, Decentraland has a grants DAO to reward people for developing its features, and the platform offers generous revenue splits with content creators in its marketplace; 2.5 per cent of revenue goes to the governance DAO, with the rest going directly to creators. It is hard to overlook that this entire online world has at most 8,000 users per day, however, when Facebook, YouTube and Instagram each have over 2 billion monthly active users.[35]

So at this point, a thriving web3 metaverse with crypto and DeFi at its core is an uncertain and distant promise, but it's too early to speak to its long-term fate.

References

1   T Elmasary, H Khan, L Yee, E Hazan, G Kelly, S Srivastava and R W Zemmel. *Value creation in the metaverse: the real business of the virtual world*, McKinsey, 2022, https://www.mckinsey.com/capabilities/growth-marketing-and-sales/our-insights/value-creation-in-the-metaverse (archived at https://perma.cc/4WVT-48QT)

2   J Peters. Meta figured out legs for its avatars, The Verge, 2022, www.theverge.com/2022/10/11/23390503/meta-quest-horizon-avatars-legs (archived at https://perma.cc/C4MD-UNJH)

3   Reuters. HSBC launches metaverse portfolio for wealthy Asian clients, Reuters, 6 April 2022, www.reuters.com/technology/hsbc-launches-metaverse-portfolio-wealthy-asian-clients-2022-04-06/ (archived at https://perma.cc/SL96-9FQY)

4   A P Pereira. UK banks HSBC, Nationwide to ban crypto purchases with credit cards, Cointelegraph, 2023, cointelegraph.com/news/uk-banks-hsbc-nationwide-to-ban-crypto-purchases-with-credit-cards-report (archived at https://perma.cc/L9K2-8LW4)

5   O Hernandez. Mastercard files 15 metaverse and NFT related trademarks, Cointelegraph, 2022, cointelegraph.com/news/mastercard-files-15-metaverse-and-nft-related-trademarks (archived at https://perma.cc/KM7U-CJQP)

6   A Brown. How hip-hop superstar Travis Scott has become corporate America's brand whisperer, Forbes, 2020, www.forbes.com/sites/abrambrown/2020/11/30/how-hip-hop-superstar-travis-scott-has-become-corporate-americas-brand-whisperer/?sh=7f6c414074e7 (archived at https://perma.cc/TA8C-BB9F)

7   M McDowell. Metaverse Fashion Week: the hits and misses, Vogue Business, 29 March 2022, www.voguebusiness.com/technology/metaverse-fashion-week-the-hits-and-misses (archived at https://perma.cc/CU93-PJVH)

8   S Lutz. And the winner of Metaverse Fashion Week 2023 is…, Decrypt, 2023, decrypt.co/125737/winner-decentraland-metaverse-fashion-week-2023 (archived at https://perma.cc/8H5Q-WVRB)

9   Gartner. Gartner identifies the Top 10 strategic technology trends for 2023, Gartner, 2022, www.gartner.com/en/newsroom/press-releases/2022-10-17-gartner-identifies-the-top-10-strategic-technology-trends-for-2023 (archived at https://perma.cc/HB3D-ZR7H)

10 Gartner, Gartner predicts 25% of people will spend at least one hour per day in the metaverse by 2026, Gartner, 2022, www.gartner.com/en/newsroom/press-releases/2022-02-07-gartner-predicts-25-percent-of-people-will-spend-at-least-one-hour-per-day-in-the-metaverse-by-2026 (archived at https://perma.cc/89G5-MEHD)

11 S Goldstein. Luxury in the metaverse? Morgan Stanley says it could become a €50 billion market, MarketWatch, 2021, www.marketwatch.com/story/luxury-in-the-metaverse-morgan-stanley-says-it-could-become-a-50-billion-market-11637058661 (archived at https://perma.cc/4A5A-6KP5)

12 B Monaghan. $1.2 billion Metaverse project, Decentraland only has '38 active users', report claims, indy100, 2022, www.indy100.com/science-tech/decentraland-metaverse-38-users-billon (archived at https://perma.cc/3QXE-NQFS)

13 C Thompson. It's lonely in the metaverse: DappRadar data suggests Decentraland has 38 'daily active' users in $1.3B ecosystem, CoinDesk, 2022, www.coindesk.com/web3/2022/10/07/its-lonely-in-the-metaverse-decentralands-38-daily-active-users-in-a-13b-ecosystem/ (archived at https://perma.cc/P7W5-DQPY)

14 M Ball. *The metaverse and how it will revolutionize everything*, Liveright Publishing Corporation, W.W. Norton & Company, New York, NY

15 L. Russell-Jones. Tech giants Alphabet, Meta and Amazon control half of ads outside China, CITYA.M., 6 December 2021, https://www.cityam.com/tech-giants-alphabet-meta-and-amazon-control-half-of-ads-outside-china/ (archived at https://perma.cc/GWV2-Y6SS)

16 J Ye. Who owns in-game items acquired by players? Tencent makes its case, inkl, 2021, https://www.inkl.com/news/who-owns-in-game-items-acquired-by-players-tencent-makes-its-case (archived at https://perma.cc/9W7D-GA5Q)

17 decentraland.org. Decentraland 2022 recap, Decentraland, 2022, decentraland.org/blog/announcements/decentraland-2022-recap (archived at https://perma.cc/M97P-VRY4)

18 T Mochizuki and V Savov. Epic's battle with Apple and Google actually dates back to Pac-Man, Bloomberg, 19 August 2020, www.bloomberg.com/news/articles/2020-08-19/epic-games-fortnite-battle-with-apple-and-google-can-be-traced-to-nintendo-tax (archived at https://perma.cc/B55Y-ADUD)

19 S Hollister. Apple and Epic both lost today, The Verge, 2021, www.theverge.com/2021/9/10/22667769/apple-epic-lost-lawsuit-verdict-ruling (archived at https://perma.cc/E5UR-9UEK)

20 I A Hamilton. Meta will charge creators fees of up to 47.5% to sell virtual wares in its metaverse, Business Insider, 2022, www.businessinsider.com/meta-metaverse-charges-creators-47-percent-sales-fee-cut-zuckerberg-2022-4?r=US&IR=T (archived at https://perma.cc/47FL-BV6E)

21 Metro. Meta Quest VR division has lost $24 billion in two years, Metro, 3 February 2023, metro.co.uk/2023/02/03/meta-quest-vr-division-has-lost-24-billion-in-two-years-18217720/ (archived at https://perma.cc/AG28-KLK7)

22 N. Lomas. Metaverse is just VR, admits Meta, as it lobbies against 'arbitrary' network fee, TechCrunch, 2023, https://techcrunch.com/2023/03/23/meta-metaverse-network-fee-nonsense/?guce_referrer=aHR0cHM6Ly93d3cucmVVkZGl0LmNvbS8&guce_referrer_sig=AQAAAATKmSfauDHH0IyzCokLtU-iaCO_JQ7SEiWi7koKLc5ybd9JiEqYCHn5AL-yKyLN-XMg-gfhuL-Pc-iKjQo-IAL83cwSUly12XgbKnu9RuzQvBTutiYIdfTKTZ1bwAq2cvLp6VurSEklHG_BE1whUVEWtJVCBDxBSFRvsEBksORC&guccounter=2 (archived at https://perma.cc/J4ZX-QDRA)

23 ethernodes.org. Ethereum Mainnet statistics, ethernodes.org, 2023, ethernodes.org/networkType/Hosting (archived at https://perma.cc/3C3E-NGAV)

24 S Higgins. $257 million: Filecoin breaks all-time record for ICO funding, CoinDesk, 2017, www.coindesk.com/markets/2017/09/07/257-million-filecoin-breaks-all-time-record-for-ico-funding/ (archived at https://perma.cc/3AW2-TKN5)

25 A R Sorkin, J Karaian, S Kessler, S Gandel, M J de la Merced, L Hirsch and E Livni. How a buzzy cryptocurrency fizzled, *The New York Times*, 28 June 2021, www.nytimes.com/2021/06/28/business/dealbook/dfinity-icp-ico.html (archived at https://perma.cc/N58H-68HP)

26 D. Choy. The promises of blockchain gaming, Bankless, 2023, www.bankless.com/the-promises-of-blockchain-gaming-2 (archived at https://perma.cc/93NK-7VZL)

27 Morgan Stanley. Here's why e-commerce growth can stay stronger for longer, Morgan Stanley, 2022, www.morganstanley.com/ideas/global-ecommerce-growth-forecast-2022 (archived at https://perma.cc/YY23-648C)

28 A Brown. Valve co-founder says half of all Steam cryptocurrency payments were fraudulent, NME, 2022, www.nme.com/news/gaming-news/valve-co-founder-says-half-of-all-steam-cryptocurrency-payments-were-fraudulent-3171111 (archived at https://perma.cc/EC6A-EQU5)

29 C Thompson. Sony files patent for NFTs to allow transfers between games and consoles, CoinDesk, 2023, www.coindesk.com/web3/2023/03/21/sony-files-patent-for-nfts-to-allow-transfers-between-games-and-consoles/ (archived at https://perma.cc/T3QM-HCAB)

30 BusinessWire. Roblox reports fourth quarter and full year 2022 financial results, Businesswire, 2023, www.businesswire.com/news/home/20230215005060/en/Roblox-Reports-Fourth-Quarter-and-Full-Year-2022-Financial-Results (archived at https://perma.cc/7VVP-9YR2)

31 A Capoot. Shares of Roblox fall 12% after company releases March update, CNBC, 2023, www.cnbc.com/2023/04/17/roblox-stock-falls-11percent-after-company-releases-march-update-.html (archived at https://perma.cc/6C3Z-W4TH)

32 P Tassi. Meta's 'Horizon Worlds' has somehow lost 100,000 players in eight months, Forbes, 17 October 2022, www.forbes.com/sites/paultassi/2022/10/17/metas-horizon-worlds-has-somehow-lost-100000-players-in-eight-months/?sh=58d9e23a2a1b (archived at https://perma.cc/Z8N9-4ESV)

33 United States Securities and Exchange Commission. Registration statement on Form S-1, SEC, 2020, www.sec.gov/Archives/edgar/data/1315098/000119312520298230/d87104ds1.htm#rom87104_12 (archived at https://perma.cc/F58U-3CS5)

34 The Sandbox. 2022 Year in review: one year in the making of the open metaverse, Sandbox, 14 February 2023, www.sandbox.game/en/blog/2022-year-in-review-one-year-in-the-making-of-the-open-metaverse/3293/ (archived at https://perma.cc/PP5R-6UTJ)

35 S Dixon. Global social networks ranked by number of users 2023, Statista, 2023, www.statista.com/statistics/272014/global-social-networks-ranked-by-number-of-users/ (archived at https://perma.cc/6AZH-QGH7)

08

TradFi enters the market: Game over for the decentralized dream?

If we look at the origins of Bitcoin, Satoshi Nakamoto is clear that his design is intended for a 'purely peer-to-peer version of electronic cash', existing independently of financial institutions. When Vitalik Buterin published the Ethereum whitepaper, he built on this concept, creating a platform for decentralized apps that perform the functions that are usually provided by financial institutions. This takes us in a clear direction, towards a new technology that pries our finances away from the control of central banks and financial giants and shifts power towards decentralized entities. DeFi, from this stance, is part of a politicized economic movement; one that presents a gateway to a new frontier for global finance, disrupting the way that governments, central banks and major institutions influence our lives. These things, however, are easy to write about but far harder to achieve. In this chapter, we will consider how institutions and governments are instead making use of this technology and integrating it within their systems and processes.

THE TECH DOES NOT BELONG TO DeFi

Despite the origins of blockchain finance, there are many reasons for financial institutions to be enthusiastic about it. It can make them more efficient, collaborative and versatile, and early adopters may well have an initial advantage over competitors. While DeFi innovations are not really built with fiat currency in mind, there are many ways that financial services providers can improve today's economy by integrating DLT and offering developments within a regulated environment. As for governments, if new technology is emerging that threatens their fiat currencies, and accordingly, their ability to set monetary policy and shape their economies, then we should expect them to integrate this technology, improve upon it, or else ban it outright. A third consideration is fintech and big tech. If money becomes entirely digital, and new currencies and applications emerge, then digital-native companies could become a more integral part of our financial lives.

Institutional investing in DeFi

Before getting into the details of blockchain and smart contract projects being led by institutions, it is worth acknowledging that some financial institutions have already attempted to capture the economic value of DeFi by investing in crypto or crypto-adjacent assets and companies. To expand on 'crypto or crypto adjacent', note the following ways that centralized organizations offer access to crypto.

Direct access

Many banks allow retail investors to buy crypto with fiat currency, and a range of fintechs and neo-banks have apps that allow users to easily exchange fiat for crypto. Institutions themselves might add cryptoassets to their balance sheets, ostensibly as a diversifier or as an inflationary hedge, although cryptoassets have generally fallen short on the second of these objectives.

However, institutional investors have been reluctant to add crypto holdings to client portfolios due to regulatory hurdles, custody requirements and volatility.

Indirect access

The challenges of adding cryptoassets to client portfolios can be partially countered with the use of an investment wrapper. Exchange-traded funds, usually referred to as ETFs, have been at the forefront of this, with Bitcoin ETFs leading the way. Regulators in some jurisdictions allow futures and spot ETFs to operate, and there is also an embryonic market for Ether and DeFi ETFs.

Futures ETFs, in this market, essentially hold and trade crypto futures contracts with the intention of mimicking the price of the underlying asset. A spot ETF, by contrast, is a fund that directly holds the underlying assets, meaning investors can invest at the asset's actual price. The use of funds is seen as desirable for several reasons, and perhaps primarily for enabling inflows to crypto without the need for large investors to manage custody of the assets (such as crypto wallets, especially where it would be logical to use more than one). The first DeFi ETF was launched in Brazil in February 2022, with mixed responses from onlookers.[1]

For those looking for regulated crypto exposure outside of an investment wrapper, a handful of exchanges allow derivatives trading. A notable example is the Chicago Mercantile Exchange (CME), and if ever evidence was needed for a blending of the old and new worlds, note that the CME was founded in 1898 as the Chicago Butter and Egg Board.

Adjacent access

Rather than investing directly in cryptoassets, funds may attempt to capture returns by investing in the companies at the forefront of crypto, or in companies that offer services to crypto, such as mining or cybersecurity. Funds are now available for a range of crypto and blockchain themes which trade shares in these companies.

To add nuance and a nod to the previous chapter, Fidelity and BlackRock (through its iShares brand) have launched metaverse ETFs, and Bitwise and SoFi have launched Web3 ETFs. These funds consist of investments in companies with a stake in the success of the metaverse and web3 respectively, and as such do not require crypto holdings.

There was a time when institutional investment in crypto seemed implausible, and even now there is likely an element of suspicion within most organizations. J.P. Morgan Chase CEO Jamie Dimon has publicly questioned the value of bitcoin, but J.P. Morgan, nonetheless, has its own blockchain business unit and has created its own permissioned blockchain coin (JPM Coin), allowed its wealth management clients in the US to access crypto funds and opened a lounge in the metaverse.[2] The surface-level conflict in these positions is indicative of another general theme. Institutions are largely, and understandably, apprehensive about the prospect of a decentralized economic system, but more enthusiastic about the technology that supports it.

Which organizations are embracing blockchain and crypto?

Deloitte's 2021 Global Blockchain Survey estimated that 50–70 per cent of financial services institutions were pursuing digital asset business opportunities.[3] There are many reasons why. Some are doing it to tokenize investments or reduce friction, security risk and cost in payments, while others are doing it to reduce processing times or the potential for human error, among other things. The urgency of this investment appears to have increased. In some markets, blockchain capabilities may even be necessary for keeping pace with competitors, rather than a whimsical or hopeful investment. Many institutions are also keen to earn revenue from the crypto and DeFi universe, provided that they can do so in a regulated and safe manner. See the following for a handful of examples of how recognized companies are embracing blockchain and crypto.

Banking

Crypto holds an unusual relationship with banks. Some banks have begun offering retail clients access to crypto trading services, generally limited to trading and custody, but banking services for crypto are peripheral. A lack of developed regulation is a deterrent, and equally, crypto holders don't necessarily need traditional banking services.

WHY EVERYDAY BANKING AND DeFi DON'T FIT

Individual crypto owners are unlikely to require the use of a conventional bank for services relating to cryptoassets. In terms of asset custody, they are served by crypto wallets, and those more immersed in DeFi will likely use protocols to generate interest or investment returns from assets. Yield farming, for example, might be regarded as DeFi's answer to interest payments.

It is also healthier for the DeFi ecosystem that assets are put to use in lending, farming and staking protocols, which provide liquidity to DeFi markets. This contrasts with traditional banking, in which a portion of client deposits is loaned out to stimulate the economy and generate profits.

Crypto banking has made greater inroads in the provision of services for crypto exchanges, institutional investors, stablecoin issuers and major lenders. These services are typically provided to allow companies to operate within regulatory frameworks and are perhaps better understood as banking services to crypto-involved firms, rather than 'crypto banking' in a DeFi sense. They allow banks to offer custody of assets, trading, staking and more.

Given the rapid growth of DeFi and crypto, demand for these services initially peaked in the early 2020s, especially in the United States. The frontrunners were Silvergate Bank and Signature Bank, who were not only willing to welcome crypto companies as clients, but also provide 24/7 on-ramps from fiat to crypto; Silvergate did so through the Silvergate Exchange Network (SEN) and Signature through a system named Signet. For a time, these services allowed crypto companies to work with fiat currency outside of traditional banking hours.

However, the past tense is used for good reason. Silvergate and Signature both encountered a dramatic rise and fall, as both were wiped out by the contagion from Silicon Valley Bank's (SVB's) swift demise. Early analysis of the situation indicates that both were brought down by bank runs as clients clamoured to withdraw funds, despite them respectively holding asset balances of $11 billion and $114 billion when the market turned.[4] Both banks had predated crypto.

These collapses left many commercial clients scrambling for banking services, with only a limited range of providers capable of catering to their needs. It was reported that several clients, undeterred by the recent disintegration of Credit Suisse, turned to Swiss banks, a claim corroborated in a CNBC interview by the chief marketing officer of Sygnum, one of the nation's biggest providers of digital asset banking.[5] Circle, which held 8 per cent of the funds backing its USDC stablecoin with SVB, briefly depegged to beneath 87 cents. It would subsequently strengthen its ties with BNY Mellon and add Cross River Bank as a commercial banking partner.

Despite this hammer blow for crypto-focused banking, its long-term prospects are likely to be brighter as sensible regulation enters the market. In the meantime, this situation may even present a lucrative opening for banks that can profitably service these relatively unique clients while performing the basic but understated duty of staying solvent.

THE CHALLENGES OF BEING A CRYPTO BANK

Crypto banks are operating in a different sphere to the rest of the banking world. There appear to be some lessons that can be learnt from the rapid client withdrawals that brought down Silvergate Bank and Signature Bank, as well as the demise of Silicon Valley Bank beforehand. Three factors for crypto bank runs stand out in this regard.

1 The speed with which clients can withdraw assets.

2 The philosophy that intermediaries should not be able to interfere with a crypto holder's decisions relating to their assets. Any exchange asked to freeze withdrawals is unlikely to respond positively, and any exchange that does will be at the mercy of its account holders.

> **3** The crypto community is well-connected and also engaged with social media. Concerns about market declines and institutional failures can be communicated at lightning speeds, so bank runs could take a matter of hours rather than months.
>
> To clarify, a bank run occurs when clients withdraw their money en masse due to fears of losing it. This, in turn, causes mass outflows for banks, putting strain on their reserves and potentially triggering bankruptcy.

At present, crypto banking remains a niche market. Where feasible and seemingly safe, major players have offered services for institutional crypto clients, and access to trading for retail ones. Even in cases where commitments don't extend far beyond lip service, it is understandable that banks have not been entirely avoidant of crypto. Crypto services can attract new clients and retain existing ones, while also helping banks present themselves as on trend, especially in relation to the next generation of customers.

The recent banking collapses, however, act as a deterrent. Silvergate and Signature might be regarded as having flown too close to the sun, though a pointed footnote to this story is that Silicon Valley Bank may have survived for at least a few more days had it been able to transfer assets and borrow money after 4pm local time on the day prior to its failure.[6] It's hard to say what difference this would have made, but the case for a 24/7 financial system can be made.

A last word on blockchain and banks is that multinational modern banks, of course, offer far more than just banking services, and their interest in crypto is more evident in other activities. To sweep crypto aside briefly, blockchain offers a chance for banks to modernize their processes in relation to payment security and fraud prevention, cross-border settlements, lending and digitizing systems that were previously paper-based.

Investment management

Direct crypto investments are generally provided by DeFi-native companies or fintechs, but as mentioned, there are a handful of banks and institutions providing such a service. Fidelity, for example, quietly launched a simplified crypto trading platform for US retail clients in 35 states in 2023.[7] In terms of investing, institutional opportunities are also relatively limited. BlackRock, the world's largest asset manager, has facilitated direct investment in Bitcoin for a handful of US institutional clients through the launch of a private bitcoin trust.[8] Franklin Templeton is also offering access to crypto funds, following its investment in Eaglebrook Advisers and subsequent launch of two funds consisting entirely of cryptoassets.[9] In Asia, there have been multiple launches of cryptocurrency and blockchain-focused funds that don't directly hold crypto, in Singapore, Hong Kong and South Korea. In Australia, several funds are offering direct access for institutional and even retail clients through investment trusts and ETFs. This is not an exhaustive list but demonstrates a burgeoning global market.

Blockchain is also being applied to the processing of investment funds. A notable example of this is the Franklin Templeton US Government Money Fund, which has used blockchain to process transactions and track share ownership since late 2021.[10] The use of blockchain for this mutual fund is a notable development. From a provider perspective, government money funds invest heavily in high-quality and short-duration debt, and from an individual investor perspective, these funds are rarely held long-term and are not designed for long-term capital appreciation. In simple terms, a lot of trading and processing is required, and blockchain should prove a vastly superior alternative to paper-based settlements.

In Europe, Société Générale piloted a €100m covered bond on the Ethereum blockchain in 2019, and in 2021 issued a structured product that was registered as a security token on the Tezos blockchain.[11] By 2022, the European Investment Bank had launched two euro-denominated digital bonds on a private blockchain in a partnership with Goldman Sachs, Santander and Société Générale (the second launch was leveraged by Goldman Sachs as an opportunity to launch its proprietary Tokenization Platform) and at the start of 2023 it launched its first pound sterling denominated blockchain bond, a £50 million issuance led by BNP Paribas, RBC Capital Markets and HSBC (the bond was accessible and operated via HSBC's Orion tokenization platform).[12,13]

Elsewhere, HSBC has used blockchain to settle bonds in a day, rather than four, and Société Générale is offering a range of services to help regulated European asset managers integrate digital assets into their portfolios.[14] China's WeBank has also introduced blockchain to support its environmental, social and governance (ESG) processes, and many industry experts believe that DLT has a crucial role to play in supporting sustainable and ethical practices, through practices such as the tokenization of carbon credits or relevant ESG data.[15]

Blockchain is also providing opportunities for providers of alternative investments. Private equity firm Apollo, following the prominent hire of Christine Moy from J.P. Morgan, announced that it will be investing in web3 and blockchain companies, citing lending, content royalties, payments and insurance as prime use cases for the technology.[16] The firm also entered into a partnership with Figure Lending LLC, bringing mortgages on-chain and reportedly cutting settlement time from weeks to seconds.[17] To extend the theme of improvements in processing accuracy and speed, WeBank's blockchain-based information verification platform should also be mentioned. It is reported that the platform, which connects the notary office and borrowers in China, has led to an increase in loan approvals for car buyers from 20 per cent to 80 per cent since its launch in April 2022.[18]

Venture capital firms have also kept a close eye on crypto markets. Andreessen Horowitz, also known as a16z, has been a prominent backer of crypto projects, launching four funds between 2018 and 2022 and raising a total of $7.6 billion.[19] The first and fourth of these were launched during bear markets (crypto winters) and taken at face value the investments represent a long-term faith in the market and a conviction in 'buying cheap' while share and coin prices are falling. The fourth a16z fund raised $4.5 billion and followed a halving of the price of bitcoin.[20]

In another novel case, at least right now, $500 billion AUM investment manager KKR & Co has tokenized part of its Health Care Strategic Growth Fund on Layer 1 blockchain Avalanche.[21] The tokenized portion of the fund acts as a quasi-feeder fund, allowing the general public to invest in it, and therefore offering access to an opportunity that would otherwise be exclusive.[22] We might see this as indicative of a step forward for alternative investing. If blockchain facilitates simple fundraising and trading for private equity and venture capital funds, it is very plausible that there will be more opportunities for everyday investors to access pooled investments that were previously reserved for institutional and high-net-worth investors. Pair this with tokenization and investors will be able to invest with far greater specificity than ever before. Putting investment returns aside for a second, this could provoke countless opportunities to align investments with ESG and ethical views, niche interests and community outcomes.

Big tech and the battle for the economy

It is not just large financial institutions circling crypto markets and deciding if, how and where to swoop in. The economic shift delivered by crypto is also of serious interest to tech giants, such as Apple, Alphabet, Amazon, Meta and Microsoft (though we may also include the likes of Alibaba, Tencent and Samsung), and they are all approaching it in different ways. In this regard, we can include decisions on whether to accept or encourage crypto payments, the use of crypto within products and services, the interoperability of tech platforms with blockchains and practical applications such as blockchain within supply chains or data storage. Given the wide range of business activities pursued by big tech, it is impossible to cover every use of blockchain and crypto, but here, several examples will be highlighted.

As with the metaverse, any discussion on this topic requires a mention of Meta. The Silicon Valley social media pioneer was one of the first household names to make a serious play on digital money, launching a stablecoin in 2019 known as Libra, with Spotify, Visa, Mastercard, Uber and Vodafone all on board as founding members with equal voting rights.[23] The upside for Meta from creating this coin, ostensibly, was access to transaction data, fees from transactions, user engagement and an opportunity to grow e-commerce within its platforms. Regulators were alive to this, not least because Facebook had over 1.6 billion daily users by the end of 2019, so Libra, later renamed Diem, faced continual scrutiny from US regulators and importantly the Federal Reserve. The project met its end in early 2022, with Meta selling Diem to Silvergate Bank. To date, this attempt to launch and manage a global currency appears to be big tech's most ambitious project in crypto; and undoubtedly, the emergence of a global currency owned by one of the world's largest and most socially embedded companies would have been an unmistakable and unintended consequence of the emergence of blockchain finance. After adjusting its plans, Meta briefly allowed users to create and share, but not buy and sell, NFTs across Facebook and Instagram before announcing plans to wind down the project in 2023.[24]

Alphabet (Google) also seeks a future in blockchain and has invested in institutional crypto platform Fireblocks, NBA Top Shot, CryptoKitties creator Dapper Labs and digital currency venture capital firm Digital Currency Group.[25] It has also partnered with crypto exchange Coinbase to allow users to pay for Google Cloud services with cryptoassets.[26] This partnership paves the way for Google to use Coinbase's custody service, Coinbase Prime, for institutional crypto services, and for Coinbase to make use of Google's cloud infrastructure and data analytics services.

Elsewhere, it is reported that Tencent has used blockchain to help 400 million users of its WeChat social media platform to pay taxes, donations and medical bills.[27] Its cloud computing arm, Tencent Cloud, even launched a 'Web3 Build Day' in Singapore in February 2023, another signal of intention within decentralized technology. Ant Group, an affiliate of Alibaba, has created its own blockchain, AntChain, and been one of the leading global blockchain patent filers. It launched its LETUS project to lower the storage costs of blockchain networks in 2022, runs a digital collectables platform named Topnod and has a stated focus on secure computing and the Internet of Things.

There are several large fintech operators involved, too. Trading app Robinhood, which positions itself as a zero-commission broker and allows crypto transactions, found itself in an unusual predicament prior to its 2021 IPO as Dogecoin accounted for 6 per cent of its overall revenues.[28] In September 2022, it went a step further, rolling out a web3 wallet for its users, and in the process allowing them custody of their own assets; a crucial distinguishing factor after the FTX debacle. The wallet was initially only compatible with the Polygon blockchain and the 0x decentralized exchange infrastructure, but plans for cross-chain compatibility have been announced. Some observed that the tool resembled a trading app and as it evolved it more closely resembled software such as MetaMask, which allows users to transact and connect with dApps.[29]

Block, created by Twitter founder Jack Dorsey, is also active in this market, partnering with Coinbase and Circle to create Verite, a decentralized identity solution. This web3-focused project is designed to allow users to verify their identity without sharing information with intermediaries. Dorsey has long been a supporter of DeFi, choosing to open source Block's (known as Square at the time) cold storage wallet in 2018, and offering access to Bitcoin for users of Square's CashApp. This Bitcoin activity generated $156 million of profit in 2022.[30]

Payments

Currency is the lifeblood of any economic system and Bitcoin would never have been such a revolutionary force had it not demonstrated any potential as a method of payment. Yes, this potential was most famously directed towards illicit dealings and astronomically priced pizzas, but payments and Bitcoin, and likewise DeFi, have a close relationship. The topic also warrants more depth as payments, and in particular international payments, have been earmarked as a prime use case for blockchain for many years.

Before going further into the use of blockchain in payments, we should first distinguish between retail and wholesale payments, and outline the shortcomings that blockchain can prove its worth against. To start, the variation between retail and wholesale payments boils down to this: retail payment involves the settlement of everyday payments between individuals and businesses. Wholesale payments are used to settle transactions between banks, major financial institutions and large corporations.

Most nations possess at least one payment set-up for low-volume and high-value transfers, and these are known as Real Time Gross Settlement (RTGS) systems. These are usually used in wholesale markets, and settlements are on a payment-by-payment basis, which is to say that these large payments are settled on a gross basis throughout the day, and not bundled with other payments. Payments are real-time in the sense that they are settled instantly once processed, though these processing systems are usually closed on evenings and weekends. High-value payment systems that exist within RTGS frameworks include, to name just a few, RITS in Australia, T2 in the Eurozone, CBN RTGS in Nigeria, BOJ-NET in Japan, CHAPS in the UK, Fedwire in the US and CNAPS in China. RTGS systems are unlikely to factor into most people's thinking where payment is concerned, though their role within the economy is fundamental. In the UK in 2021, CHAPS payments accounted for 0.1 per cent of the total payments volume, but 90 per cent of value.[31]

Retail payments by contrast handle a high volume of low-value payments and transactions, before being settled via the RTGS system on a Deferred Net Settlement (DNS) basis. As the name suggests, these payments are deferred, bundled together and then settled, usually once per day but sometimes less frequently depending on the type of DNS being used. These systems do, however, sometimes operate on a 24/7 basis. There are occasional overlaps between retail and wholesale banking, and each framework operates in different ways with some containing a plethora of systems to serve different functions.

THE MANY TYPES OF PAYMENT SYSTEM

The payments systems of all nations have developed gradually as economies and technology have developed. For various reasons, this has led to the emergence of numerous payment systems in some nations, handling different types of transactions. The Bank of England has several DNS systems, which may help elaborate on this:

1 Bacs: for direct debits and credits

2 The Faster Payments Service: for standing orders, internet and telephone payments, and credit transfers

> **3** The Image Clearing System: for settlements based on images of cheques and paper credits
>
> **4** LINK: the UK's ATM network
>
> **5** PEXA: a service for remortgaging and other residential property transactions

Each nation's payment infrastructure has evolved in its own way and very few, if any, were created with international standardization as a priority. International bank transfers, important to so many, are accordingly something of a flag-bearer for inefficiency and layers of cost. To look at cross-border payments on the whole, they are typically processed in one-to-five working days and may need to pass through several intermediaries. They are sometimes straightforward, like when two payment service providers (PSPs) are involved, with one originating the payment and the other the beneficiary. However, if the PSPs do not hold accounts with each other, a correspondent bank, with which both hold an account, will be required. In a circumstance where the currency pairs involved are not commonly traded, yet more correspondent banks might be required to complete the payment, and of course, with each bank added to the process more time and expense are added. In some cases, a cross-border payment will cost ten times the amount of a domestic one (relative to a UK domestic payment).[32] There are other factors to consider, too, such as legacy technology platforms used by some nations, some of which were originally built to handle paper-based processes. On top of this there are time zones to consider, which may present further problems where settlement systems only operate during certain times, and to name a few more challenges there are compliance procedures, documentation requirements, inconsistent data formats and lengthy transaction chains to contend with.

If you think this sounds slightly crazy, you are not alone. In 2023, the G20 laid out quantitative targets for cross-border payments to be met by 2027, aiming to harmonize payments between banks and remove frustrations for those moving money.[33] There appears to be a consensus that cross-border transactions suffer from opacity, low transaction speeds, restricted access and high costs. To look at the entirety of the market, cross-border payments are expected to total $250 trillion in 2027, so the introduction of blockchain could be transformational.[34] To look at blockchain's potential to right the wrongs of existing systems, we can note that remittance payments to low- and middle-income countries totalled $626 billion in 2022, at an average cost of 6 per cent for transactions worth $200 (the United Nations' Sustainable Development Goals has set a target for this to be beneath 3 per cent by 2030). For some nations, most notably Tonga, where remittances received were 50 per cent of GDP in 2022, a reduction in costs would have a huge impact.[35] Other nations that stand to benefit significantly include Lebanon (38 per cent), Samoa (34 per cent), Tajikistan (32 per cent), Kyrgyz Republic (31 per cent), The Gambia (28 per cent), Honduras (27 per cent), El Salvador (24 per cent), Haiti (22 per cent) and Nepal (22 per cent). In terms of remittance volumes, rather than GDP percentages, India ($100 billion), Mexico ($60 billion), China ($51 billion), the Philippines ($38 billion) and Egypt ($32 billion) lead the way.

Some might look at this inefficiency and layered cost and see a pivotal role for cryptocurrencies. Equally, we can observe that the Financial Stability Board's list of actions for achieving the G20 target makes no mention of decentralization.[36] This does not mean that serious attempts are not being made to bring blockchain to payments networks. For example, a major development is the move towards Central Bank Digital Currencies (CBDCs), which will be explored later. Besides CBDC projects, there are many other organizations and projects attempting to overhaul the payments network, with much of this work focused on wholesale payments. Organizations such as R3, RTGS.global, Fnality, Partior and the Regulated Liability Network (RLN) are at the forefront of this.

R3

R3 brings DLT functionality to financial services with its own blockchain, Corda. The intention of R3 is to deliver 'digital trust' between parties, or in crypto parlance, to automate complex processes with smart contracts. This should improve the speed and scale of global trading and settlement, while reducing counterparty, operational and market risks, especially in regard to reconciliation and settlement times. R3 is actively engaged in establishing CBDCs, though the international firm and its blockchain have a broader remit encapsulating payments, reconciliation, digital assets and global trade.

RTGS.GLOBAL

RTGS.global is an aspiring financial market infrastructure (FMI), designed to enable banks holding central bank reserves in their local jurisdiction to deploy the high-quality liquid assets (HQLA) part of their reserves to settle FX (foreign exchange) cross-border wholesale payments. The business considers itself a global switchboard for interbank liquidity, complemented by tools that support better payments and banking.

The company has built a central ledger, which can allow banks that have central reserves to transact with each other across borders. The system enables banks to exchange liquidity in one currency for that in another, without the liquidity itself needing to move over local RTGS rails. HQLA in one currency can atomically settle for that in another and an immutable ledger manages the ownership of assets. This system may eventually facilitate reliable international wholesale transactions in milliseconds.

REGULATED LIABILITY NETWORK

The RLN intends to connect all regulated money to a shared ledger in order to protect the sovereignty and monetary control of nation-states. This network brings together central bank money, commercial bank money and e-money with the intention of integrating many of the features that give cryptoassets a potential advantage over regulated currency. The network's whitepaper included contributions from senior figures at SWIFT, Citi, BNY Mellon, HSBC, Lloyds, ANZ, TD Bank, Wells Fargo and US Bank.

FNALITY INTERNATIONAL

Fnality was created by a consortium of major financial institutions for the establishment of a network of decentralized infrastructures for financial markets. In doing so, it is creating several national systems, each built within their own regulatory framework, to facilitate tokenized and peer-to-peer markets. In addition to providing a network, Fnality intends to deliver the pay leg of wholesale transactions, offering payments that are Ethereum-based, permissioned and settled via the Fnality settlement asset. This is neither a CBDC nor a stablecoin, but Fnality has been working with numerous central banks and anticipates that its UK payment system will go live in the second half of 2023.

PARTIOR

Founded in 2021 as a collaboration between J.P. Morgan, DBS Bank and Temasek, and later incorporating Standard Chartered as a backer, Partior is an interbank network designed to support multi-currency payments. Importantly, it is designed as a network rather than a payment or settlement system.

Partior was originally spun out from Project Ubin, a CBDC initiative from the Monetary Authority of Singapore, and began with the US Dollar and the Singapore Dollar. It now operates in 20 countries across North America, Europe, the Middle-East, Asia and Australasia, working with a range of commercial banks, central banks and market and technology infrastructure partners. Partior has initially positioned itself as a network for wholesale payments, though the network allows for retail payment applications to be integrated.

TASSAT

Tassat intends to modernize the US banking system through its private and permissioned blockchain offering, focused on business-to-business (B2B) payments. It launched in October 2022, completing over $500 million of transactions within its first eight hours.[37]

USDF CONSORTIUM

The USDF Consortium is applying blockchain to offer a digital dollar for US banks, and accordingly to apply blockchain efficiencies to payments. Its intention is to extend the existing model for US banking and prepare it for an environment where transactions are tokenized. This model would align central bank money with new technology, while upholding the current regulatory framework and continuing to facilitate fractional reserve banking.

> **FRACTIONAL RESERVE BANKING**
>
> Fractional reserve banking is the process whereby banks lend out a percentage of the money that has been deposited by clients.

In relation to wholesale payment, we might also note the activity of J.P. Morgan, which launched its JPM Coin to represent fiat currencies on blockchain for members of its private client network. This allows for Payment versus Payment (PvP), Delivery versus Payment (DvP) and machine-to-machine payments to occur, and it can also be used in traditional cross-border payments. As well as application in cross-border payments and foreign exchange, it is anticipated that this will help with corporate treasury solutions, too. Intriguingly, Onyx's head of digital assets, Tyrone Lobban, expressed interest in bringing trillions of dollars of tokenized assets into DeFi when speaking to CoinDesk at Consensus 2022.[38]

> **PAYMENT VERSUS PAYMENT**
>
> PvP is a settlement mechanism for foreign exchange to ensure that a payment in one currency only occurs if the corresponding payment in another currency, or currencies, also does. Delivery versus Payment, similarly, dictates that the exchange of securities and payments between parties is simultaneous. Both of these mechanisms are regulated in most markets, ensuring that settlement is final.

Blockchain in wholesale payments

The use of blockchain in PvP and DvP payments could add efficiencies and lower costs for a whole range of domestic and international wholesale payments. To reframe this, it offers an opportunity to provide billions in annual savings and disrupt operations that handle trillions of dollars of payments every day. The reason why blockchain is so relevant here is that smart contracts allow for simultaneous trades of information on a peer-to-peer basis, and via atomic swaps this may even take place cross-chain. If the assets being traded can be tokenized and traded for a mutually agreeable asset like a stablecoin, it may follow that a whole range of banks, clearing houses and other intermediaries will find themselves with a diminished role.

ATOMIC SWAPS

Atomic swaps allow trades to be made between blockchains without the need for an intermediary.

To better see where blockchain and cryptoassets could fit in, let's consider the use of the Continuous Linked Settlement (CLS) Bank, which is used primarily by investment funds and banks, and is presently the most efficient method in many nations for international wholesale PvP and DvP payments (these are FX payments), handling over $6 trillion of volume on a typical day. The CLS was founded in 2002 and currently offers a huge amount of value to cross-border wholesale payments, adding risk mitigation and efficient settlement processes for its members. Its key security feature is that it negates Herstatt risk by ensuring that all parties to a transaction have posted collateral. (Herstatt risk is the risk that only one party sends their payment, and is named after the 1974 bankruptcy of Germany's Herstatt Bank, which blocked the dollar interbank payment system.) The key efficiency feature is multilateral netting, which is the process whereby institutional transactions are accrued and bundled, before eventually settling. Loosely described, multilateral netting takes every transaction into account before determining how much actually needs to be sent to each bank involved. This process ensured that on its busiest day in 2021, where it handled $15.4 trillion of payment instructions, the CLS only required $72 billion to fund settlements.[39]

MULTILATERAL NETTING

Here's a basic example of how multilateral netting works. If a bank sends 20 separate $1 million payments to other banks using CLS, and receives 21 payments of $1 million during the same processing cycle, the CLS will aggregate the transactions and send this bank $1 million rather than send funds back and forth for every transaction.

This system works well, and transaction times are typically two days. However, these will be two days in which asset and currency prices can change, numerous intermediaries may be required, collateral may need to be posted back and forth in relation to price swings and liquidity costs will rack up. If this same process were to occur on blockchain, one might expect transfers to be unbundled and instantaneous once parties are ready to transact. It is likely to be far less burdensome from an administrative perspective, margin fees will be minimized and transactions will be possible on a 24/7 basis.

Sadly, the solution is not so simple as 'just do a blockchain'. There are legal, regulatory and stakeholder issues to be resolved, and no doubt some practical ones, too. Collaboration between banks, governments and financial institutions, at the very least, is required. Furthermore, coding an agreement into a smart contract does not settle a payment where currencies and assets are not native to the blockchain. This is where Fnality's attempt is particularly interesting. The organization currently works with 17 major institutions (who are shareholders) and has been engaging with central banks, with some success, in Britain, Canada, Japan, Europe and the United States. This issue of central banks will be particularly crucial as banks begin to make their stances clearer on the topic of CBDCs and digital money. Further, there will be localized issues to deal with, and it is possible that some banks will refuse to engage with the concept at all. Equally, some central banks will take a hands-on approach to managing digital currencies, whereas others will prefer for initiatives to arise from the private sector.

To go back to Fnality, and the topic of on-chain currency, the organization presents a route to this via its Fnality Payment System, which uses tokens that are directly exchangeable for fiat currency. This differs from a CBDC in the sense that it is only for use by members of the system, and different from a stablecoin in that the asset, if a dollar or a pound, is designed to be considered as exactly that by the central bank. Stablecoins, on the other hand, are assets designed to be equivalent to a fiat value, but their value is maintained by a securitized basket of holdings (usually cash and short-dated government debt) rather than a central bank promise. This is not to endorse Fnality above other wholesale banking projects, but rather to show how blockchain and crypto-inspired technology might over-haul a major industry.

Interestingly, Fnality CEO Rhomaios Ram says:

> 'I don't perceive what we're doing as payments. We're essentially helping financial institutions optimize their balance sheets and their treasury function… for example if you imagine more than half of all capital markets were settled on some form of blockchain, in all major jurisdictions, there could be billions upon billions of dollars of balance sheet savings for the banks, which hopefully would get passed on to their customers. And I think it will get passed on.'

There is a lot to be thrashed out as we move towards a future for digital and likely blockchain-based payments. For instance, assets other than fiat currency can be tokenized, and this might factor into institutional payments, too. There will also be discrepancies between national systems and legal issues to overcome, not to mention a need for banks using the system to be capable of doing so. And so the future is unclear, but it looks like wholesale domestic and interna-tional payments could, at least in part, be considerably improved thanks to the rise of crypto and DeFi.

Blockchain in retail payments

The landscape for retail payments is a little different. An immedi-ate distinction is that transaction volume is far higher. The European

Central Bank, to outline this, reported that 114.2 billion non-cash transactions were made in the euro area in 2021, though the challenge for blockchain-based payments is more than a numbers game.[40] Complexity is a factor, too. Transactions in retail can be fraught with issues that disrupt the simplicity of a payment, such as consumer protection, fraud and chargebacks, so we can see why wholesale payments have been the first frontier for digital currency. It is easier to code for transactions with trusted parties, fewer variables and lower volumes. In fact, when things do occasionally go wrong in wholesale, such as when Deutsche Bank mistakenly sent $35 billion to an exchange (its market capitalization at the time was $5 billion shy of this), issues are fixed with urgency and typically without dispute.[41]

So far, there has been a mismatch between the needs for retail payments and the traits of cryptoassets. This is partly due to cryptoasset volatility, which renders many of them unsuitable for everyday payments. It has also not helped that Bitcoin and Ethereum, the blockchains for the two largest coins by market cap, were not originally suited for processing transactions in such quantities. Nonetheless, other Layer 1 blockchains may emerge and host the currencies of the future, and similarly, Layer 2 solutions might expand the capabilities of Bitcoin and Ethereum, such is the benefit of composability. To a large extent, the issues of volatility and scale are well on their way to being addressed. On volatility, the private market solution is stablecoins, provided they can hold their value, and the central bank solution is CBDCs, provided that governments welcome them. It is entirely possible that other cryptoassets will have widespread use in payment, too.

Payment service providers are watching this space with interest, and in this regard we should note PayPal's recent activity. PayPal has been accepting a limited range of cryptocurrencies as payments since October 2020 and closed out 2022 with $604 million of client crypto holdings.[42] More tellingly, it had intended to launch a stablecoin in 2023 but has since tempered expectations, putting the launch on ice and saying instead that the option of a stablecoin is being explored.[43] The eBay-owned company appears to have a strategy in relation to blockchain solutions, too, and was one of several investors in a $200 million funding round for Aptos Labs, the company behind Layer 1 blockchain Aptos. The Aptos blockchain is designed for ultra-fast settlements, and while it is yet to be exposed to robust testing in crypto markets, PayPal will have taken note of its developers' claims that it can complete over 130,000 transactions per second.[44]

If technology and currency are capable of delivering crypto payments in retail, there is arguably just one more hurdle to jump, which is customer adoption. In this respect, payment service providers are beginning to offer variety and flexibility for users. Mastercard and Visa have both issued numerous debit and credit cards for crypto-related companies. The cards each offer differing functionalities, including cashback in fiat or bitcoin, cutting intermediaries from transactions involving both fiat and crypto, waiving FX fees, and the ability to use crypto as collateral for credit cards used to spend fiat currency. Mastercard has issued 35 of them for companies such as ByBit, Nexo and Binance, while Visa is utilizing its cards to position itself as the 'network of choice for crypto wallets', championing connections with Circle, Coinbase, Wirex and Crypto.com on its website. In terms of fraud prevention and identifying suspicious transactions on block-chain, Mastercard also acquired crypto tracing business CipherTrace in 2021. To look purely at fiat to crypto transactions, the activities of payments and processing multinational FIS can be included. The company handled $30 billion of card-to-crypto transactions for Binance and Kraken in 2021.

There are now more ways to spend crypto, but what can you actually buy with it? And do retailers want to accept crypto? In the early-to-mid 2020s, purchases with crypto remain a fringe activity but the sands are shifting. Visa's 2022 'Back to Business' study, conducted in nine nations and surveying 2,250 small business owners with 100 employees or fewer (Brazil, Canada, Germany, Hong Kong, Ireland, Russia, Singapore, the United Arab Emirates and the United States), found that 24 per cent of them plan to accept digital curren-cies such as bitcoin.[45]

An investigation of larger retailers, published by Deloitte in collab-oration with PayPal in 2022, might inspire a more bullish outlook.

This study of 2,000 senior executives at consumer goods and services retailers in the United States, with annual revenues ranging from under $10 million to $500 million and above, found that 85 per cent of organizations are giving high or very high priority to enabling cryptocurrency payments, and 83 per cent are doing the same for stablecoins. 87 per cent of respondents agreed that organizations accepting digital currencies currently had a competitive advantage in the market, and 85 per cent agreed that the use of digital currencies for everyday purchases will increase exponentially over the next few years. The adoption of crypto payments is not entirely about attracting customers. 39 per cent of respondents cited in-house treasury and finance management as a boon, and 40 per cent agreed that immediate access to funds is a motivating factor. This study hints at powerful tailwinds for crypto adoption in retail payment, though it would be remiss to overlook that the study is focused solely on America, and took place prior to the crypto winter. Confidence relating to legal acceptance and payment security may have been dented since. Respondents had listed payments platform security (43 per cent), the changing regulatory landscape (37 per cent) and the instability of the digital currency market (36 per cent) as their three biggest concerns.

That said, there are good reasons why merchants might not be so quick to turn their backs. Crypto transactions offer a handful of potential benefits to card payment networks, in that they are settled immediately once processed and can be considerably cheaper, too. The most popular option for retailers so far has been to use the services of a crypto payment gateway, and these will generally charge a 1 per cent flat fee to cover their processing costs, comparing favourably with typical credit card processing fees of 1.5–3.5 per cent. Those with a crypto-savvy client base may also prefer to deal directly in crypto. In this case, gas and transaction fees for Ethereum and Bitcoin will be a deterrent for most smaller transactions, although large one-off payments could be considerably cheaper, and Layer 2 networks may offer a workaround for smaller payments by reducing fees and increasing processing speeds.

STRIKE

On the topic of Layer 2s, the launch of Layer-2 bitcoin payments network Strike could be an important development. Strike uses the Bitcoin Lightning network to facilitate cross-border and remittance payments, switching local currencies to Bitcoin, transferring it, and then switching it back to the recipient's local currency. This may sound like the work of an industry outsider, but Strike can count Visa, Fiserv and Clover as partners.[46]

Merchants need to put thought into their plans to accept crypto payments. They will need to find a suitable payment gateway or wallet, integrate their crypto payments with any accounting software that they have, and be mindful of the tax implications for receiving payments this way. For those in e-commerce, additional work will be needed to integrate crypto into the checkout process, though some gateways offer this as a service. Merchants may also choose to immediately convert any cryptoassets they receive into cash, especially where falls in crypto value could threaten financial stability.

Starbucks, Shopify, BMW, Balenciaga, Chipotle and Microsoft are now among the major brands that accept payment in crypto in some shape or form. But is there significant customer demand to buy goods and services with cryptoassets? Visa published *The Crypto Phenomenon: 2022 Consumer Attitudes & Usage* to gauge consumer interest across a range of developing and emerging national markets.[47] The survey of 16,865 adults found that 34 per cent of crypto-aware respondents were also crypto owners, but also found that 12 per cent of this cohort was sceptical and a further 36 per cent unengaged (95 per cent of respondents reported an awareness of crypto). Ownership and curiosity in crypto, interestingly, was more pronounced in emerging markets, with 41 per cent of respondents claiming to own crypto. This may be linked to the instability of fiat currency in some of those markets, users' ability to access the dollar or Euro via stablecoins and the prospect of international payments without incurring exchange fees. This does not mean, however, that respondents are itching to make purchases in crypto. The survey concludes that most who own cryptocurrencies view them as wealth-building assets to be held as investments. There is, nonetheless, an expectation that digital assets and cryptocurrency will be a viable payment for most goods and services by the late 2020s.

A tokenized future

When looking at these developments in retail and wholesale payments, it appears that we are moving towards a tokenized future. If the value of a wide range of assets can be demonstrated on-chain, then we are moving towards a system that allows value to be easily exchanged with immediacy and at huge volume both domestically and internationally. Several influential executives appear to be positioning themselves for this shift. Speaking at a Dealbook event in November 2022, BlackRock CEO Larry Fink declared that the next generation for markets and securities will be tokenization, and similarly, Mastercard CEO Michael Miebach stated in a Forbes interview that we are moving to a world in which everything is tokenized and safely passed around.[48] Mastercard has been processing north of two billion 'tokenized' transactions per month. While blockchain has not initially been used to achieve this, Mastercard has been working on tokenization of multiple assets that will eventually be tracked across a variety of public and private chains.

Another implication of tokenization is the relative ease with which a wide variety of assets, many of which might be fractionalized, can change hands. Ricardo Correia, global head of digital currencies and payments at R3, says:

'The dematerialization of everything, I love that space… Cars, houses, anything that's of value, you should be able to tokenize and exchange in real time.'

As an aside, Correia points out that tokenization is a practice as old as time.

'Money is just a token. It's an IOU and it used to be backed by gold.'

All of this tokenization presents a need for a common denominator of value. Fiat currency would typically be used but its suitability is slightly limited as it is off-chain. This, again, is where stablecoins and CBDCs offer value. Stablecoins have received interest from several traditional firms. FIS has partnered with Circle to allow merchants to make and receive settlements in USDC on the Polygon blockchain, BlackRock has a partnership with Circle to manage a portion of its reserve funds and the majority of Tether's reserves are managed by Wall Street firm Cantor Fitzgerald.[49] CBDCs, meanwhile, offer a representation of fiat currency on-chain in the truest sense.

What does all of this mean?

This chapter shows that the technology for decentralization can also be used to the benefit of centralized organizations. As suggested earlier, the same tools that were supposed to erode the power of traditional intermediaries have also been used to make them more efficient. In a sense, this is to be expected. Decentralized technology doesn't belong to anyone and by its nature is largely open sourced. It is nevertheless staggering that cryptocurrency and decentralized finance have inspired so much change, and could eventually leave their mark on billions of dollars of annual cost savings and revenues, and potentially trillions of dollars of daily institutional and retail payments. From one pseudonymous whitepaper, blockchain and other types of DLT may go on to become the rails for much of institutional finance.

Where does this leave DeFi? In a sense, we can note that its first-mover advantage over TradFi is close to expiration, but DeFi's composability and open-sourcing offers a platform from which it can evolve, persist and reestablish its revolutionary clout. DeFi's distinguishing factors in the future seem likely to be the things that make it a web3 entity; open sourcing, democratized access and self-sovereignty. To take a hopeful perspective, and this may be too hopeful, this could also be a prompt for DeFi innovators to make good on promises such as financial inclusion, funding small businesses that don't usually receive access and banking the unbanked, or something to that effect.

The relationship between DeFi and TradFi is often viewed in an antagonistic sense, but it may also be helpful to view the two as complementary. Many in TradFi speak of DeFi's achievements with admiration; Dutch banking multinational ING even published a whitepaper stating that 'the best of both worlds is achieved if centralized and decentralized financial services cooperate'.[50] There is increasing use of DeFi by institutions, too. J.P. Morgan, for instance, used a modified version of the Aave protocol on the Polygon mainnet to execute its first DeFi trade, using fiat from its balance sheets. Aave founder Stani Kulechov says:

> 'It shows that when there is a base layer of infrastructure available to everyone, you can build custom markets or solutions for institutions within private markets. I think that's very valuable.'

DeFi innovations may continue to inspire developments in TradFi, too. We might look at Project Mariana, an initiative between the Bank for International Settlements and several central banks, which intends to apply automated market maker technology for cross-border exchanges.[51] There may yet be opportunities to apply concepts like yield farming, perpetual futures or anything relevant that can be programmed. Consider, in a more digitized economy, that it may even be possible to apply a flash loan where an immediately settleable trading opportunity exists, thus enabling someone with zero on their balance sheet to capitalize on a huge arbitrage opportunity between two or more assets. With any such development, we cannot expect reputable and regulated institutions to go near them until they are truly considered safe.

It should also be accepted that DeFi is still a new addition to finance. There may be an inclination to look at the increasing adoption of blockchain and tokenization in traditional and centralized finance and to reach the conclusion that DeFi had a nice run. However, a reason why DeFi excited many people is that it presented a model for finance that can create new products and serve new markets. TradFi's success in adopting these ideas may even be considered as proof of concept. Naturally, the next steps taken by regulators and important decision-makers will have a significant influence on what comes next, but one thing remains; DeFi is a shared platform, and so long as there is interest in building upon it, it can continue to transform finance.

References

1 S Johnson. World's first DeFi ETF to launch in Brazil next month, *Financial Times*, 31 January 2022, www.ft.com/content/2d00d0e4-0297-484d-aaa5-069bf4df64b7 (archived at https://perma.cc/C36B-NBVW)

2 CNBC Television. JPMorgan's Jamie Dimon: Bitcoin is a 'hyped-up fraud', CNBC Television, 2023, www.youtube.com/watch?v=qdIooHrQeK8

3 Deloitte Insights. Deloitte's 2021 global blockchain survey: a new age of digital assets, 2021, www2.deloitte.com/content/dam/insights/articles/US144337_Blockchain-survey/DI_Blockchain-survey.pdf (archived at https://perma.cc/K8SC-KA7T)

4 M Sigalos. Crypto-focused bank Silvergate is shutting operations and liquidating after market meltdown, CNBC, 11 April 2023, www.cnbc.com/2023/03/08/silvergate-shutting-down-operations-and-liquidating-bank.html (archived at https://perma.cc/8W4C-E78Q)

5 A Kharpal. 'Inundated with requests': Digital currency firms look to Swiss banks after crypto-friendly lenders fail, CNBC, 2023, www.cnbc.com/2023/03/22/crypto-firms-look-to-swiss-lenders-after-silvergate-signature-bank-fail.html (archived at https://perma.cc/R2KJ-VSDN)

6 H Miao, G Zuckerman and B Eisen. How the last-ditch effort to save Silicon Valley Bank failed, *The Wall Street Journal*, 22 March, 2023, www.wsj.com/articles/how-the-last-ditch-effort-to-save-silicon-valley-bank-failed-89619cb2 (archived at https://perma.cc/D92E-W83B)

7, 8, 9, 10, 14, 15, 17, 18, 25, 26, 27 N Bambysheva and M del Castillo. Forbes Blockchain 50 2023, Forbes, 2023, www.forbes.com/sites/ninabambysheva/2023/02/07/forbes-blockchain-50-2023/?sh=1d2568ac319d (archived at https://perma.cc/MG7V-PNY5)

11 Societe Generale. Societe Generale issues the first structured product on public blockchain, Société Générale, 2021, www.societegenerale.com/en/news/press-release/first-structured-product-public-blockchain (archived at https://perma.cc/UP8Z-78L9)

12   Reuters. EIB launches second euro digital bond with Goldman, SocGen, Reuters, 29 November 2022, https://www.reuters.com/markets/rates-bonds/eib-launches-second-euro-digital-bond-2022-11-29/ (archived at https://perma.cc/UM56-6ZPH)

13   European Investment Bank. EIB issues its first ever digital bond in pound sterling, EIB, 2023, www.eib.org/en/press/all/2023-030-eib-issues-its-first-ever-digital-bond-in-british-pounds (archived at https://perma.cc/YZD7-FKPE)

16   S Basak. Apollo hires JPMorgan's Christine Moy in digital-assets push, Bloomberg.com, 28 April 2022, www.bloomberg.com/news/articles/2022-04-28/apollo-hires-jpmorgan-s-christine-moy-in-digital-assets-push#xj4y7vzkg (archived at https://perma.cc/4EM3-LKGP)

19   A Konrad. A16z Crypto's record new $4.5 billion fund doubles down on Web3 amid market crash, Forbes, 2022, https://www.forbes.com/sites/alexkonrad/2022/05/25/a16z-crypto-record-4th-fund-doubles-down-on-web3-amid-market-crash/ (archived at https://perma.cc/6GS4-3T6Q)

21, 22   J Melinek. KKR dives into Avalanche blockchain to tokenize and 'democratize' financial services, TechCrunch, 2022, https://techcrunch.com/2022/09/13/kkr-dives-into-avalanche-blockchain-to-tokenize-and-democratize-financial-services/ (archived at https://perma.cc/W5HK-LX9H)

20   K Rooney. Andreessen Horowitz raises $4.5 billion crypto fund to take advantage of bargains in down market, CNBC, 2022, www.cnbc.com/2022/05/25/andreessen-horowitz-raises-4point5-billion-crypto-fund-in-down-market.html (archived at https://perma.cc/FA82-BD9D)

23   S Schroeder. Facebook announces Libra cryptocurrency with a massive list of partners, Mashable, 2019, mashable.com/article/facebook-libra (archived at https://perma.cc/CA75-BD9C)

24   J Peters. Meta gives up on NFTs for Facebook and Instagram, The Verge, 13 March 2023, www.theverge.com/2023/3/13/23638572/instagram-nft-meta-facebook-quits-digital-collectibles (archived at https://perma.cc/YU6U-A8BY)

28   United States Securities and Exchange Commission. Registration Statement: Robinhood Markets, Inc., SEC, 2021, www.sec.gov/Archives/edgar/data/1783879/000162828021013318/robinhoods-1.htm (archived at https://perma.cc/57NQ-PV2Q)

29   K Irwin. Robinhood rolls out its MetaMask wallet competitor to 1 million users, Decrypt, 2023, decrypt.co/119594/robinhood-wallet-metamask (archived at https://perma.cc/8JZ3-KX8W)

30   N Wang. Block's Q4 bitcoin revenue fell 7% year over year to $1.83B, CoinDesk, 2023, https://uk.style.yahoo.com/block-q4-bitcoin-revenue-fell-213625764.html (archived at https://perma.cc/UJ58-HP4Q)

31 UK Finance. UK Payment Markets Summary 2022, UK Finance, 2022, www. ukfinance.org.uk/system/files/2022-08/UKFPaymentMarketsSummary2022.pdf (archived at https://perma.cc/MY5N-PFNA)

32 Bank of England. Cross-border payments, Bank of England, 2023, www. bankofengland.co.uk/payment-and-settlement/cross-border-payments (archived at https://perma.cc/JX25-F6B9)

33 36 Financial Stability Board. G20 roadmap for enhancing cross-border payments: priority actions for achieving the G20 targets, FSB, 2023, www.fsb. org/2023/02/g20-roadmap-for-enhancing-cross-border-payments-priority-actions-for-achieving-the-g20-targets/ (archived at https://perma.cc/ 7VYM-47NR)

34 Bank of England. Cross-border payments, Bank of England, 2023, www. bankofengland.co.uk/payment-and-settlement/cross-border-payments (archived at https://perma.cc/JX25-F6B9)

35 Knomad. Remittances brave global headwinds Special focus: climate migration, World Bank Group, 2022, www.knomad.org/sites/default/files/ publication-doc/migration_and_development_brief_37_nov_2022.pdf (archived at https://perma.cc/Q5JB-KSWE)

37 BusinessWire. Tassat® successfully completes launch of The Digital Interbank Network™, Business Wire, 2022, www.businesswire.com/news/home/ 20221003005347/en/TassatpercentC2percentAE-successfully-completes-launch-of-The-Digital-Interbank-NetworkpercentE2percent84percentA2 (archived at https://perma.cc/PJ7P-MWN3)

38 I Allison. JPMorgan wants to bring trillions of dollars of tokenized assets to DeFi, CoinDesk, 2022, www.coindesk.com/business/2022/06/11/jpmorgan-wants-to-bring-trillions-of-dollars-of-tokenized-assets-to-defi/ (archived at https://perma.cc/J6ZQ-9H2L)

39 CLS. CLS celebrates 20 years of trusted market solutions, CLS Group, 2022, www.cls-group.com/news/cls-celebrates-20-years-of-trusted-market-solutions/#ftn1 (archived at https://perma.cc/5D54-MBPF)

40 European Central Bank. Payments statistics: 2021, ECB, 2022, www.ecb. europa.eu/press/pr/stats/paysec/html/ecb.pis2021~956efe1ee6.en.html (archived at https://perma.cc/4BML-RH4K)

41 M Egan. Oops! Deutsche Bank accidentally sent a $35 billion payment, CNNBusiness, 2018, money.cnn.com/2018/04/19/investing/deutsche-bank-35-billion-mistake/index.html (archived at https://perma.cc/3W4U-FUXA)

42 J Crawley. PayPal held $604M of customers' crypto as of year-end 2022, CoinDesk, 2023, www.coindesk.com/business/2023/02/10/paypal-held-604m-of-customers-crypto-as-of-year-end-2022/ (archived at https://perma.cc/ Z5X3-P9GH)

43 Reuters. PayPal pauses stablecoin work amid regulatory scrutiny of crypto – Bloomberg News, Reuters, 10 February 2023, www.reuters.com/technology/paypal-pauses-stablecoin-work-amid-regulatory-scrutiny-crypto-bloomberg-news-2023-02-10/ (archived at https://perma.cc/7U4D-VGP4)

44 B Munster. What is Aptos? The 'Solana Killer' created by Diem Developers, Decrypt, 2022, decrypt.co/resources/what-is-aptos-the-solana-killer-created-by-diem-developers (archived at https://perma.cc/T4LV-DH7Q)

45 Visa. Visa study: small businesses optimistic, looking to digital payments for growth in new year, Visa, 2022, usa.visa.com/about-visa/newsroom/press-releases.releaseId.18711.html (archived at https://perma.cc/67YS-4KJ8)

46 J Melinek. Bitcoin and the Lightning Network are moving payments globally, TechCrunch, 2023, techcrunch.com/2023/03/11/bitcoin-and-the-lightning-network-are-moving-payments-globally/ (archived at https://perma.cc/6A3Z-SDZ3)

47 Visa. The crypto phenomenon: 2022 consumer attitudes & usage, Visa, 2022, usa.visa.com/content/dam/VCOM/regional/na/us/Solutions/documents/visa-cryptocurrency-a-and-u-2022-final-white-paper.pdf (archived at https://perma.cc/57P3-RCQH)

48 N Bambysheva and M del Castillo. How Mastercard, Goldman Sachs and other 'TradFi' titans are using blockchain to rewire global finance, Forbes, 2023, www.forbes.com/sites/ninabambysheva/2023/02/07/how-mastercard-goldman-sachs-and-other-tradfi-titans-are-using-blockchain-to-rewire-global-finance/?sh=37db1275339f (archived at https://perma.cc/G7S8-DWDG)

49 CoinDesk. FIS subsidiary Worldpay to enable USDC settlements on Polygon, Business Insider, 2022, markets.businessinsider.com/news/currencies/fis-subsidiary-worldpay-to-enable-usdc-settlements-on-polygon-1031863034 (archived at https://perma.cc/W6NK-A5BC)

50 X Meegan and T Koens. Lessons learned from decentralised finance (DeFi), ING, 2021, www.ingwb.com/binaries/content/assets/insights/themes/distributed-ledger-technology/defi_white_paper_v2.0.pdf (archived at https://perma.cc/85HB-J45U)

51 Bank for International Settlements. Project Mariana: CBDCs in automated market-makers, BIS, n.d., www.bis.org/about/bisih/topics/cbdc/mariana.htm (archived at https://perma.cc/GVW7-6WQ8)

09

CBDCs: The central bank's answer to crypto

Governments and central banks were never going to stand idle as investment in DeFi snowballed and fiat money flowed into cryptoassets. Instead, while working to build regulatory frameworks around blockchain-based assets, they have also been investigating the launch of their own Central Bank Digital Currencies (CBDCs). These currencies are mostly in the developmental stage but the rush to research and launch CBDCs is well underway.

Most major economies have either researched, designed a proof of concept or piloted a CBDC and the Atlantic Council's CBDC tracker counts 102 countries and currency unions as being actively engaged in doing so in Q2 of 2023.[1] Of these projects, 11 CBDCs have launched, with 18 pilot projects ongoing and 32 CBDCs in development. Those to have launched include the eNaira in Nigeria, JAM-DEX in Jamaica, the Sand Dollar in Bahamas and DCash, incorporating member nations of the Eastern Caribbean Central Bank (Grenada, Anguilla, St. Kitts & Nevis, Antigua & Barbuda, Montserrat, Saint Lucia, Saint Vincent and the Grenadines and Dominica). These projects and launches are not uniform, but the vast majority are making use of DLT and blockchain. The one early exception is JAM-DEX.

While the launches show a commitment to the concept, at present the ongoing pilots are a more prominent display of potential impact. The nations currently running pilot schemes include China, India, Russia, Australia, Saudi Arabia, Singapore, South Korea, Japan, the

UAE, Ukraine, Sweden, Malaysia, Ghana, Hong Kong, South Africa, Iran, Kazakhstan and Thailand. More generally, 18 of the G20 nations are now deemed to be in advanced stages of CBDC development.

These developments are not without motive. The friendly ones to include would be consumer safety, enabling a more efficient economy, financial inclusion and building a partly composable currency platform that private sector participants can work with and build upon. There are macroeconomic trends that encourage the growth of digital money too, such as the growth of e-commerce, contactless payments, and the use of cards, smart devices and digital wallets. And then, of course, there is the possibility of making use of new technology to provide a more versatile and secure payments framework.

However, it is no secret that CBDCs might be a response to the threat provided by cryptoassets and other private digital currencies. Increased supply of digital currencies could dilute the strength of domestic currency and hinder the ability of central banks to influence their economies through monetary policy. This issue of economic sovereignty was brought into sharp focus by the debate that played out during Meta's failed Diem project, which was perceived by many as a poorly disguised attempt to replace the dollar.

In nations that are already highly dollarized (i.e. nations where the US dollar is widely accepted as a substitute for a domestic currency), the threat posed by cryptoassets, or even foreign CBDCs, to economic sovereignty is likely to be greater.[2] In these nations there is already a reliance on foreign currency, limiting the influence of central banks to varying degrees, and many nations fit this description. In 2020, one-third of countries used foreign currency for more than 30 per cent of all deposits and loans, and foreign currency accounted for more than half of total deposits in 17 per cent of countries.[3] There is also a correlation between inflation and dollarization and we might reasonably suspect a foreign CBDC to be among the options for someone looking to reduce their holdings of a currency that loses value at speed.[4]

The programmable possibilities for CBDCs may negate these risks, especially in relation to linking expenditures with identification. Central banks may be able to implement these digital currencies in a manner that controls spending, with the intention of preventing outflows, encouraging domestic spending and reducing the risk of wild swings in foreign exchange rates.

We cannot overlook the political nature of finance either, and the role of money in political and economic arrangements, both formally and in terms of soft power. The Federal Reserve's 2022 paper, *Money and Payments: The U.S Dollar in the Age of Digital Transformation* directly observes that a CBDC could be used to preserve the US dollar's role as the most widely used currency for payments and investments, as well as its function as the world's reserve currency.[5] As things stand, the US holds a sizable influence over standards within international monetary systems; and its citizens, companies and government all benefit from lower transaction and borrowing costs as a result of its dominant position.

From another international relations perspective, digital currencies such as Russia's digital rouble, apparently designed for mutual settlements with e-CNY (China's digital yuan), can be positioned as a means for bypassing international sanctions.

WILL CBDCs DIMINISH THE DOLLAR'S STATUS AS THE GLOBAL RESERVE CURRENCY?

Global reserve currencies are foreign currencies held in large amounts by central banks and monetary authorities. These reserves play an important role in international investments and transactions.

In today's economy, the US dollar operates as the global reserve currency. In the decade leading to 2023, it accounted for roughly 60 per cent of global reserves, and the Euro for 20 per cent. A number of other currencies are often held as reserve currencies, including Japanese Yen, pounds sterling, Australian dollars, Canadian dollars, Swiss francs and Chinese Yuan.[6]

There are some who believe this order might be disrupted by CBDCs or stablecoins. Demand for new digital currencies may increase if they are deemed advantageous for facilitating international trade, and if there is reason to believe they might reduce costs and increase settlement speeds. It has even been suggested that a private stablecoin, if backed by a social media or other international digital platform, could create an informal currency zone.

There are mixed opinions about whether CBDCs put the US's status at risk. Some believe the risk is minimal as the economic reasons for using the dollar extend far beyond the digitalization of currency, and include its stability, global acceptance and deep liquidity. Further, most stablecoins are pegged to the dollar, so their proliferation may even strengthen the dollar's position by increasing demand for dollar-denominated reserve assets.

There have been suggestions that governments with larger economies, and in particular China, may seek to replace the US dollar as the global reserve currency. China's launch of a CBDC, e-CNY, may even be a motivating factor for the CBDC initiatives of other nations, and some regard its launch of the Renminbi Currency Arrangement (this is not a CBDC arrangement) across the Asia-Pacific region and Chile as evidence of its longer-term aims.[7]

Retail vs wholesale

As with the payment discussion in the previous chapter, CBDCs are being designed with either retail, wholesale or both types of payment in mind. There is ample opportunity for digital currencies to build efficiencies into both, but the role of central banks will come under particular scrutiny where individual rights or commercial interests are deemed at risk.

Before looking at how these CBDCs might impact payments, it is sensible to look at a fundamental classification of money within banking systems. In doing so, we can consider money as taking the following forms.

Central bank/Public money

This money is issued by the central bank and is available to the general public in the form of coins and banknotes. The vast majority of it, however, is held in digital commercial bank balances at central banks. This includes the money used in wholesale payments, and it has been argued that this use of central bank money may already constitute a type of wholesale CBDC (this point was made by Fabio Panetta, member of the executive board of the European Central Bank, at an event hosted by the Deutsche Bundesbank in 2022).[8]

Commercial bank/Private money

This is typically money held by individuals and businesses with regulated commercial banks. This is the money that changes hands during non-cash transactions, such as card, mobile or online payments. It is also the money that fintech apps interact with via application programming interfaces (APIs), which might add saving, investing, FX or other capabilities.

The distinction between these two types of money is important. Hypothetically, if central banks choose to directly handle retail accounts, in effect taking on roles usually held by commercial banks, this is likely to lead to reductions in transaction fees and retail deposits in the commercial banks.

Nations and collaborators who are designing CBDCs also need to consider the attributes that are coded into them. For a CBDC to serve the needs of its users, it should be interoperable with other currencies and systems, have robust security and fraud prevention capabilities, and a decision should be made over whether or not it is interest-bearing. A CBDC that pays no interest is likely to be suited for spending unless it exists in a negative interest rate environment. A relatively high interest rate, conversely, may incentivize users to hold the currency for savings purposes.

Wholesale CBDC

As mentioned in the previous chapter, there is scope for DLT to remove delays, costs and intermediaries from the process of wholesale payments, especially cross-border. If such changes can be achieved through the use of tokenization (possibly stablecoins) and atomic swaps, and with settlement possibly even provided on-chain by a third party, then central banks may want to fulfil these roles instead.

Even so, central banks are not obligated to jump on the bandwagon, and we should not consider any of this as inevitable. Banks may choose to improve their existing systems in a way that does not involve DLT, and this will not necessarily set them back. Research from Banque de France found that banks might still be able to access DLT benefits via third parties, though there may be a tariff involved with using a less standardized approach.[9] Central banks might also engage with the private sector to deliver a wholesale payment solution that falls within their regulation.

As with the use of CLS, international collaboration and integration will greatly improve the benefits of any wholesale CBDC. In theory, a wholesale CBDC delivers the benefits of digital finance to wholesale payments in a manner that central banks can manage and control directly.

Retail CBDC

Retail CBDCs are designed for use by people and businesses for everyday payments, and some central banks are exploring them as a viable option. The use of blockchain ostensibly delivers safety, security, regulatory protection and transparency for end users, and programmability could be used to build new features into transactions. Economic sovereignty can be appreciated as a worthwhile attribute here, too, in relation to the benefits of being able to receive money directly from the central bank. This might take on use within a welfare system, or the form of an emergency payment that goes directly to those in need. This might also offer a direct alternative to monetary policies designed to stimulate growth, such as quantitative easing.

QUANTITATIVE EASING

Quantitative easing occurs when central banks purchase government bonds or other assets to lower long-term interest rates. This, in turn, encourages spending.

Despite the potential upsides, retail CBDCs come with a warning. There is the aforementioned risk of bank disintermediation, but concerns over user privacy and government overreach have taken centre stage. If the central bank can programme your money, then it can potentially control and freeze it, monitor your spending activity, and create incentives or disincentives to save or spend your money. And even if there is no stated intention to do any of this, once the door is open to CBDCs, can it really be closed?

The initial response to the European Commission's public consultation on the digital euro placed privacy as the number one concern, ahead of the need for secure payment and being able to use the digital euro without additional costs.[10] This observation requires a caveat. Rather unusually, 87 per cent of respondents to this survey were male, and one-third of professional respondents worked in tech, so this is not necessarily a sample of the general public (although the tech skew may imply that it's a sample that understands the issue relatively well). What's more, this is a hot issue among crypto enthusiasts and libertarian groups. Privacy concerns around China's digital yuan (e-CNY) are often brought up in relation to this. A senior representative of the People's Bank of China has described its approach to CBDC privacy as a combination of anonymity and managed anonymity.[11]

WHAT DO PEOPLE WORKING ON CBDC PROJECTS SAY?

Ricardo Correia from R3 says that concerns are warranted to a degree, but challenges the notion that CBDCs send us towards an Orwellian future:

'Your bank [already] sees every single payment that you make using your apps and your credit and debit cards, so it won't be any more or any less private than what you already do. If you're really unhappy about this, you probably should not be in the banking system at all.

Your money today is 95 per cent digital, and so 95 per cent of it can be surveilled, but there are laws in place. Banking acts and so on, that prevent the banks from tampering with and surveilling your payments to a degree... and the policies that we see coming through from central banks say that the money they issue into commercial banks will provide

> absolutely no traceability of who gets that money. The central bank will never be able to say that you got this particular CBDC token, only the commercial bank whose wallet you're using. And that's what we do today.'

The counter-narrative to this is that central banks disintermediate commercial banks and eventually manage your account.

> 'You wouldn't imagine that the central bank would set up bank accounts for us – some have tried and they failed. It's non-trivial, and managing AML, KYC and CFT [anti-money laundering, know your client and countering the funding of terrorism] is hugely expensive and comes with a hell of a lot of risk.
>
> Direct issuance is not something we are seeing as a common mode. The issuance of a CBDC through digital wallets that are managed and maintained by commercial banks is a model that seems quite obvious.'

R3 has worked with numerous central banks and key collaborators on the implementation of CBDCs.

It is impossible to say how governments will apply CBDCs in the long run, but the use of DLT in currency could make it very easy for those with access to a database to trace your financial activities. This is the same technology that allows for immutable records and transactions that can be publicly verified, only the pseudonymity of a private key may be replaced with a digital identifier.

For reasons not limited to privacy, early adoption of retail CBDCs has been underwhelming. In the first year of its launch, less than one in 200 Nigerian citizens used the eNaira.[12] (Uptake increased in 2023, but this may be due to shortages of cash.) Similarly, e-CNY transactions were valued at $14.5 billion in Q3 of 2022, in comparison to the $12.5 trillion of value processed through private digital systems, and in 2022, more than a year after its launch, it was reported that Bahama's Sand Dollar made up less than 0.1 per cent of currency in circulation and has struggled to gain the approval of merchants.[13, 14] This is to say nothing of its longer-term trajectory, however. Consumer confidence, incentives, smoother interfaces and familiarity or necessity could enhance CBDC usage by magnitudes.

THREE CONCEPTS FOR RETAIL CBDC OPERATIONS[15]

The International Monetary Fund has put forward three possible systems for operating a CBDC, and the Atlantic Council uses a similar distinction. The three models are:

1 **Unilateral CBDC:** The central bank issues money and directly interacts with the end user.

2 **Intermediated CBDC:** The central bank issues money, but intermediaries (including wholesale banks) handle interactions with end users.

3 **Synthetic CBDC:** The central bank does not issue money. Instead, intermediaries issue money that is backed by central bank assets that they acquire from the central bank.

CBDC projects have so far upheld the role of intermediaries, and of the 42 CBDC projects to take a stance on using a direct or intermediated approach, only three chose to develop a CBDC where wholesale banks would be excluded from the process. Of these, two projects are inactive (in Iceland and Denmark) and the other is cancelled (Senegal).[16]

In terms of the importance of private money and cash, which some fear will be eroded by CBDCs, it is also possible to place limits on the amounts in circulation and the amounts that individuals and businesses are able to hold. For example, the eNaira has tiered daily transaction limits and eNaira wallet limits, with greater levels of identity verification required as the tiers progress. In Q2 of 2023, the Tier 3 wallet equates to $10,750 and daily spend cannot exceed $2,150. The e-CNY, Sand Dollar and ECCU (Eastern Caribbean Currency Union) have implemented their own versions of tiered spending limits.

TABLE 9.1 eNaira spending limits[17]

Category	Daily transaction limit	Balance/eNaira speed wallet limit
Tier 0	N 20,000	N 120,000
Tier 1	N 50,000	N 300,000
Tier 2	N 200,000	N 500,000
Tier 3	N 1,000,000	N 5,000,000
Merchant	No limit	No limit

These limits are set to preserve financial stability and also hint that central banks don't intend, at least yet, for CBDCs to be used for everything. Digital currencies may eventually become one segment of a diverse currency landscape.

ADDITIONAL POINTS ON FINANCIAL STABILITY

Retail CBDC interest rates, if set at a relatively high level, could incentivize people to move their funds to a CBDC. This would most likely decrease retail deposits held at commercial banks. Also, some nations have investigated the possibility of a CBDC that works offline. This, while proving hard to achieve, might be preferable in regions where internet access is limited, or where natural disasters or armed conflict harm national infrastructures.

Early explorations of retail CBDCs have focused on domestic payments, though they could reasonably play a valuable role in cross-border payments. The cost-saving benefits are an immediate incentive for making it happen but there are also substantial risks associated with providing this functionality. Cross-border CBDC functionality could lead to enhanced currency substitutions and shocks (a currency shock is where the value of a currency spikes rapidly in relation to another). There would also be a need for some amount of CBDC standardization and mutual agreement on AML/KYC/CFT rules and how currencies can be used and shared. International relations will also be a factor in CBDC collaborations.

CROSS-BORDER COLLABORATION

There is an appetite for international collaboration, and several projects have been launched to smooth the flow of wholesale and retail payments. They include:

- **mBridge:** Thailand, China, Hong Kong and the UAE (Wholesale)
- **Project Dunbar:** Australia, Singapore, Malaysia and South Africa (Wholesale)

- **Project Sela:** Israel, Hong Kong and BIS (Retail)
- **Project Icebreaker:** Israel, Norway and Sweden (Retail)
- **Project Mariana:** France, Singapore, BIS and Switzerland (Wholesale)
- **Project Jura:** Switzerland and France (Wholesale)
- **Project Rosalind:** United Kingdom and BIS (Retail)
- **Project Aurum:** BIS and Hong Kong (Retail and Wholesale)
- **Project Helvetia:** Switzerland and the BIS (Wholesale)
- **Project Jasper:** Canada, Singapore and the UK (Wholesale)
- **Project Aber:** The UAE and Saudi Arabia (Wholesale)

The Bank for International Settlements has acknowledged an opportunity for multi-CBDCs, or mCBDCs, which would involve collaboration between central banks.[18] This could ease some of the biggest CBDC concerns for central banks, in particular those relating to international tax avoidance and the spending and accepting of CBDCs abroad. Greater harmonization could also mitigate foreign exchange volatility, especially if CBDCs facilitate immediate and accessible currency exchange. This could also lead to efficiencies in increasingly globalized markets.

Disintermediation in the age of CBDCs?

In the previous chapter, it was suggested that TradFi's usage of crypto and DeFi tools offered a subversion of Satoshi's original vision. It would be an ironic twist if government adoption of digital currency were to lead the way towards removal of intermediaries instead. Is this actually going to happen? At first glance, it is perhaps best to avoid hyperbole. While some central banks, The Bank of England for example, have publicly claimed to have no interest in upholding the status quo or protecting business models within the commercial banking sector, it remains the case that CBDCs are being introduced tentatively and carefully, often with account limits and no interest payments.[19]

Despite this, a CBDC could present an existential threat if positioned to do so. You could even encounter a financial crisis scenario in which account holders move their money as quickly as possible into CBDCs, provided there are no limitations on doing so, trusting the central bank above commercial ones. This seems the obvious dramatic use case, but a threat is posed even if money switches across gradually. The problem is this: banks need those deposits to finance loans, such as mortgages, and to make investments. In a system with no limits on CBDC accounts and where CBDC provision and account management are handled entirely by a central bank, a sharp removal of deposits could alter the provision of banking. Banks would require a new supply of funds in order to carry out activities. This might be doable and banks might borrow heavily in long-term funds in order to subsequently finance their loans, but it would present a new paradigm for commercial banks. Likewise, central banks might lend CBDC deposits back to banks. The risk here is that governments could influence or interfere with bank lending decisions.

There are also questions to ask about what CBDCs mean for the future of payment service providers. If central banks were to maximize their digital currency plans, it is possible that they would offer some of the services that are provided by private entities. The crux of this issue is whether or not central banks would actually want to take this route. It could mean taking full responsibility for a swathe of compliance (AML/CFT/KYC), customer service and cybersecurity roles. It could also require central banks to achieve greater interoperability with international banks (central or commercial), design user-friendly payment journeys and find ways to innovate and improve in line with other economies. PSPs are far better equipped to do all of this. It is also very naive to dismiss the private sector as a lame duck here. Public–private partnerships, which have received support from the likes of ECB President Christine Lagarde, will be the desired choice for some governments that roll out a CBDC plan.[20]

When looking at disintermediation we should consider the full range and complexity of services offered by banks and other important intermediaries. There is much work to be done before these services can be substituted for smart contracts and DLTs. It would also be a huge task for a central bank to recreate the user experience that customers are used to, taking trends like embedded finance and payment verticals into account (embedded finance involves the integration of financial services within a business's products and services), while facilitating acceptable levels of customer service and seamless online checkout processes.

To circle back to privacy concerns, we might conclude on retail payments by noting the importance of trust. If the general public is strongly opposed to the use of CBDCs and does not trust central banks to manage their money and respect their rights, then retail CBDC adoption in many places could well be halted.

Legislation and regulation: the next step for governments

CBDCs are a lucid demonstration of governments taking inspiration from DeFi. However, they may be less enthusiastic about DeFi itself, or at the very least suspicious of it, and consequently, there is now a race to build suitable regulatory frameworks around cryptoassets. From the outside looking in, it might look as though governments and regulators have been slow to respond, but it is fair to say that crypto and DeFi present a range of consequential and complicated issues.

In creating legal and regulatory frameworks, questions we can ask include:

- Do existing legal and regulatory frameworks provide instruction on how DeFi issues should be tackled?
- Where DeFi mimics traditional financial markets, should activities and assets be treated the same?
- Are regulated institutions involved in the activities?
- How should tokens or coins be classified for tax and regulatory purposes?
- What is the legal status of different types of cryptoassets?
- What is the contractual status of various DeFi transactions?

- Who is liable if smart contracts, protocols, wallets or asset prices are compromised?
- How can pseudonymous parties be held accountable?
- Are creative solutions required?
- How should international transactions be handled, especially where the entities involved are in jurisdictions with incompatible rules and regulations?
- Which parts can we actually regulate?

This list is far from exhaustive, which serves to outline the depth and breadth of the task ahead.

THE DIFFICULTIES OF REGULATING DECENTRALIZED PROTOCOLS

DeFi creates a range of legal headaches. Hugo Hoyland, chief strategy officer at Asset Reality, drew upon his experience to offer a novel and hypothetical example involving a flash loan attack:

'What duty does a developer have when writing open source code and releasing it to the wild? In a flash loan attack, you might have a developer release a smart contract that manages a liquidity pool for a swap from Token A to Token B. If someone's able to read the smart contracts very, very carefully, and ultimately manipulate them without breaking them; to just manipulate the way they function by putting too much liquidity in at one point, so they can take a far, far greater share of the liquidity out at another point, is that breaking the law? Is that a theft? Is that a hack? What is it, legally speaking? And that becomes a really interesting question because a smart contract is just a series of "If this then that statements", and you have someone who's read the "if this then that" very carefully and found a way to "if this, then I get a big bit of that", and they've just been clever.

A lot of them who do these flash loan attacks out themselves publicly as soon as they've done it. They say, "look, it's me. The funds are there. I've taken them. Come get me." Sometimes they're a bit ruder than that but it's basically, "you guys wrote a bad code, I've exploited it." But is it an exploit? Is it just someone manipulating it? Is it just someone being clever? Those are really interesting questions, which I don't think anyone has really answered yet.

And if you were one of the funders of the liquidity pool, and suddenly your funds are gone because someone used the smart contract, who do you go after? Do you go after the developers for initially writing a smart contract that was wrong? Do you go after the person who manipulated it? Do you go after the governance token holders, who should have also noticed that the smart contract was wrong and made changes to the protocol going forward? All of these people are just addresses on a blockchain and they're pseudonymous. It's really hard to get some form of legal recourse.'

International efforts to set standards for crypto and DeFi

While individual nations are determining their own rules and standards for DeFi and cryptoassets, there have been several endeavours from international standard setters to provide overarching guidelines. These will not necessarily all be followed by each jurisdiction but could help introduce an element of standardization. Guidelines include the following.

1. Basel Committee on Banking Supervision: Prudential Treatment of Cryptoasset Exposures

This paper sets out a prudential standard relating to bank exposure to cryptoassets. It splits cryptoassets and stablecoins into two categories.

GROUP 1

These cryptoassets need to meet a set of classification conditions, and include tokenized traditional assets, provided that they carry the same level of credit and market risk as they would in non-tokenized form. This category also includes stablecoins with values tied to effective stabilization mechanisms (this broadly means stablecoins with historically safe assets such as cash and treasuries, rather than riskier assets or algorithms).

GROUP 2

These assets fail to meet any of the classification conditions and are therefore deemed to be riskier. Banks holding these assets need to heighten risk management procedures to comply with the standard.

This standard provides some thought-provoking positions. The inclusion of tokenized 'real-world assets' may provide a reference point for other on-chain assets, and the identification of Group 2 assets leads to a practical risk-management-focused method for integrating esoteric assets.

The paper also explains that the classification of assets on permissionless blockchains, such as Bitcoin and Ether, can only enter Group 1 if risks can be sufficiently mitigated.

2. Financial Stability Board: International Regulation of Crypto-asset Activities

In October 2022, the Financial Stability Board (FSB) put forward a set of proposals to the central bank governors and finance ministers of the G20. These proposals offer guidance but produce no legal rights or obligations.

The FSB generally recommends that nations achieve greater consistency in regulatory and supervisory approaches, and advocates that its recommendations apply to any type of cryptoasset, cryptoasset issuer or intermediary whose behaviour may weaken financial stability. It also calls for greater transparency and stronger governance requirements for stablecoin issuers. Final recommendations for G20 members are expected to be published by the end of 2025.

3. Financial Action Task Force: Virtual Assets and Virtual Asset Service Providers: Updated Guidance for a Risk-Based Approach

This guidance from the Financial Action Task Force (FATF) was published in October 2021 to offer greater clarity around the definition and supervision of virtual assets (VA) and service providers (VASP), setting out principles to help develop regulatory and supervisory directives. The paper also examines the role of peer-to-peer (P2P) transactions within virtual assets, and how regulators and supervisors might respond if illicit P2P activity increases.

The FATF's guidance is impactful. One of its key additions has been the extension of the 'travel rule' to VAs, which recommends that service providers share customer information when engaging in higher-value transactions. Nations are adopting this rule at different speeds and applying different thresholds (e.g. €1,000 across Europe and $3,000 in the United States), but this is considered an important step towards minimizing money laundering, and payments to illegal operations or sanctioned entities. These recommendations also introduce government oversight and threaten the potential anonymity of future crypto transactions that pass the threshold.

4. *International Organization of Securities Commission: Crypto-Asset Roadmap for 2022–2023*

The International Organization of Securities Commission (IOSCO) is a fintech task force with 27 members from board member jurisdictions, chaired by the Singapore Monetary Authority. It has created two workstreams for crypto and DeFi. The crypto workstream will focus on issues that impact market integrity and investor protection. The DeFi equivalent also explores these topics, as well as financial stability risks presented to broader financial markets by DeFi protocols, stablecoins, exchanges and trading platforms. Both workstreams intend to provide policy recommendations in Q4 of 2023. This work could deliver important findings on the interconnectedness of DeFi and regulated markets, and hint at the future of DeFi's relationship with regulation.

5. *Board of the International Organization of Securities Commissions/ IOSCO: Applications of the Principles for Financial Market Infrastructures to Stablecoin Arrangements*

This guidance applies the Principles for Financial Market Infrastructures (PFMI) to stablecoin arrangements that are systemically important. It offers a range of key considerations around governance, risk management, settlement finality and money settlements. The paper does not introduce new standards but offers some guidance on identifying structurally important stablecoins and the principles they should adhere to.

International frameworks for regulation

Regulation for cryptoassets is a certainty; if there were any doubt over this, it was effectively quashed by the collapse of FTX and Terra Luna, and more formally by the European Union's decision to green-light its MiCA regulatory framework. Regulators in numerous other jurisdictions, but not all, are now considering how to create rules around cryptoassets that provide greater consumer safety while helping registered businesses in the crypto space operate with confidence and clarity. This is no small task and requires immediacy, expertise and careful wording, and there will also be demand for regulators to clamp down on nefarious conduct and to respond to a market that is evolving at lightspeed. In nations where regulation is introduced, it will be important to find a balance between strictness and leniency and to introduce suitable reporting requirements for businesses to adhere to.

To speak to the complexity of regulating this environment, consider issues such as decentralization and the variety of tokens available. As discussed in the chapter on DAOs, the legal classification of decentralized organizations presents grey areas and there is debate over how far they can or should be regulated. Many decentralized organizations, exchanges or protocols will facilitate the pseudonymity of users and protocol founders, international transactions and P2P dealings. Should a decentralized protocol user seek legal recourse, it is unclear where liability rests. Regulators can speak more confidently of CeFi organizations, and potentially of DeFi protocols where the founders and developers are identifiable, but the latter is a murkier area. As for token varieties, there are differences between fungible tokens and NFTs to navigate. There is also work required to classify how and where a token might qualify as a security or asset, and where tokens should not be the concern of a financial regulator. Not all tokens are financial instruments.

While regulation does not marry up with decentralization, those in CeFi have good reason to welcome legal clarity. An effective regime can help deter the launch of ill-conceived crypto projects and should bolster consumer confidence and the reputation of their businesses. Further, it should increase the likelihood of professional connections. Crypto firms in some nations have been unable to find insurers and banks willing to work with them, but regulation should foster greater collaboration and remove an element of regulatory risk from partnerships.[21]

Markets in Crypto-Assets Regulation (MiCA)[22]

The European Union made the first move to bring cryptoassets within regulation through MiCA, a cross-border initiative tabled in 2020 and expected to roll out in 2024. Its goal is to support the potential of digital finance and encourage innovation and competition while mitigating risks. It names four core objectives:

1 to provide legal certainty

2 to support innovation

3 to instil appropriate levels of consumer and investor protection and market integrity

4 to achieve financial stability.

MiCA will apply to the following types of token and asset:

- **Asset-Referenced Token (ART):** Essentially a stablecoin that is backed by multiple assets, which may include fiat currencies, commodities or cryptoassets.
- **Electronic Money Tokens (EMTs):** These are stablecoins backed by a single fiat currency.
- **Utility Tokens:** Cryptoassets that grant a user rights to a service or product provided by the issuer.
- **Other Cryptoassets:** Other tokens that are stored and transferred electronically, which offer a digital representation of value or rights, will fall under MiCA.

The following are digital assets not covered by MiCA:

- NFTs
- DeFi protocols
- CBDCs
- assets that fall under existing EU regulations
- assets that are free of charge or cannot be used in transactions.

The MiCA regulation presents a series of obligations for those who provide services and issue assets in crypto markets:

Cryptoasset issuers are expected to be legally registered and to share necessary financial information. Issuers are required to publish a whitepaper that outlines technical information and adheres to at least a minimum standard. Issuers need to make several disclosures available to the general public, including information on the key characteristics of the token or asset, token utility, risks and restrictions.

Cryptoasset service providers need to have a registered office in an EU Member State and be authorized to provide regulated services by a national competent authority. They also need to abide by capital requirements rules, and are required to meet a set of conduct requirements to ensure that they act fairly and in the interest of clients. Organizationally, cryptoasset service providers must be effectively managed in the EU and demonstrably maintain a range of national and EU regulatory standards relating to risk management, safekeeping of assets, complaints procedures and location of management.

CAPITAL REQUIREMENTS

Some regulated entities are required to hold liquid capital on their balance sheets. Requirements will vary based on the chosen regulated activity and the level of risk involved, and these rules are designed to help banks meet withdrawal requirements in a downturn or to deter companies from taking on excessive amounts of high-risk assets relative to their regulated activities.

For those offering custody or safekeeping of cryptoassets, the new rules require that they produce daily reports of holdings, establish a suitable custody policy and are liable for client losses relating to cybercrime and code failures. Trading platforms, meanwhile, must take action to ensure that their systems are safe and secure, and that settlements are completed within 24 hours of a trade.

A safer market environment?

As well as placing requirements upon asset issuers and service providers, MiCA defines rules to prevent market abuse such as insider trading and market manipulation. This regime, backed up by potential sanctions, fines and public censures, runs in contrast to the unchecked influence of crypto whales and wash trading (there may also be consequences for anyone looking to replicate Elon Musk's support of Dogecoin. A $258 billion lawsuit was brought against the business magnate for allegedly using his influence to lift the price of the memecoin by over 36,000 per cent).[23]

If printed, the MiCA regulations would not be a dissimilar size to this book, so for brevity this is all of the detail provided.

'CAN'T WE JUST BAN CRYPTO?'

One question that doesn't go away is 'what if crypto gets banned?' Charles Kerrigan, crypto expert and partner at international law firm CMS, explains that governments will have a hard time banning it.

'From a policy perspective, you've got a kind of binary position. A country can ban crypto or not ban crypto. So before you get into analyzing the position in a country, the first question is "has the country in question banned crypto?". And the second bit is, even if the answer is "yes", it just tends not to work. So China has at times banned crypto and that's proven to be a good case study of the fact you can't ban crypto: using VPNs and various other techniques, citizens reach it. The reason for that is that crypto is a technology. It's a how, not a what. So it's a bit like trying to ban the internet. You definitely can't do that. And then in terms of regulation, we've seen how hard it is to regulate the internet when people have tried.

The balancing point to this view, which is correct, is that crypto will get regulated and it will get more regulated, and that will be one of the characteristics of the next couple of years.'

What happens next?

While many crypto firms are already regulated in the EU, albeit without uniformity, the arrival of MiCA will offer the most illuminating insight to date on how a bespoke crypto legal framework might impact crypto businesses and markets. Other jurisdictions will now have the opportunity to borrow from it or stand in contrast to it. We can expect the scope of regulation to expand from here.

Before moving on, it should be acknowledged that legal frameworks go far beyond what is described here. In relation to activities originating from DeFi, we can pick out rules around crowdfunding, which could influence DAO activity. In relation to the loud and partisan FUD and FOMO attached to cryptoassets, instruction on the marketing and promotion of cryptoassets could reshape some of the discourse around coins and projects.

FUD, FOMO, WAGMI AND NGMI

FUD (meaning fear, uncertainty and doubt) and FOMO (fear of missing out) are mentioned frequently in online forums, often in relation to crypto prices and their rises and falls. Several projects have openly embraced the terminology, also adopting terms like WAGMI (We're All Gonna Make It) and NGMI (Not Gonna Make It) to show support for projects and fellow investors, or to goad someone for missing out on an opportunity. These acronyms are deployed with varying levels of sincerity.

In time, we will also see other nations strengthen their regulatory frameworks for cryptoassets. As with CBDC projects, most major economies are working to build out plans for the sector. These frameworks are likely to expand and gain specificity as DeFi and crypto evolve and may intertwine with other developments in technology such as generative AI and embedded finance. The EU, for example, is aiming to produce a set of standards for the metaverse, particularly around digital identity. It will be intriguing to see how far this goes, and also how regulators respond when market risk is introduced by the activity of crypto whales, or even hackers, who operate outside of their legal reach. There could also be issues where crashes in unregulated corners of crypto present contagion risks to regulated markets. In several ways, the persistence of regulated activity within partially regulated markets and currencies could keep regulators on their toes.

References

1 16 Atlantic Council. Central Bank Digital Currency Tracker, Atlantic Council, 2023, www.atlanticcouncil.org/cbdctracker/ (archived at https://perma.cc/8925-PA7D)

2 S Brooks. Staff discussion paper/document d'analyse du personnel-2021-17 Revisiting the monetary sovereignty rationale for CBDCs, Bank of Canada, 2021, www.bankofcanada.ca/wp-content/uploads/2021/12/sdp2021-17.pdf (archived at https://perma.cc/V7JT-WUPP)

3 International Monetary Fund. 'Digital Money Across Borders: Macro-Financial Implications', IMF Policy Paper, 2020, No. 2020/050.

4, 18 Bank for International Settlements. CBDCs: an opportunity for the monetary system, BIS Annual Economic Report 2021, 2021, www.bis.org/publ/arpdf/ar2021e3.pdf (archived at https://perma.cc/N6SN-BTHA)

5 Board of Governors of the Federal Reserve System. Money and payments: the U.S. dollar in the age of digital transformation, Federal Reserve, 2022, www.federalreserve.gov/publications/files/money-and-payments-20220120.pdf (archived at https://perma.cc/MLB2-HYJA)

6 International Monetary Fund. Currency composition of official foreign exchange reserves (COFER), IMF, 2023, data.imf.org/?sk=E6A5F467-C14B-4AA8-9F6D-5A09EC4E62A4 (archived at https://perma.cc/Y3BD-YSAU)

7 Bank for International Settlements. BIS announces Renminbi liquidity arrangement, BIS, 2022, www.bis.org/press/p220625.htm (archived at https://perma.cc/8HZ2-GLR6)

8 European Central Bank. Demystifying wholesale central bank digital currency, www.ecb.europa.eu, 2022, www.ecb.europa.eu/press/key/date/2022/html/ecb. sp220926~5f9b85685a.en.html (archived at https://perma.cc/B462-3GPP)

9 Banque de France, Wholesale central bank digital currency experiments with the Banque de France, 2021, Banque de France, www.banque-france.fr/sites/ default/files/media/2021/11/09/rapport_mnbc_0.pdf (archived at https://perma. cc/Q554-B6SN)

10 European Commission. Consultation document: targeted consultation on a digital euro, 2022, European Commission, finance.ec.europa.eu/system/ files/2022-06/2022-digital-euro-consultation-document_en.pdf (archived at https://perma.cc/D3KM-C3WR)

11 PYMNTS. China central bank governor says digital yuan has 'managed anonymity', www.pymnts.com, 2022, www.pymnts.com/cryptocurrency/ 2022/china-central-bank-governor-digital-yuan-managed-anonymity/ (archived at https://perma.cc/GAD5-44VQ)

12 International Monetary Fund. Nigeria: 2022 Article IV consultation-press release; staff report; and statement by the Executive Director for Nigeria, IMF, 2022, www.imf.org/en/Publications/CR/Issues/2023/02/16/Nigeria-2022- Article-IV-Consultation-Press-Release-Staff-Report-and-Statement-by- the-529842 (archived at https://perma.cc/N9B2-WDCJ)

13 M Muir. Central banks' digital currency plans face public backlash, Financial Times, 13 March 2023, https://www.ft.com/content/e0b7f134-c935-4cd6- bf27-460c37db1512 (archived at https://perma.cc/5HDM-AL8Q)

14 International Monetary Fund. The Bahamas: 2022 Article IV consultation - press release; staff report; and statement by the Executive Director for the Bahamas, IMF Country Report, May 2022, No. 22/121.

15 G Soderberg et al. Behind the scenes of central bank digital currency: emerging trends, insights, and policy lessons, IMF, 2022, Washington, DC

17 Central Bank of Nigeria. Regulatory guidelines on the eNAIRA, 2021, www.cbn.gov.ng/Out/2021/FPRD/eNairaCircularAndGuidelinesFINAL.pdf (archived at https://perma.cc/9DQ9-236G)

19 Bank of England and HM Treasury. The digital pound: a new form of money for households and businesses? Consultation paper, Bank of England, 2023, www.bankofengland.co.uk/-/media/boe/files/paper/2023/the-digital-pound- consultation-working-paper.pdf (archived at https://perma.cc/Q99H-SR4S)

20 C Lagarde. Winds of change: the case for new digital currency, IMF, 2018, www.imf.org/en/News/Articles/2018/11/13/sp111418-winds-of-change-the- case-for-new-digital-currency (archived at https://perma.cc/9R9Q-78TJ)

21 A Baydakova. MiCA at the door: how European crypto firms are getting ready for sweeping legislation, CoinDesk, 2023, www.coindesk.com/consensus- magazine/2023/01/24/european-union-mica-crypto-regulation/ (archived at https://perma.cc/X3PN-5FZT)

22 European Commission. Proposal for a regulation of the European Parliament and of the Council on Markets in Crypto-assets, and amending Directive (EU) 2019/1937, EUR-Lex, 2020, https://eur-lex.europa.eu/legal-content/EN/TXT/?uri=CELEX%3A52020PC0593 (archived at https://perma.cc/D3BW-B3R6)

23 J Stempel. Elon Musk seeks to end $258 billion Dogecoin lawsuit, Reuters, 3 April 2023, www.reuters.com/legal/elon-musk-seeks-end-258-billion-dogecoin-lawsuit-2023-04-01 (archived at https://perma.cc/2JFJ-SXKZ)

10

The long road ahead: Can DeFi fulfil its promise?

The story so far has shown how DeFi and the innovations behind it have had several major implications. To look at the material and financial side, we can see that it has inspired a new investment market and encouraged the creation of a $50 billion DeFi space (this number will no doubt have changed significantly by the time you read this). It has also given traditional institutions reason to invest directly in it on behalf of their clients, or even to take tools such as blockchain and smart contracts and use them for the betterment of TradFi and real-world assets, bringing us closer to a tokenized economy.

Governments and central banks have had plenty to chew on as well. The arrival of cryptoassets, currently worth about 1 per cent of the world's GDP (and at one point it was greater than 3 per cent), has provoked difficult and confusing conversations about the future of economic sovereignty and the threats and opportunities posed by a borderless and alternative currency. These conversations are not just about monetary policy, FX rates and international relations; they also require projections for the future health of our financial infrastructure, with a view to concerns around the disintermediation of TradFi and the consequences this might have for financial stability. Looking at the material impact of DeFi and crypto, it has clearly made waves.

The part that hasn't been explored so closely is the philosophy that underpins DeFi, and the many ambitious claims that have been made in relation to it. For some, crypto was a punt made during a dull or desperate moment but for others it was much, much more. This was the financial system that would bank the unbanked, provide genuine financial inclusion, and remove us from the relative tyranny of centralized power structures and lead us to a better, fairer system. But is there any truth in this? And do crypto and DeFi even stand for these things?

Does DeFi stand for anything?

Many believe that DeFi has a distinct political slant. Its basic traits and early adopters have a noticeable alignment with libertarianism (Satoshi acknowledged the libertarian appeal of Bitcoin in 2008 in an email to renowned developer Hal Finney), and to build on this we can add that crypto's first significant marketplace was the darknet's Silk Road.[1] Despite this, it's a fool's errand to ascribe definitive political views to DeFi as a whole. Decentralization is better understood as the 'how' for reaching a destination, rather than a reason for the destination itself. As the DeFi marketplace currently shows, crypto and DeFi can be used to achieve a wide range of goals, and funds can be raised and allocated towards any number of things. DeFi is pretty much a blank canvas on which developers and communities can paint vistas that might be libertarian, socialist, progressive, conservative, anarchist or something in between or very different. Putting it another way, technology doesn't really possess any fixed morality or political bias. Outputs are relative to the inputs.

We might have more luck if we ascribe political values to specific crypto and DeFi projects. In 2018, CoinDesk surveyed 1,200 members of the crypto community, finding that 52 per cent of respondents identified as right-wing and 45 per cent as left-wing.[2] When burrowing beneath this even(ish) split, political differences emerged between users of different coins. The responses of Bitcoin users were described as most closely following the general population, but altcoin Dash (Dash is a privacy coin and was formerly known as Darkcoin – its name change reflects an attempt to distance itself from darknet markets) skewed 78 per cent right-wing, Ether skewed 55 per cent left-wing, and 36 per cent of monero (another privacy coin) users identified as anarcho-capitalists. The undercurrent of libertarianism, or any political ideology, is diluted in popular coins where people have bought in on the basic premise of hoping for an investment return. Still, we can draw crude lines for how cryptoassets and DeFi align with political values. Coins and protocols that uphold individual privacy, freedoms and free market capitalism usually have a stronger pull with right-wing followers. Similarly, there may be more appetite for regulation and consumer protection on the left, and also for DAOs and community governance models that tackle wealth inequalities and offer financial aid and assistance. Again, this is a crude distinction but we should realize that decentralization of our financial ecosystem, and the technology that allows it, offers new mechanisms through which to support political agendas. With regulation looming, there are also indications that bold political statements on crypto regulation will become a vote winner.

Is it destroying the planet?

This is a topic where morality and material factors combine. Climate change is the biggest threat to our future, and crypto and DeFi are not helping. Digiconomist's Bitcoin Energy Consumption Index, in June 2023, reported that the carbon footprint of bitcoin alone is similar to that of the entirety of Libya, and that its energy use is comparable to that of Kazakhstan.[3] Inefficiency is as much an issue as volume. Digiconomist also claims that a single bitcoin transaction carries the same carbon footprint as watching over 60,000 hours of YouTube videos, and the same amount of energy required to power a US household for 22 days. What's more, mining hardware generally becomes obsolete every 18 months, and the resulting hardware disposal is similar to the entirety of small IT equipment waste in the Netherlands. This is something to address.

To stop the analysis there would be to overlook the efforts made to foster a more climate-conscious crypto sector. First, as mentioned previously, the shift to proof-of-stake validation has dramatically reduced the energy intensity of transactions on Ethereum, and the use of PoS for other blockchains is widespread. Ethereum transactions still have the carbon footprint of 44 Visa transactions (or 3 hours of YouTube, to maintain the comparison), but energy requirements have been cut by 99.84 per cent.[4] There have also been improvements in our ability to measure the impact of blockchain finance. The CCRI Crypto Sustainability Indices, for example, track the CO_2 emissions and carbon footprints for more than 20 cryptocurrencies, with plans to expand its remit to tokens.[5] In a slightly different vein, the World Economic Forum has published guidelines to help blockchain finance activities meet ESG standards, and in terms of private sector commitment, MicroStrategy executive chairman Michael Saylor created the Bitcoin Mining Council, a voluntary forum to encourage transparency in energy reporting.[6, 7]

Crypto is also benefiting from the world's gradual shift to a greener energy grid, with tools being designed to help blockchains, validators and miners track and match renewable energy on a 24/7 basis.[8] This improves the likelihood that the energy used for blockchain activities will be from renewable sources, and also helps power grid operators understand daily and hourly demands for renewable energy. It is also likely that providers will emerge to offer a greater range of certifications and awards to acknowledge adherence to sustainability standards. Energy Web, for example, is introducing a renewable bitcoin mining certificate, designed for crypto producers, buyers and intermediaries.[9]

Geographical variances in crypto activity also need to be considered. At present, many large economies including the United States, China, India and Russia are largely reliant on fossil fuels, so the location of activity matters. There are limitations on how accurately miner locations can be measured but CoinShares research from 2022 indicates that the nations using the most power through crypto mining are the United States, Kazakhstan, Canada, Russia and China.[10] (China's contribution to mining has dropped significantly since its ban on the activity was introduced in May 2021.) The current outlook is not ideal, though there are two hopes. One is that block-chain finance relocates mining activity towards areas with greener energy mixes, and it is becoming easier to identify these through sources like Electricity Maps, which identifies regions and nations with lower carbon intensity and higher renewables dependency.[11] There is potential to do this on a more granular level, too. Cornell University published a 2022 report to assess the viability of each US state as a mining hub, based on the ability to mine with renewable energy and carbon capture.[12] The second hope is a continued global shift away from fossil fuels. The International Energy Agency reports that renewables accounted for 28 per cent of global energy genera-tion in 2021.[13]

A greener crypto economy is likely but not a foregone conclusion. There are many vested interests in maintaining a role for fossil fuels, and economic reasons for individuals to overlook environmental concerns. Putting it another way, would emissions be your first thought if mining offered a way out of a depressing financial position? Crypto mining can be lucrative, so regions with all manners of energy mixes have rushed to embrace it. Take the example of Kentucky, a coal-dependent US state, where 38 of its 120 counties are in the bottom 10 per cent for economic performance nationwide. The state has become one of the most popular locations for bitcoin mining in the US, offer-ing a package of tax incentives to encourage this, and while there is an expectation that Kentucky, like the rest of the nation, will become more reliant on renewables and that this will mitigate the long-term impact of mining, there have also been several instances across the US of fossil fuel plants being restored or revitalized as a result of increased bitcoin mining activity (for an example, look to the Hardin coal plant in Montana).[14, 15] In any case, Kentucky's bitcoin network has been estimated to have the highest carbon footprint among all US states.[16]

Limiting carbon emissions, energy consumption and waste in crypto will require sustained effort and patience, not least because of the global scale and limited visibility of participants in the ecosystem. There are other concerns, too. International energy grids are far from being ready for 24/7 sustainable power and electricity generated this way remains a finite resource. This has caused concerns in Sweden, where the director generals of both the Swedish Financial Supervisory Authority and the Swedish Environmental Protection Agency spoke out against rising electricity consumption in Sweden caused by mining, and how it has restricted the nation's ability to electrify its transport sector and develop fossil-free steel and battery manufacturing.[17]

It's fair to say that sustainability is a problem for all of finance and not just DeFi. The implementation of ESG standards in regulated markets has proven tricky due to a lack of reporting standardization, reporting blind spots and greenwashing (greenwashing is the practice of making misleading claims or offering deceptive branding and marketing to embellish your sustainability credentials). There have also been corporate cultural barriers to ESG investing and practices, and prior to the late 2010s, very few TradFi organizations demonstrated a thorough commitment to sustainability and positive impact activity.

All considered, it is reasonable to say that crypto is having a substantial and negative impact on climate change, but this may gradually be mitigated by the presence of private and public sector interest in improving the situation, and a worldwide energy network that is edging towards a more sustainable future. To zoom out a little, we can also say that crypto is not single-handedly destroying the planet, and also that it is not the only energy-intensive process in modern life. To borrow from NYDIG's Bitcoin Net Zero paper, bitcoin's energy consumption is similar to that of domestic tumble dryers (counting OECD member nations, China and India), and is far smaller than that of air conditioning and fans, and domestic refrigeration.[18] This does not mean we should be blasé about crypto's climate impact, though it does provide perspective.

Is crypto really inclusive?

It is often claimed that crypto and DeFi will foster financial inclusion through the provision of a more transparent and accessible financial system, available all day every day with minimal barriers to entry. This inclusion narrative has nuance to it, cutting along gender, ethnicity and geographical lines to name just a few, and through this story DeFi is held up as a bold alternative to a TradFi system that has underserved those without wealth, and driven a wedge between the haves and the have nots. It is a powerful idea, but to what degree has it been truly achieved? We can get a rough idea by looking at some of the biggest claims attached to crypto. These include projections that it will allow cheaper remittances, bank the unbanked, help owners build wealth and democratize finance. There is reason to believe it can do these things, to various extents, but it currently looks like there is a long way to go.

Remittances

To start with remittances, crypto has not yet transformed the market in the manner that had been hoped. A combination of gas fees and costs for on-ramps and off-ramps have so far countered the cost benefits of using blockchain payment rails, and at times of high network traffic, crypto remittances may even be disproportionately expensive. There is genuine potential for blockchain payments to meet this need but no evidence that it has substantially managed to do so. In fact, a much-quoted 2021 estimation suggests that a $200 payment from US dollars in the US to Euros in Europe, via a stablecoin, could cost anything between $5.98–$86.44. The same transaction via Western Union at the time had fees of $4.88.[19] The problem here, generally, is the on- and off-ramps. Remittances are usually paid in cash, and those receiving them will rarely be spending in crypto. As such, there is still a requirement for middlemen and, additionally, the unclear legal regulatory status of stablecoins has been a hurdle. Change could be on the way. There are indications from those in the remittance business that the technology for a cheaper remittance system, on blockchain rails, is more or less ready.[20] As discussed earlier, there are also indications that retailers and merchants are moving to accommodate crypto payments, which would remove a layer of cost and move us closer to a world where crypto remittances are commonplace.

Will crypto bank the unbanked?

Another claim linked to crypto is that it will provide banking services to the 1.4 billion people who are still without them.[21] Given the proliferation of global internet services and smartphone ownership, we might expect most people's first banking experience to be a digital one. This is a trend that could lean towards a decentralized future but as with remittances, we should not jump the gun. The GSMA's State of Mobile Internet Connectivity Report highlights some shortcomings in online adoption, showing that 5 per cent of the global population is without internet access. More tellingly, it found that in 2021 there were 3.2 billion people, 40 per cent of the world's population, facing barriers to online access including a lack of literacy and digital skills, access to relevant content and services, safety and security concerns and affordability (especially in relation to handsets).[22] Digitalization is bound to have an impact on the underbanked and unbanked, but this will clearly not reach all corners overnight.

Analysis needs to focus on the needs of the unbanked, too. Basic needs include a place to safely store money, access services and grow wealth. In terms of safe storage, crypto wallets do offer the potential benefits of self-custody and ostensibly high security. Even so, this requires users to become familiar with an entirely new process, to be capable of self-custody and to trust this new method. Users of any type of wallet will also find that there are costs associated with using their funds. Transaction fees can be unsavoury, asset price volatility (depending on the assets held) may be unwelcome for those needing to reliably pay rents and bills, and for now, notwithstanding the earlier commentary, the range of merchants accepting crypto payments is rather limited in most locations.

As for access to services, commentary on DeFi often presents the ability to engage with protocols, dApps and cryptoassets via smartphone as a harbinger for financial inclusion, and this may mirror trends in TradFi and fintech where banking and investing services can be accessed via apps. There is a further discussion presented by the lack of regulation in crypto. The lack of need for identification and verification may enable people to interact with DeFi in scenarios where TradFi would exclude them, and while this may seem like a fringe position on first inspection, oppressive regimes, wars, systemic biases, difficulties in obtaining documentation and the need for privacy may provide necessary context for it. It can also be said that DeFi democratizes access to all areas, in contrast to TradFi's tendency to offer more nuanced and varied services and opportunities to wealthier clients only.

There are very reasonable points to make around consumer protection and education nonetheless, and abundant benefits from safeguarding users from a system with unverified actors and no right to recourse. At a basic level, DeFi serves a potent cocktail of scams, hacks and poorly formulated projects, keeping headline writers well-occupied. Web3 is Going Just Great, a site tracking such incidents, currently reports a cost to society in excess of $12 billion on its 'Grift Counter'.[23] Democratized access or otherwise, we might also look at some of DeFi's more creative protocols and challenge the wisdom of allowing newcomers to make exotic trades in unregulated markets with evident imbalances of knowledge and wealth.

Wealth building is another issue. On one hand, the meteoric rise of bitcoin, and to a lesser extent Ether, has given hope that previously excluded investors can get a vital foot on the ladder. The problem here, in a scenario where crypto is held in the expectation of investment returns, is that these are risky investments, and this is before we consider running them through DeFi protocols. This isn't a comprehensive argument against investing, nor activities that might generate an income such as yield farming, but we can't assume that speculative cryptoassets will accumulate value in the long run or even be sustainable. There is also the danger that cryptoassets appeal to vulnerable investors. The previous wild upswings in crypto prices will be hard to ignore for people whose ambitions for financial freedom will not be met by steady and gradual annual returns. This points to failures in the traditional system, too.

Another factor is that a lack of credit history often prevents people from accessing banking services, and DeFi negates this by not requiring any. To use a decentralized and public protocol you can be anyone, in theory, and a corresponding thought is that DeFi microloans might enable individuals and small businesses to receive the funding that they need, which TradFi won't provide, to invest in a healthier financial future. It is hard to see how this squares with DeFi's lending processes, however, which are usually collateralized. Collateralized debt is of no use to the many who are unbanked because they are unlikely to meet minimum deposit requirements. The alternative is that DeFi lending services crop up that are willing to take on borrowers with limited or no collateral. The feasibility of sustainably offering such a service, without implementing restrictive terms or interest rates, is low (and even these caveats might not be enough), especially in a crypto market where it would be impractical to chase a borrower who has missed deadlines. To offer a silver lining here, DAOs may eventually take on a role for identifying community lending projects, and as the technology evolves, borrowers may be able to collateralize assets and services other than currency. We also can't rule out improvements or creative (and hopefully reliable) new approaches to credit scoring.

Democratizing finance?

Crypto enthusiasts often talk of its ability to democratize finance and there are signs that it's made some inroads. It is internationally available, has no real cost barrier to entry and has inspired a swathe of new investors. With the possibility of a tokenized future in mind, it can also be said that fractionalization of investments will give people newfound access to assets that were previously exclusive, and this could involve crypto or real-world assets. (Even if the bulk of this activity were to involve real-world assets, we can draw a line from crypto that leads to this eventuality, and in this regard, crypto will have helped deliver new asset classes to the masses.) DeFi has also provided platforms for international marketplaces and competition. If we look at NFTs as an example, there is an opportunity for people from all walks of life to create something unique and sell it conveniently in an online marketplace. There is also the prospect of jobs being created by NFTs, NFT gaming and the metaverse. A word of caution is required here: the NFT market in some locales is a rigged game, with wash trading accounting for a reported 35–58 per cent of transactions, and an easily identifiable wealth gap between projects and buyers.[24, 25] This does not mean that smaller users are all getting scammed, as wash trading is somewhat minimal in some markets and more pronounced in expensive trades, although it does demonstrate that the wealth-creating potential of the NFT market is presently overstated. A handful of smaller projects will no doubt do tremendously well, but this is unlikely indicative of general upward mobility at this moment in time.

The early days of DeFi Gaming spawned some novel activities in relation to wealth distribution, too. Axie Infinity, formerly a dominant force in this market, once hosted a lucrative play-to-earn market where wealthier players more or less loaned out their in-game characters so that other players could play with them and earn revenue. This created an unusual form of employment in which teams of players in the Philippines and Venezuela were playing the game on behalf of 'managers' who were receiving 50–60 per cent cuts of their revenue. This led to some fascinating stories, including one involving a rice feed seller, also a caregiver, tripling his income by playing an hour of Axie Infinity per day.[26] This arrangement offered employment and empowerment to the rice feed seller, though there are many reasons to be uneasy with a system in which players in wealthier nations earn a passive income from the playing time of those in poorer nations, not to mention the lack of meaningful economic activity taking place. Axie Infinity has since shifted from a play-to-earn model to a play-and-earn model.[27]

Claims of inclusion in DeFi and crypto, as we can see, need to be vetted. Genuine inclusion does happen in these markets, but sometimes the inclusion is illusory, other times it benefits a select few but perpetuates an increasingly unequal market, and at other times it is outright predatory. To clarify the third of these possibilities, predatory inclusion involves offering access to goods, services and opportunities to marginalized groups in a manner that destabilizes their long-term prospects. TradFi versions of this might include payday loans or subprime mortgages (which played a role in the 2007–2008 global financial crisis). While the relationship between predatory inclusion and DeFi is young, it could be said that those with crypto riches stand to benefit by bringing people into the system who will never achieve the same. Conversations on inclusion can extend to the culture within crypto companies and online forums, too. Silicon Valley has a chequered reputation for diversity, equity and inclusion, and a number of crypto companies have been the subject of journalistic investigations on this front.

This is not to say that crypto won't or can't foster financial inclusion. There are many bright people, emerging DAOs and well-intentioned projects that intend to do just that, and an array of grassroots and community-based projects that deliver positive outcomes despite not necessarily achieving mainstream attention.

The concentration of crypto ownership

We also need to get an idea of who owns and controls cryptoassets and DeFi. An initial observation is that ownership and mining are concentrated in the hands of relatively few accounts. To start with Ethereum, an early 2022 Morgan Stanley note claimed that the top 100 addresses held 39 per cent of Ether, and blockchain analytics platform Nansen found that 64 per cent of staked Ether was controlled by only five entities.[28, 29] As for mining, it has been suggested that 0.5 per cent of individual miners in Ethereum's old proof-of-work system received 30–50 per cent of the rewards, and within hours of the move to PoS, it was identified that two addresses, one belonging to decentralized staking solution Lido and the other to centralized exchange Coinbase, had built over 40 per cent of Ethereum blocks.[30] This latter finding doesn't undeniably prove concentration of ownership but certainly hints at it.

To look at crypto's most valuable coin, bitcoin has been found to possess similar ownership traits. A study from Igor Makarov (London

School of Economics) and Antoinette Schoar (MIT Sloan) is illustrative here, showing that in January 2021, 0.014 per cent of bitcoin owners held 26 per cent of all bitcoin wealth.[31] This may sound exaggerated but the study takes several clear steps to offer a conservative estimate while accounting for addresses owned by exchanges. It even counts the earliest minted bitcoins, held in 20,000 addresses, as being individually owned in spite of widely held suspicions that they all belong to Satoshi. (The study also finds that 90 per cent of bitcoin mining is undertaken by only 10 per cent of miners, and that 0.1 per cent of miners control half of the total capacity, though we should observe that 60–80 per cent of mining capacity was located in China according to Makarov and Schoar, and this is surely no longer the case since the introduction of China's mining ban.) If there is any mitigating factor here, it might be that a large number of small and mostly dormant accounts inflate user numbers and amplify the appearance of wealth concentration. We also have no idea of knowing what the off-chain wealth of market participants might look like.

Crypto wealth and control are concentrated it seems. While there has been a great influx of owners, corresponding with spikes in the price of bitcoin, it does not change the fact that not all crypto owners are equal.[32] Those who got in at the ground floor and stayed in have enjoyed outsized benefits compared to anyone who wants in on the action now. Who were the early adopters? A comprehensive analysis isn't really possible but we can be confident that they were mostly men. The link is not conclusive, but any 'rich list' for crypto will generally contain few if any women, and there does not appear to be a single female crypto billionaire. (And here, I acknowledge the uneasy link between inclusion and billionaires.) Looking beyond the super-rich, in November 2013, a year-and-a-half after its launch, Coinbase reported that 87.5 per cent of its users were men.[33] To make one more point on the gender divide in crypto, of the 121 publicly listed crypto businesses in 2021, only five had female founders and each of these five entrepreneurs had launched their business with at least one male co-founder.[34] Besides gender, there are many other demographic splits that can surely be observed in relation to crypto ownership and concentration.

From this limited analysis, we can see that crypto and DeFi have so far been hindered as inclusion gateways for underrepresented or marginalized groups, which again is not to say that decentralization doesn't or won't provide opportunities. This analysis of wealth concentration is also very broad and centred on the two largest blockchains in crypto.

MANAGING HOPES AND EXPECTATIONS

The DeFi and crypto communities are not oblivious to the imperfections mentioned here. Ines Illipse, host of the Cryptophobia podcast and member of the Bankless DAO community, says:

> 'Blockchain today is full of scams and there's so much noise and hype to filter through to understand what's going on. I worry that the high barriers to entry into the web3 space in its infancy might lead to the space evolving to benefit a specific group of people, just like our financial system does today. I'm basically afraid that we will have the problems we have in our system today but at a higher and more complex level.'

Nonetheless, Illipse has seen firsthand how blockchain can be beneficial to society, especially while working on a recent research project with ChromaWay, a leading Swedish blockchain company. The research centred on blockchain use cases for social entrepreneurs and NGOs. She adds:

> 'I learned so much during the project about actual use cases of blockchain technology that also have a positive impact on the world. For example, the role of blockchain in crisis management. I was amazed that Syrian refugees can purchase food using aid provided by the World Food Program by scanning the iris of their eyes at checkout. This program is built on the blockchain combined with pre-existing biometrics technology used by the UNHCR.' (United Nations High Commissioner for Refugees)

Is it even decentralized?

The answer to the above question might be mostly, faintly or not at all, depending on the protocol being analysed. As discussed earlier, decentralization is best understood as a North Star for DeFi rather than an endpoint. While coins, protocols and projects sit on different ends of the decentralization spectrum, the idea of fully decentralized finance is a long way off if it can even be achieved. We might witness centralization in various forms due to the use and need for leadership teams, key developers, mining pools, exchanges, network infrastructure, hardware and software. In many cases, there will be an individual or small group of people who are able to terminate or halt actions on a blockchain. Concentration of ownership may also impact validation methods and give individual players the power to influence markets at will. Likewise, a concentration of ownership within certain geographies could be identified as a weakness; there is a risk of adverse effects if internet access is shut off due to a natural disaster, or perhaps even a crypto ban.

The presence of centralization is not necessarily damning. Those using CeFi to store or make transactions with cryptoassets would be naive to think that transactions are fully decentralized, especially as regulation expands. There are many who are using these services, and likewise many working in crypto, who instead welcome the appearance of regulatory oversight, governance standards and consumer protection. As for DeFi, there are abundant benefits to retaining an element of centralization when a protocol is new. These benefits are largely practical, such as the ability to make changes to code and for developers to action relevant strategies quickly, rather than wait for the outcomes of DAO votes. It is also typical for DeFi protocols to retain an element of centralization as they grow. Open sourcing and community governance can empower a protocol but there are instances where centralized intervention, or at least thought leadership, will be preferable. A legal incident could even force such an action.

So casting the ideological purity aside, it is more appropriate to say that DeFi is making finance more decentralized rather than entirely so. Even if its execution is imperfect, DeFi offers an alternative to centralized ownership and governance and can operate in a very different manner to TradFi. A senior decision-maker in a DAO, for example, will be in place to enact the will of voters rather than to dictate decisions from the top down. There will be instances where a protocol's lack of decentralization muddies this ideal, but the ethos of DeFi can often be enforced without perfect community control.

This does bring a final issue to the table, which is democracy as a means of governing financial systems. While DAO failures were explored earlier, especially in relation to centralization, we might also reasonably ask if a fair voting system with equally weighted votes is what finance has always needed. The early days of DeFi were populated with protocol enthusiasts who favour the democratic system, but might this change if user bases grow and attract members who are disengaged with governance? Or even engaged with governance but misaligned with the original philosophy of the DAO? As touched upon previously, voters will also be exposed to outside influences and may even be incentivized to vote certain ways. Democracy sounds like the fairest way to operate. That does not mean that it's the most efficient for finance nor its best mode of governance.

Towards a better future

What has been the point of all of this? DeFi isn't fully decentralized, DAOs aren't necessarily democratic, crypto has a wealth inequality problem and is bad for the planet, and the sector has an absolute Grand Canyon of a gender gap. This is before we mention the rugpulls, scams and frauds that have lifted billions from investors. Shall we pack it up and go home? What if we don't? As stated earlier, the technology is not to blame for how it is used, nor should we expect an entirely new global financial system to be fully and smoothly operational within 15 years of the whitepaper that inspired it. There could be greater things to come – new coins, new communities, new validation methods and new visions.

There is also good reason to step back from the metanarrative that DeFi and crypto will run the world. Regardless of the insinuations of its earliest visionaries, DeFi now represents many different things for many different people. This notion also holds DeFi to a level of adoption and financial revolution that its ecosystem, and society at large, is not ready to accommodate. But can it change the world? That seems more realistic, and in many ways it already has. There are plenty of positives that can already be celebrated. To view DeFi as a sandbox of financial experimentation within a new paradigm for finance, it has introduced technology that can, at least to some extent, disintermediate and automate processes and remove paperwork, going some way towards its founding ambitions. Decentralization has also inspired new forms of governance, and it has promoted tokenization, both in a unique sense through NFTs and in a fungible manner through fractionalized investment. DeFi has already been a tremendous catalyst for financial services modernization and if it continues to flourish it will achieve much more.

Financial and technological innovation aside, we can also view DeFi as a tool for alleviating TradFi's socioeconomic shortcomings or creating more inclusive platforms for the underrepresented. Cleve Mesidor, a former presidential appointee for Barack Obama, and now executive director of the Blockchain Foundation, explains that this was exactly her intention:

'I think a lot of the earliest folks who came into crypto came to solve a problem that they saw within society and I'm no different.'

And the reason why?

'For at least 95 per cent of people, money never works for you. That's why I went into public policy and that's why I was attracted to crypto. How do you change society?

Traditional finance never worked for me specifically. I'm a Gen Xer, I have a master's degree, I make good money, I'm a reputable professional, but I'm the customer the bank would give the subprime loan to. Wealth managers are not interested in my money. So traditional finance has always been biased against the value that I bring to the table. I, like many, have had to look outside of traditional finance.

I believe we can change the world. I think we have new tools. What we have now is people saying, "technology doesn't change things, people do. Government doesn't change things, people do." So policy and innovation have to be tools that we get into the hands of people to solve their own problems, and decentralization is the only way to effectively do that.'

There is a strong empowerment narrative here with technology and community at its heart. Mesidor is not the only person who feels this way, and we can see this 'let's do things differently' initiative in groups such as the DADA Collective, a web3 group that takes its name from the early twentieth-century anti-bourgeois artistic movement of Dadaism.[35] The female founders of this collective, Beatriz Ramos and Judy Mam, have stated an intention to stand in contrast to the 'winners and losers' model that they perceive in the traditional art market, and to subvert the power structures that exist presently in the creator economy. The DADA digital platform has made use of blockchain since 2017, building royalties into Ethereum smart contracts, and its ecosystem now has over 175,000 participants, has curated a portfolio with more than 115,000 works and presents an example of how DeFi can encourage equitable practices within the creator economy.

The desire to create something better was also a motivation for Tavonia Evans, a software engineer who felt excluded by the financial system when she was unable to raise capital for a startup business in 2014. Three years on, Evans launched Guapcoin, a cryptocurrency aimed at creating economic opportunities for the African diaspora. Beyond the coin, Guapcoin intends to, and already does, work with merchants who accept it as payment. The long-term goal is for Guapcoin and its community to support and invest more heavily in business and community projects. Evans says:

'My case with Guapcoin is that it's to be used as money. In America, we always talk about the black dollar, which is this fictional thing that symbolizes our spending. But a problem that has not been solved [is that] the wealth gap has just been growing. So my thoughts were "how can we solve this problem? Why can't we just invest the social capital that we have, which I know we have large reserves of, into our black dollar?"'

We can see a departure from DeFi's libertarianism here, and unsurprisingly Evans offers a different perspective on how to utilize this

new form of finance. She explains that community projects and finan-
cialized DAOs will benefit from a persisting element of centralization:

> 'Decentralization is fine for people who've already had power. But for
> people who haven't, to disrupt the power they haven't had could be
> really tragic, because they're on a journey to reclaim it.'

This thought process also takes us away from the idea of a single
overarching solution, towards an ecosystem with space for a multi-
tude of interconnected communities.

> 'When you're targeting a certain community, you have a whole different
> set of needs… You can't just take one brush and paint it across and
> be like "this is the solution that's going to help everybody", because
> it's not. The issue of empowerment is not just a financial issue, it's a
> psychological issue.'

So here, just like corporations and governments are exploring crypto,
NFTs and CBDCs to explore their goals, we see how DeFi's technologies can be reconfigured to achieve different ambitions. This entire
market is nascent, and again it needs to be said that there is no significant evidence that DeFi has done much to fix the socio-economic
shortcomings of TradFi. Even so, for as long as financial systems are
exclusionary, there will surely be an appetite for alternatives and the
work is just beginning.

Can regulation help crypto?

If carried out effectively, the regulation of CeFi will vastly reduce
fraudulent crypto activities, offer consumer protections, and make the
providers and users of cryptoassets and services more accountable for
their actions (regulators appear hesitant to act on DeFi, and MiCA
introduces no rules for it). When regulation is formalized, as MiCA in
the EU is likely to demonstrate, it should also encourage the provision
of banking services for crypto businesses and offer much-needed legal

clarity for all involved. This, in turn, will be welcoming for institutional investors. It will no doubt assuage the concerns of many retail investors, too; centralized exchanges have to date proven far more popular than DEXs with everyday consumers, with Binance alone holding $64 billion in client money relative to an entire DeFi market of $50 billion.[36] With regulatory protections, these retail consumers can now make transactions with their cryptoassets with more confidence and faith in the system. It is hoped that this regulatory framework will minimize the impact of, or better yet prevent, another FTX, Terra Luna, Three Arrows Capital, and so on.

Regulation will also seek to bolster the general safety of crypto markets. MiCA enforces stringent measures against manipulating markets, and in relation to this, those making transfers in excess of €1,000, even from self-hosted wallets, will now be subject to the travel rule. The travel rule will give crypto firms the ability to trace, and potentially block, any suspicious activity, and reduces the likelihood of registered entities being used to launder money or fund terrorism. Early indications are that those in CeFi are welcoming of the upcoming MiCA implementation, and some believe other regimes will follow suit, especially if crypto businesses, unsure of their legal position in their current location, head to Europe in search of certainty.

This offers a promising start for CeFi, and further regulation and iterations of MiCA seem inevitable. And yet there is an itch to scratch, as unregulated DeFi protocols can still thrive, and these protocols may use the exact same assets that flow through CeFi. This poses a contagion risk, but how do you regulate DeFi in situations where leaders can't be identified? Can it even be done, and should it be done? Who is liable if things go wrong, who is responsible for an open-source protocol, and how do we identify pseudonymous entities and in particular those using privacy coins? If users eventually flock to CeFi in their droves this issue may take care of itself, largely. If they don't, this could be a regulatory headache.

Given DeFi's roots, anti-regulatory stances might be considered, too. Some believe that MiCA will hinder the ability of DeFi to create new solutions. In this regard, MiCA requires any new asset issuance to be accompanied by a whitepaper to inform potential holders of the attributes of the asset, but seeing as there is no requirement for this documentation to be approved by an authorizing body, this might not be particularly stifling. A weightier drawback for innovation, one might expect, is that those operating under regulation will be less brazen in getting new code and projects to market. A lot of people have been burned by the Wild West Wall Street, but in harbouring new ideas, be they good, bad or ugly, it has been a potent force. There are some who feel that crypto should be left to self-regulate, on the terms that the market will decide which aspects of DeFi win out.

Between legality and morality

Regulation seems inevitable and generally popular. Nonetheless, there are times when DeFi has served as a lifeline for people who have been failed by regulations and legal systems. This aspect of DeFi will be more valuable to someone who doesn't, or can't, trust the authorities and institutions they might otherwise be expected to depend upon. There are big questions we can ask. Where do we turn when legality and morality are at odds? What do we do when political, regulatory or bureaucratic processes prevent us from carrying out actions made in good faith?

We can apply this to extreme but very real scenarios, like the earthquakes that hit Turkey and Syria in 2023, killing 50,000 and injuring another 100,000. $12.5 million of aid in cryptocurrency was sent via fundraisers, crypto exchanges and figureheads, as Turkey temporarily lifted its restrictions on the use of crypto for payments, and global charities such as Save the Children advertised their ability to accept crypto donations. The use of blockchain here built transparency and speed into the donations, giving donors confidence that their funds ended up in the right hands.[37] It also prompted the possibility of getting money directly to those who need it, which is promising as senders may have little or no say in how aid is used when donations are made through traditional channels.[38] However, the viability or lack thereof of spending crypto, especially in a crisis, should not be overlooked.

There are also instances where it may be crucial to have custody of an asset with enduring international value. On this topic, Roya Mahboob, co-founder of the Digital Citizen Fund in Afghanistan, created upsides beyond investment returns when she decided to pay staff and freelancers in bitcoin from the early 2010s. This payment method initially had utility as cash payments were neither feasible nor safe, and most girls and women were either not allowed to open a bank account or lacked the required documentation to do so. Following the Taliban's capture of Kabul in 2021, several of the women to have opened crypto wallets, including those who had been taught how to do so at the Digital Citizen Fund's learning centres, were able to use their cryptoassets as they fled the country, helping their families to evacuate and start life elsewhere.[39]

The war in Ukraine offers a final example. By March 2023, over $210 million of cryptocurrency had been donated to fund the Ukrainian relief and resistance, of which $60–65 million had been raised by a crypto fund led by Michael Chobanian, president of the Blockchain Association of Ukraine and founder of Kuna Exchange. Chobanian believes that crypto offers a more efficient alternative to fiat currency, which he says takes at least three days if Swift and the Ukranian banking system is involved. In fact, he is highly critical of the entire financial system in Ukraine, and its limited stock market, high inflation and insufficient pension provision (including private options). Here, he tells the story of how crypto enabled him to quickly mobilize funding for the resistance:

'The war started at 5am. I was online non-stop until 3pm, and I was looking at how the situation was unveiling. It was obvious to me that a lot of people require help evacuating. A lot of military personnel were asking for help saying; "Listen, we don't have anything apart from old AK-47s back from the 50s and 60s".

It was clear to me that we needed to organize help and do it fast. The fastest way is crypto, because receiving fiat in the highly regulated world is virtually impossible to set up in minutes. We launched the fund as an infrastructure provider more than an exchange. And, yeah, it took us a couple of minutes and with a few clicks we created the page for the crypto fund, and we started collecting money and immediately spending it. The most important thing is not actually collecting money. It was to spend it immediately.

The reason was obvious. The soldiers were standing on the front line without helmets, without bulletproof vests, without any food rations for the next couple of days, without anything to be honest apart from the AKs. And our role was also to get humanitarian aid in as quickly as possible. And with crypto you can do it in, well – it depends on the blockchain. So bitcoin is 30 minutes, with Ether, it's a minute, with Tron, it's even less.

So people were buying petrol. The soldiers that were verified were texting us, "please can we buy some petrol because we don't have any in our tanks or in our SUVs". So they're standing at the petrol stations: "could you send us some money so we can fill up and go on the front line?"

We were selling crypto, converting to local currency, to Ukrainian hryvnia, and immediately sending that money to the parts and people who could top up and continue doing whatever they were supposed to do. And the same for the volunteers. People had for example a bus or minivan, they were evacuating people from places like Mariupol. We were sending hryvnia to them, we were buying food in Mariupol. We could do it within minutes. Not hours, not days.'

As these scenarios make clear, the existence of a currency that operates independently of financial institutions and governments will not always be a bad thing. If strict regulation is brought in globally, then relief efforts like this could be diminished. It's true also that crypto does not take sides. As sanctions kick in against Russia, it has been suggested that it will use cryptoassets to evade them, and several Russian entities have been identified as trying to do exactly that.[40] Nothing in crypto or DeFi is ever straightforward.

References

1 Buttonwood. The complicated politics of crypto and web3, The Economist, 2022, www.economist.com/finance-and-economics/2022/04/16/the-complicated-politics-of-crypto-and-web3 (archived at https://perma.cc/9NFD-NLQW)

2 P Ryan. Left, right and center: crypto isn't just for libertarians anymore, CoinDesk, 2018, www.coindesk.com/markets/2018/07/27/left-right-and-center-crypto-isnt-just-for-libertarians-anymore/ (archived at https://perma.cc/BN4Y-FHUH)

3 Digiconomist. Bitcoin Energy Consumption Index, Digiconomist, 2023, digiconomist.net/bitcoin-energy-consumption (archived at https://perma.cc/92L9-5GRT)

4 Digiconomist. Ethereum Energy Consumption Index (beta), Digiconomist, 2023, digiconomist.net/ethereum-energy-consumption (archived at https://perma.cc/8ACQ-4BGF).

5 CCRI. CCRI Crypto Sustainability Indices, 2023, indices.carbon-ratings.com/ (archived at https://perma.cc/AX68-VE6W)

6 C Mulligan and E Cheikosman. World Economic Forum – Guidelines for improving blockchain's environmental, social and economic impact: insight report, World Economic Forum, April 2023, https://www3.weforum.org/docs/WEF_Guidelines_for_Improving_Blockchain%E2%80%99s_Environmental_Social_and_Economic_Impact_2023.pdf (archived at https://perma.cc/J5P3-LH6Y)

7 Bitcoin Mining Council. Welcome to the Bitcoin Mining Council, Bitcoin Mining Council, 2023, bitcoinminingcouncil.com/ (archived at https://perma.cc/RFG2-5CF9)

8 Energy Web. Case Study – 24/7 track and match, Energy Web, 2023, www.energyweb.org/case-study-24-7-track-and-match/ (archived at https://perma.cc/XY78-6TSN)

9 Energy Web. Case studies – green proofs, Energy Web, 2023, www.energyweb.org/case-studies-green-proofs/ (archived at https://perma.cc/LX6C-DH2M)

10 CoinShares. The bitcoin mining network: energy and carbon impact, 2022, coinshares.com/research/bitcoin-mining-network-2022 (archived at https://perma.cc/E5A5-83ZU)

11 Electricity Maps Live. 24/7 CO_2 emissions of electricity consumption, 2023, app.electricitymaps.com/map (archived at https://perma.cc/2N9Y-QR3E)

12 16 L Schwartz. These are the top U.S. states for Bitcoin mining, according to an Ivy League study, Fortune, 2022, fortune.com/crypto/2022/09/26/top-u-s-states-bitcoin-mining/ (archived at https://perma.cc/95FE-4ACN)

13 IEA. Renewables, IEA, 2023, www.iea.org/fuels-and-technologies/renewables (archived at https://perma.cc/3Q27-STN5)

14 A Asher-Schapiro. UPDATE 1-INSIGHT-Coal to crypto: The gold rush bringing bitcoin miners to Kentucky, Reuters, 2022, https://www.reuters.com/article/usa-bitcoin-environment-idUKL5N2VO4WT (archived at https://perma.cc/3YFP-P3YR)

15 O Milman. Bitcoin miners revived a dying coal plant – then CO_2 emissions soared, *The Guardian*, 2022, www.theguardian.com/technology/2022/feb/18/bitcoin-miners-revive-fossil-fuel-plant-co2-emissions-soared (archived at https://perma.cc/X394-KVEC).

17 Finansinspektionen. Crypto-assets are a threat to the climate transition – energy-intensive mining should be banned, Finansinspektionen, 2021, www.fi.se/en/published/presentations/2021/crypto-assets-are-a-threat-to-the-climate-transition--energy-intensive-mining-should-be-banned/ (archived at https://perma.cc/LV28-S3XG)

18 R Stevens and N Carter. Bitcoin net zero, NYDIG, 2021, nydig.com/bitcoin-net-zero (archived at https://perma.cc/Y4PW-26GP)

19 Full Committee Hearing. Stablecoins: How do they work, how are they used, and what are their risks?, United States Senate Committee on banking, housing, and urban affairs, 2021, https://www.banking.senate.gov/hearings/stablecoins-how-do-they-work-how-are-they-used-and-what-are-their-risks (archived at https://perma.cc/H7LJ-3XCR)

20 A Navarro and M Reyes. A Mexican crypto startup wants to make cash remittances cheaper, Bloomberg, 30 November 2021, www.bloomberg.com/news/articles/2021-11-30/crypto-news-bitso-helps-turn-dollars-into-pesos-with-bitcoin (archived at https://perma.cc/5QCA-UL5X)

21 The World Bank. COVID-19 boosted the adoption of digital financial services, The World Bank, 2022, www.worldbank.org/en/news/feature/2022/07/21/covid-19-boosted-the-adoption-of-digital-financial-services (archived at https://perma.cc/S6NM-7DHV)

22 GSMA. The State of Mobile Internet Connectivity Report 2022 – Mobile for Development, 2022, GSMA, www.gsma.com/r/somic/ (archived at https://perma.cc/LC5B-TWYW)

23 M White. Web3 is going just great, 2023, web3isgoinggreat.com/ (archived at https://perma.cc/ZR3P-J83Z)

24 NFTGo. NFT Annual Report 2023, NFTGo.io, 2023, nftgo.io/research/reports/2023-nft-annual-report (archived at https://perma.cc/4RYS-DLY6)

25 hildobby. NFT wash trading on Ethereum, Dune, 2022, community.dune.com/blog/nft-wash-trading-on-ethereum (archived at https://perma.cc/9BKC-K75A)

26 V Elliott. Workers in the Global South are making a living playing the blockchain game Axie Infinity, Rest of World, 2021, restofworld.org/2021/axie-infinity/ (archived at https://perma.cc/2U4P-VTDA)

27   E Nicolle. Axie Infinity to be 'even more aggressive' with crypto after hard
     year, Bloomberg, 25 February 2023, www.bloomberg.com/news/articles/
     2023-02-25/axie-infinity-axs-to-be-even-more-aggressive-with-crypto-
     after-hard-year (archived at https://perma.cc/VW42-2LQQ)

28   W Canny. Morgan Stanley says Ethereum less decentralized, Ether more
     volatile compared to Bitcoin, Yahoo Finance, 2022, finance.yahoo.com/news/
     morgan-stanley-says-ethereum-less-113816777.html (archived at https://
     perma.cc/K4NK-X2AQ)

29   G Jenkinson. 64% of staked ETH controlled by 5 entities — Nansen,
     Cointelegraph, 2022, https://cointelegraph.com/news/64-of-staked-eth-
     controlled-by-five-entities-nansen (archived at https://perma.cc/T6DA-54DJ)

30   AP Pereira. 40%+ of Ethereum PoS nodes are controlled by 2 addresses, says
     Santiment data, Cointelegraph, 2022, cointelegraph.com/news/40-ethereum-
     pos-nodes-are-controlled-by-two-addresses-says-santiment-data (archived at
     https://perma.cc/5XDD-MLH4)

31   I Makarov and A Schoar. Blockchain analysis of the Bitcoin market, Social
     Science Research Network, 2021, doi: doi.org/10.2139/ssrn.3942181
     (archived at https://perma.cc/T99E-6WGV)

32   C Wheat and G Eckerd. The dynamics and demographics of U.S. household
     crypto-asset use, JPMorgan Chase & Co., 2022, www.jpmorganchase.com/
     institute/research/financial-markets/dynamics-demographics-us-household-
     crypto-asset-cryptocurrency-use (archived at https://perma.cc/HN3Y-DJZ3)

33   N Hajdarbegovic. Coinbase passes 650,000 users in less than a year,
     CoinDesk, 2013, www.coindesk.com/markets/2013/12/19/coinbase-passes-
     650000-users-in-less-than-a-year/ (archived at https://perma.cc/99ZV-9B58)

34   Crypto Head. The Cryptocurrency Company Index, Crypto Head, 2023,
     cryptohead.io/research/cryptocurrency-company-index/?msID=5717aa95-
     8a58-4454-9210-9f72fa4cd4a0 (archived at https://perma.cc/V3UN-EKLZ)

35   C Mesidor. Crypto artists share how Web3 tools enable diverse art market
     experiments, Forbes, 2023, www.forbes.com/sites/digital-assets/2023/05/01/
     crypto-artists-share-how-web3-tools-enable-diverse-art-market-
     experiments/?sh=42872b9864b0 (archived at https://perma.cc/2UER-B7G5)

36   S D Young. Binance's on-chain balance stands at $64B, Nansen data shows,
     Binance, 2023, www.binance.com/en/news/flash/7478050 (archived at https://
     perma.cc/9A7K-AQ59)

37   Elliptic Connect. Turkey and Syria earthquakes: crypto exchanges and donors
     raise $12.5 million in aid, Elliptic, 2023, hub.elliptic.co/analysis/turkey-and-
     syria-earthquakes-crypto-exchanges-and-donors-raise-12-5-million-in-aid/
     (archived at https://perma.cc/8U7Q-CMYY)

38 E Cheikosman. How blockchain-driven humanitarianism can help people, World Economic Forum, 2023, www.weforum.org/agenda/2023/03/blockchain-driven-humanitarianism/ (archived at https://perma.cc/AK6H-86WV)

39 R Chandran. FEATURE-Salaries to remittances: Afghans embrace crypto amid financial chaos, Reuters, 11 October 2021, www.reuters.com/article/crypto-currency-afghanistan-idUSL8N2QU39A (archived at https://perma.cc/8UH2-WGGR)

40 U.S. Department of the Treasury. U.S. Treasury designates facilitators of Russian sanctions evasion, 20 April 2022, home.treasury.gov/news/press-releases/jy0731 (archived at https://perma.cc/9L23-94ZE)

11

Why does DeFi matter? Concluding thoughts

Has any financial disruption created as much noise and hype as crypto? If it has, I'm happy to be corrected, but I can think of nothing quite so polarizing and attention-grabbing in modern finance. It has provided a clash of cultures, vibrant imagery and novel discussions of what our financial lives and institutions should look like. It's easy to look at the worst excesses and write it off as a passing fad or a Trojan horse for illegal activity, but there is something much, much deeper going on. It is perhaps reductive to weave every aspect of this into one narrative, so instead I'd like to conclude with a series of observations. Here goes.

DeFi and crypto have transformed money

A large and increasing share of global money today is digital. It is data, not banknotes and coins, and it is held on centralized and private ledgers (think databases and Excel). Crypto matters because people figured out that you can create new digital currencies (crypto), and that you can manage these currencies on a public and shareable database (distributed ledger technology, usually blockchain) without the involvement of any centralized financial intermediary like a central bank. DeFi matters because people demonstrated that this new digital money can be programmed to do things that regular digital money can't do, and that entire financial ecosystems can be built around it. If we cast aside issues of legality for a second, this delivers a software update to money itself. It allows money to undergo processes that once required an intermediary and adds versatility to how we exchange value on a peer-to-peer basis. I'll leave it to you to decide if it makes money better, but it certainly makes money more capable. It tokenizes it, essentially.

This alone would be plenty but it's not all. Fungibility, the sort of word you'd play in a game of Scrabble in the hope that it's real, has taken centre stage as it allows us to tokenize unique items. If we can tokenize forms of money, and also tokenize asset ownership within the same database (or a connected one), we now have a platform that could facilitate the immediate and accurate exchange of most things. If you then acknowledge the ability to fractionalize assets, or to programme them to pay royalties to original creators, and more, you open the door to a world where money takes new forms and extends its reach by magnitudes. This allows us to be very creative with what we financialize and how we financialize it, and its implications for individual and shared ownership are considerable.

Implications for traditional finance

Satoshi's Bitcoin whitepaper, and the subsequent flow of trillions of dollars into crypto, should be considered a shot across the bows of TradFi. A society conducting peer-to-peer transactions and programming its own financial functions may eventually decide that its need for financial services providers is greatly reduced. There are four things I would say in response to this.

The first is that TradFi is not sitting on its hands and waiting to be disintermediated. It is instead, in various ways, getting skin in the game by investing directly and indirectly in cryptoassets, DeFi infrastructure and the companies that are trying to bring crypto to the masses. Financial institutions are also utilizing the opportunities provided by blockchains and smart contracts to improve their efficiencies and offer new and better services for their customers, and in this respect a development like the tokenization of assets could be fantastic news for many intermediaries, especially where the trade of real-world assets is made simpler. These strategic decisions all appear to bolster the longevity of TradFi. Let's also remember that transactions involving real-world assets need to be settled once tokens have been traded, and this will help maintain a role for intermediaries and off-chain operations.

Secondly, I would observe the practical barriers to mainstream crypto adoption. While the crypto market has inspired many people to buy in, typically using a centralized exchange, many if not most of these people have bought cryptoassets, usually bitcoin, as a store of value or a speculative investment. It is a huge jump to go from buying a singular asset, usually in the hope of eventually claiming a fiat currency reward, to interacting with a decentralized and bankless environment as the focal point of your personal finances. Most people are not familiar with these tools either, and they are unlikely to agree with DeFi maximalists on how important the protocols are. For those willing to take a look at the universe of cryptoassets, the interfaces of decentralized protocols often leave a lot to be desired, and while we can expect improvements, this is, for now, a deterrent.

Financial education is relevant here, too. While trends are pointing towards greater adoption of financial apps and investment products, many will prefer to invest or access services via an intermediary, or they will at least want their app to have the backing of a reputable and regulated name. As DeFi is new, these names will usually belong to TradFi institutions. There are also moments where, due to complexity or a desire for convenience, intermediaries will be preferred, as people don't necessarily want custody of their own assets, for example. So long as people trust TradFi institutions and believe that its services add value, we can expect it to remain dominant.

A third point is that TradFi and the current capitalist mode of finance are very effective. Despite its ills, centralization and modern finance can be considered alongside the stupendous growth in world GDP that has occurred since its emergence. World GDP, adjusted for inflation, is believed to have been $430 billion in 1500, $1.2 trillion in 1820, and now, roughly 200 years on, sits above $100 trillion.[1]

There have been occasions where DeFi's failures have highlighted the relative strengths of centralized ownership and governance. There are competing histories on modern capitalism, and far more nuance to this stream of thought, but ultimately it requires seismic activity to reshape social expectations of finance in favour of DeFi and web3. In many nations, the roots of traditional finance are deeply and culturally embedded.

The fourth and final thing to raise in its own right is regulation. TradFi sits on the right side of regulation, and this enhances user confidence and builds confidence in the longevity of institutions. The mixed regulatory response to crypto and DeFi, however, will be off-putting to many would-be users, and will stifle its growth in many regions. Even in nations where clearer regimes are brought in, there may be long-term concerns around the continuing use of non-sovereign currencies, and there may be limits to the amount of growth that regimes are genuinely willing to foster.

So while the existence of a decentralized economy offers a challenge to TradFi, I believe these four factors, presently, uphold the status quo.

The importance of economic sovereignty

The rise of crypto and DeFi have also produced unexpected discussions around economic sovereignty. What might the impact be of a cryptocurrency, or a handful of them, that displaces central bank currencies? The likelihood of this seems slim, and yet the prospect of it, among other things, has spurred central banks and governments into action. Not all nations and regions have taken the same approach. China has clamped down hard on crypto, while El Salvador now accepts bitcoin as legal tender. The US is making tentative steps towards regulation, and Europe has approved a regulatory framework. Meanwhile, several nations are attempting to make themselves appealing to crypto operators through clear and accommodating tax and legal regimes.

To look at the question of economic sovereignty, it currently seems unlikely that crypto will displace major currencies. While many nations have been accommodating or ambivalent towards cryptoassets, expect a mood shift if the popularity of crypto weakens domestic currencies or the ability of central banks to influence economies. This is not simply about power. Central banks carry out a number of activities designed to maintain the health of national economies, like controlling the money supply, setting and influencing interest rates, and taking measures to promote financial stability and jobs markets. They may even step in as the lender of last resort at times of crisis. Most governments will not want their central banks to lose these intervening powers, especially as they can be used to manage economies around domestic interests. We might note that nations with low economic sovereignty are more at risk of losing economic sovereignty to a digital currency. But nonetheless, the conditions required for 'crypto takes over the world' are extreme.

Now that money does more, however, CBDCs might be the vessel through which DeFi innovations are delivered to the masses. There are clear benefits to upgrading the capabilities of central bank money, and yet the perceived threat to individual liberty and privacy will be discouraging for governments looking to implement them. This isn't a straightforward issue. There's an extent to which anyone with a bank account, or anyone using digital transactions within the current financial system, has already compromised their privacy. The same could even be said of anyone using a smartphone. Governments who wish to introduce CBDCs may do their utmost to address these concerns, and yet there will likely be a lingering doubt that digital currency might be updated to introduce intrusive features. There are widespread concerns, for instance, about the prospect of government-led money that ties people's freedoms, spending power and options to a social credit score or something else of a suitably dystopian nature. The reality is that permanent surveillance is a violation of liberty.

There are several uncertainties to untangle from here. We might ask if CBDCs will smooth international trade to the point where economies that lack one lose influence. It's also reasonable to ask if programmable currency is a step in the right direction. This issue is ethical and social as much as it is technological.

Widening and persisting inequalities in wealth and access

This book began by charting the rise of Bitcoin in tandem with a global financial crisis. It's only right to observe, admittedly at a very surface level, what's been happening in global economies since then. On one hand, let's be clear, most users of TradFi have generally encountered a far smoother ride than those in DeFi. Even so, given that the focus here is on the enduring appeal of DeFi, let's look at the persisting sentiment, especially within developed Western economies, that the financial system has fundamental flaws.

Seeing as the concentration of crypto wealth was noted in Chapter 10, it's reasonable to point out similar developments in the economy at large. An immediate starting point would be to observe the acceleration in wealth inequality that occurred during the Covid-19 pandemic. Oxfam research finds that the world's 10 richest men doubled their wealth during this time, at a rate of $1.3 billion per day, while 99 per cent of the global population suffered a reduction in income. These 10 men, as of October 2021, have six times more wealth than the poorest 3.1 billion people, and if they lost 99.999 per cent of their combined wealth, they would still be in the top 1 per cent of the world's richest.[2] It has also been found that the richest 10 per cent in the world own 76 per cent of the wealth, and that CEO pay soared by 1,460 per cent from 1978, meaning that in 2021, CEOs earned 399 times as much as a typical worker.[3,4] Wealth inequality will, of course, take on different levels and traits depending on where people are based. There are hints, however, that globalization may be reshaping the order of things. To that end, note that the income gap between the richest 10 per cent of countries and the poorest 50 per cent dropped from roughly 50× to a little below 40×. This is still massive, but consider also that the average income gap between the top 10 per cent and bottom 50 per cent of individuals within nations has gone from 8.5× to 15×. Should this path continue, though we should not assume that it will, it would blur historical international inequalities and deliver something more akin to a divide between the global rich and the global poor. With gender inequality being a concern in crypto, consider also that women's overall share of global income was recorded as slightly beneath 35 per cent in the World Inequality Report 2022.[5]

These numbers and percentages reflect general economic trends, some of which have a connection to cultural or historic imbalances of economic opportunity. They don't quite encapsulate lived experiences nor speak to the exclusion that people have felt in relation to the economic system. For a glimpse of this, look to the US, where startup businesses with all-women teams received 1.9 per cent of all venture capital funding in 2022.[6] Mixed-gender teams received 17.2 per cent of the funding, and these trends have been consistent for over a decade. It has also been shown that black founders received about 1 per cent of US venture capital funding (relative to 13.6 per cent of the population) in 2022.[7,8] It can also be highlighted that 15 per cent of venture capital general partners in Europe are women, and only 14 per cent of UK angel investors are women.[9,10] To go back to the US, reports have indicated that racial minority-owned business enterprises typically encounter higher interest rates and increased loan denials. There were also racial divides linked to US business failures resulting from Covid-19, including a 41 per cent drop in black-owned businesses and a 32 per cent decline in Latinx businesses, relative to a 17 per cent loss of white-owned businesses.[11] We could also acknowledge that 53 of the Fortune 500 CEOs in 2023 were women, marking the first time in 68 years that women had achieved 10 per cent representation on the list.[12] These examples have been cherry-picked but they offer substantive reasons why people have felt excluded from finance. People are not served as equals.

Inequalities aside, we might also ask if the global economy, to generalize, is being sensibly managed. On that front, global debt has reached $300 trillion, translating to $37,500 of average debt per person, relative to an average GDP per capita of $12,000.[13] Government debt has risen over 25 per cent since 2007 and in 2022 sits at 102 per cent of GDP. Interest rates have risen, too, which exacerbates this. The World Economic Forum has suggested that fixing the global debt issue may even form part of a 'Great Reset', in which communities accept a culture of more cautious spending. It is reasonable to say that this will be both incredibly challenging and probably unpopular, and it possibly doesn't help that the Great Reset has already been targeted by conspiracy theorists.

Opinion is split on what the gargantuan global debt truly means and what its consequences will be (debt is not always bad, but on this scale we might feel confident that it is), but for individual nations that don't meet their debt obligations, there is the risk of default, which results in higher interest rates and, potentially, serious economic damage. As I write this, in May 2023, the US Congress is debating an elevation of its debt ceiling, an artificial debt limit agreed by Congress that sits at $31.4 trillion. This limit is on course to be exceeded, and the options available are to raise the ceiling or default on the debt. Should a default occur, the Congressional Budget Office and Treasury Department project that 500,000 Americans would lose their jobs within a week, and should such a default last more than three months, that more than 8.3 million Americans would lose their jobs, and stock markets could fall by 45 per cent.[14] Further, damage to the creditworthiness of US debt would devalue the dollar, harm the US's credit rating, lift interest rates and likely encourage foreign investors to sell US assets. All of this would have major implications and threaten US economic hegemony, and yet a potential raise of the debt ceiling is being delayed and used as a bargaining chip to introduce new policies, and not for the first time.

By the time you read this, a decision will be distant in the rearview mirror, but the fact that the conversation is even happening is significant. Rather fittingly, some economists have offered a clever solution to the problem involving a loophole that allows the U.S. Department of the Treasury to mint a $1 trillion platinum coin, a solution that was also discussed by commenters during the Obama administration. However, Treasury officials and the White House have ruled out the idea that they might do this, so don't expect the US to YOLO on 'GovCoin' just yet (YOLO, meaning 'you only live once', is often used in crypto to accompany a risky investment. GovCoin is not an official terminology).[15]

Independently of recent events, there are countless reasons why people may have antipathy towards traditional financial systems. There are plenty of very good things about them, too, but motivations to seek out a new order have not disappeared after 2008. They may even be exacerbated.

NFTs, artworks and financialization

Going back to the nature of money and value, there is plenty that can be said about the explosion of NFT trading, especially in 2022 where monthly trading volume briefly reached $17 billion per month.[16] I'll concede that I was torn on what to read into this. At first, I mulled over the $900 million valuations that have been placed on the Mona Lisa, and if this might contextualize the fact that sky-high art valuations are nothing new. I then thought about the $2 million sale for one of 17 replicas of Marcel Duchamp's Dadaist peculiarity *Fountain*. For clarity, this 1917 artwork was a urinal that was laid on its back and signed pseudonymously. I wondered if NFTs might just be another opportunity for people to be astounded by seemingly worthless items selling for stupendous sums. However, neither of these examples really fit. I don't claim to be an art critic, but the Mona Lisa is widely regarded as an excellent painting, is unique, and has also taken on a depth of cultural and social relevance. Duchamp's urinal, meanwhile, was presented at a New York exhibition as a thumb in the eye to art critics and a prompt to reconsider our perceptions of what constitutes art. If I were saying anything about the initial NFT boom, then it would probably be that it represented a hyper-financialization of art. The NFTs that provide ownership of artworks are often designed to provide exclusive access to a group or events, commercial rights and status, and the success of the most successful projects can be tied to the teams behind them and their track record, sustained social media activity, celebrity endorsements, notable investors and the promise of future developments.[17] Marketing, FOMO and resale value are at the heart of these collections. Even the valuable collections that were less premeditated were fuelled by a desire to find 'the next big thing' and to profit from it.

NFT collections are not all the same, and they are not all designed primarily as investments (though many clearly are). In time, NFTs can play an important role in the evolution of digital art and can enhance the ownership rights of artists within the creator economy. This may take on greater importance if the metaverse and AR/VR experiences become more commonplace.

As the hype wears off, the underlying value of NFTs will likely become more evident to casual onlookers, and so, too, will the importance of new monetization methods for artworks, collectives and communities. The financialization of NFTs in art presents promising offshoots for a wide range of projects where community engagement and support can be leveraged and rewarded. Incentives attached to Proof of Attendance Protocols, for instance, might produce financial models to reward activities that benefit ecosystems. To go back to Chapter 6, it's also important that art is just one of many possible manifestations of NFTs.

The myth of perfect money

Blockchain and smart contracts have changed what money can do, and this gives rise to an incredibly big question: what sort of money do we want? While writing this, it was challenging to juggle the various pros and cons of crypto, DeFi, CBDCs and fiat money. Can there be a perfect type of money?

It makes sense to reflect on our options. Banknotes and cash are simple and actually quite brilliant. In today's digital and global economy, they are woefully outmoded at times, but for domestic transactions that balance security with the right to privacy, they are very useful. Conventional digital money, as most people use today, is also highly effective. It offers relatively immediate consumer payments, is easily used and can facilitate better and more efficient user experiences (i.e. chargebacks). It remains imperfect though. Interbank cooperation and payment service providers are required, adding layers of cost. Also, debit and credit card transactions are traceable, so rights to privacy could theoretically be breached.

Cryptoassets, in their various forms, may provide privacy, efficiency and speed. Even so, complete privacy would be a win for anyone looking to run a criminal enterprise. People generally need internet access to use crypto, and it can't be used if merchants don't accept it. With crypto, users also expose themselves to market and security risks that appear elevated when compared to those in TradFi.

And then we might consider CBDCs, which merge the digital benefits of crypto with legal rights and protections. This could be great, but how much do you trust your government and agree with your domestic legal system? And if you do trust your government, how confident are you that subsequent ones won't infringe on your rights and place limits on your financial freedoms?

There are so many disputes locked up in these pros and cons. A substantial one is the balance between consumer protections versus individual liberties. At a protocol level, this might play out over a discussion on whether people should be allowed to engage with the sorts of financial instruments that were previously only available to 'sophisticated' investors, and to look at it in regard to money, we can see a struggle between the right to privacy and the ability to identify fraudulent behaviour and theft. This creates an uneasy situation. Perfect privacy isn't expected, but basic privacy should be considered a human right. Similarly, most people don't want an economy where people are free to scam, but any alternative requires a compromise on privacy. There are exciting developments in DeFi that may improve the situation. Soulbound Tokens and zero-knowledge proofs may eventually allow us to prove the credibility of our identities during transactions without needing to share any information, but the long-term implications and adoption of such tools are hard to predict. For the foreseeable future, a privacy trade-off will remain where consumer protection is introduced.

There is a more complicated and unmoveable barrier to perfect money, however, and this is the subjectivity of human experience and context. As discussed earlier, laws, politics and procedures might stand in the way of a necessary and righteous course of action. It's important to consider who creates the laws, what the laws are designed for and why someone would want privacy within a transaction. This is not simply about war zones and disasters. What would we make of economic oversight in regions, either in historic or present-day contexts, where people are subjugated and marginalized based upon sexuality, religion, gender, ethnicity, race or belonging to an otherized group? There are countless reasons why privacy remains important, why programmable money could be concerning and why transaction histories could cause concerns. These are very human questions and they will be solved by neither technology nor money. Perfect money doesn't exist. It can't.

The organizational aspect of DeFi is important too, and in relation to the challenges of running DAOs and introducing democracy to finance, perfect governance can't exist either. What's more important is how people make use of these advancements and what they add to the financial system.

Technology alone won't fix our problems, but DAOs and DeFi may in time offer better platforms for incentivizing activity that helps encapsulate the ambitions, skills and creativity of people from all walks of life.

References

1   Our World in Data. World GDP over the last two millennia, Our World in Data, 2015, ourworldindata.org/grapher/world-gdp-over-the-last-two-millennia (archived at https://perma.cc/UX9Z-ESZ7)

2   Oxfam. Inequality kills: methodology note, Oxfam, 2022, oxfamilibrary. openrepository.com/bitstream/handle/10546/621341/tb-inequality-kills-methodology-note-170122-en.pdf (archived at https://perma.cc/C88Z-5JDZ)

3 5 World Inequality Report. The World Inequality Report 2022, wir2022.wid. world/executive-summary/ (archived at https://perma.cc/CVZ2-CHEK)

4   J Bivens and J Kandra. CEO pay has skyrocketed 1,460% since 1978: CEOs were paid 399 times as much as a typical worker in 2021, Economic Policy Institute, 2022, www.epi.org/publication/ceo-pay-in-2021/ (archived at https://perma.cc/6EE9-BDXG)

6   D-M Davis. Women-founded startups raised 1.9% of all VC funds in 2022, a drop from 2021, TechCrunch, 2023, techcrunch.com/2023/01/18/women-founded-startups-raised-1-9-of-all-vc-funds-in-2022-a-drop-from-2021/ (archived at https://perma.cc/SKB6-XFBR)

7   D-M Davis. Black founders still raised just 1% of all VC funds in 2022, TechCrunch, 2023, techcrunch.com/2023/01/06/black-founders-still-raised-just-1-of-all-vc-funds-in-2022/ (archived at https://perma.cc/2NPK-ZDCE)

8 United States Census Bureau. QuickFacts United States, 2022, www.census. gov/quickfacts/fact/table/US/PST045222 (archived at https://perma.cc/46YX-ZXSN)

9 A Lewin. Only 15% of VC general partners in Europe are women, Sifted, 2022, sifted.eu/articles/vc-general-partners-europe (archived at https://perma.cc/8DYA-JBPK)

10 M Partington. Only 14% of angel investors in the UK are women, report finds, Sifted, 2022, sifted.eu/articles/female-angel-investors-in-the-uk (archived at https://perma.cc/6J8S-EXKH)

11 C Costa. Minority entrepreneurs at a tipping point as Black-owned banks dwindle in the U.S., CNBC, 2020, www.cnbc.com/2020/08/25/minority-entrepreneurs-at-tipping-point-as-black-owned-banks-dwindle.html (archived at https://perma.cc/24MZ-BE8F)

12 E Hinchliffe. Women CEOs run more than 10% of Fortune 500 companies for the first time in history, Fortune, 2023, fortune.com/2023/01/12/fortune-500-companies-ceos-women-10-percent/ (archived at https://perma.cc/XH92-RYE8)

13 T Chan and A Dimitrijevic. Global debt leverage: is a great reset coming?, S&P Global, 2023, www.spglobal.com/en/research-insights/featured/special-editorial/look-forward/global-debt-leverage-is-a-great-reset-coming (archived at https://perma.cc/X6DP-JKKV)

14 CEA. The potential economic impacts of various debt ceiling scenarios, The White House, 2023, www.whitehouse.gov/cea/written-materials/2023/05/03/debt-ceiling-scenarios/ (archived at https://perma.cc/958V-TSCG)

15 A Kiersz and J Zeballos-Roig. The Biden administration could sidestep McConnell's refusal to pay America's bills by minting a $1 trillion platinum coin, Business Insider, 2023, www.businessinsider.com/mint-1-trillion-platinum-coin-debt-ceiling-2021-9?r=US&IR=T (archived at https://perma.cc/PX47-5PK8)

16 S Shukla. NFT trading volumes collapse 97% from January peak, Bloomberg, 2022, www.bloomberg.com/news/articles/2022-09-28/nft-volumes-tumble-97-from-2022-highs-as-frenzy-fades-chart (archived at https://perma.cc/3MBP-Q378)

17 S Baloyan. Marketing was key to Moonbirds becoming a super successful NFT, HackerNoon, 2022, hackernoon.com/marketing-was-key-to-moonbirds-becoming-a-super-successful-nft (archived at https://perma.cc/N9LR-TSWA)

INDEX

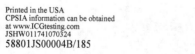
Printed in the USA
CPSIA information can be obtained
at www.ICGtesting.com
JSHW011741070324
58801JS00004B/185